The New Diversity of Family Life in Europe

Banu Çitlak · Sebastian Kurtenbach
Megan Lueneburg · Meglena Zlatkova
(Eds.)

The New Diversity of Family Life in Europe

Mobile Ethnic Groups
and Flexible Boundaries

Editors
Banu Çitlak
Dortmund, Germany

Megan Lueneburg
Plovdiv, Bulgaria

Sebastian Kurtenbach
Bielefeld, Germany

Meglena Zlatkova
Plovdiv, Bulgaria

ISBN 978-3-658-17856-7   ISBN 978-3-658-17857-4 (Ebook)
DOI 10.1007/978-3-658-17857-4

Library of Congress Control Number: 2017937301

Springer VS
© Springer Fachmedien Wiesbaden GmbH 2017
This work is subject to copyright. All rights are reserved by the Publisher, whether the whole or part of the material is concerned, specifically the rights of translation, reprinting, reuse of illustrations, recitation, broadcasting, reproduction on microfilms or in any other physical way, and transmission or information storage and retrieval, electronic adaptation, computer software, or by similar or dissimilar methodology now known or hereafter developed.
The use of general descriptive names, registered names, trademarks, service marks, etc. in this publication does not imply, even in the absence of a specific statement, that such names are exempt from the relevant protective laws and regulations and therefore free for general use.
The publisher, the authors and the editors are safe to assume that the advice and information in this book are believed to be true and accurate at the date of publication. Neither the publisher nor the authors or the editors give a warranty, express or implied, with respect to the material contained herein or for any errors or omissions that may have been made. The publisher remains neutral with regard to jurisdictional claims in published maps and institutional affiliations.

Printed on acid-free paper

This Springer VS imprint is published by Springer Nature
The registered company is Springer Fachmedien Wiesbaden GmbH
The registered company address is: Abraham-Lincoln-Str. 46, 65189 Wiesbaden, Germany

Table of Contents

Introduction 1
The new diversity of family life in Europe.
Mobile ethnic groups and flexible boundaries
*Banu Çıtlak, Sebastian Kurtenbach, Megan Lueneburg
and Meglena Zlatkova*

Studying transnationalism 7
On the empirical assessment and the overarching connections between
diverse transnational activities
Sascha Riedel

**Spatial Transnationalism:
An analytical approach** 29
Sebastian Kurtenbach

**Spatial segregation
and the unequal educational pathways
of children in urban areas** 45
Banu Çıtlak

**Development of participation in early childhood education
and care in Europe in relation to social inequality and migration** 61
Nora Jehles

V

Moving in together and marrying for the first time 81
A comparison between European countries
Barbara Elisabeth Fulda

Migration, family life and cultural inheritance 99
Perspectives from both sides of the Bulgarian-Turkish border
Meglena Zlatkova and Stoyka Penkova

Socialist family as a biopolitical dispositive 123
Rositsa Lyubenova

More than to Raise a Child from a Distance 135
Mobile Parents and Their Children Left Behind in Bulgaria
Svetlana Antova

Women and Families:
Mobility Strategies 149
Aneliya Avdzhieva

Children and Socialization:
Crossing Social and Cultural Boundaries 163
Svetoslava Mancheva

Parents' neighborhood integration
in two ethnically diverse low-income neighborhoods 181
Banu Çıtlak

Comparing seemingly different living environments 195
Focusing on children's perspectives
Maren Hilke

Growing up in a disadvantaged neighborhood 211
Preventing neighborhood effects and promoting positive youth development through sports using the example Plovdiv-Stolipinovo
Ina Schäfer

Authors.. 233

Introduction

The new diversity of family life in Europe. Mobile ethnic groups and flexible boundaries

Banu Çıtlak, Sebastian Kurtenbach, Megan Lueneburg and Meglena Zlatkova

As a consequence of the free movement legislation within Europe and a continuing migration to Europe, an increasing share of people is embedded in transnational social spaces today. These include formal and informal transnational networks and particularly networks of the nuclear and extended family members. Transnational social spaces are defined as "dense, stable, pluri-local and institutionalized frameworks composed of material artifacts, the social practices of everyday life, as well as systems of symbolic representation that are structured by and structure human life." (Pries 2001: 8). In this book, we focus primarily on families, who live in transnational social spaces in a legally plural world. Some of them are children of former immigrants (e.g. people of Turkish origin in Germany), others are trans-border citizens holding two citizenships (e.g. at the Turkish and Bulgarian border), or they are citizens of a member state, organizing their life's in more than one European country (e.g. Roma people in Bulgaria and Germany). Therefore, constituting a trans-border life is not limited to a small group of international elites, like managers, scientists or diplomats anymore. Transnationalism and diversity became the new normality in Europe.

Beyond the current political and medial discussion about the "new asylum crisis", families in Europe live already in plural worlds and experience different kinds of (formal and informal) boundaries during their everyday live. These boundaries are drawn by social inequality, discrimination and political exclusion. Under conditions of poverty and discrimination, transnational processes and biographical projects are often conflicting, painful and bound up with personal sacrifices, but they also open opportunities for migrants as well as societies as a whole. In addition, research neither underlies the fact, that the decision to immigrate is a singular and ultimate operation nor immigration a historically new process. Return migration, temporal patterns of stays and commuting between different nations are a common part of live for many families and their members. It is a challenge for contemporary social sciences to investigate the chances and risks rising from the fact that an increasing proportion of the next European generation will grow up within transnational patterns and flexible social boundaries, while holding only limited resources. Particularly the fact that national integration programs are still underfunded and the potential of "global social work" in supporting these families are still overseen, leads to rather pessimistic future expectations.

The new diversity has also an impact on the social environment of families, predominantly in urban areas of the western European nations. As a consequence of segregation and limited job opportunities, immigrants are often concentrated in a few specific neighborhoods of cities. New social coalitions and figurations of established-and-outsider relations are created, new forms and signs of cohabitation are observable, e.g. through written multilingualism, and a migration related economy and Non-Governmental Organizations run by immigrants on the local level. As a consequence, even if social actors constitute their lives in transnational social spaces, the local level becomes an important unit to understand migration.

Beside the interplay between transnational family life and transnational social spaces, this book is also a contribution to the ongoing development of a European perspective on migration. In contrast to traditional nations of immigration like the USA, Canada or Australia, European countries – in the east as well as in the west – are territorially more or less closed nations with relatively less immigration experiences. As has been visible through the "asylum crisis" lately, a common positive understanding of immigration and integration is not rooted so deeply in the self-understanding of all parts of European societies. Conservative nationalist rightwing positions rose up dramatically in nearly all European countries during the last years. Despite these political dispositions, immigration has become more common in the everyday life of families. However, nowadays family life is characterized rather by transnational social practices, than through clear processes of assimilation.

The goal of this book is to discuss current developments in migration, beyond economically and political perspectives. It is also a contribution to link Western and Eastern European perspectives as well as sociology and anthropology. About all articles in this book are concerned with different ways and perspectives of describing, empirically measuring and explaining these patterns. It was not our intention to prefer a methodological way for research, but rather put together the whole spectrum how to study transnational families and social spaces.

The book is divides in 13 contributions. First, basic assumptions and concepts about transnational family lives are presented. *Sascha Riedel* reviews the empirical literature on transnational behaviors and highlights the interconnections within this diverse field of research. Particularly, the contribution outlines different measurements of transnationalism. Subsequently, two distinct strategies of empirical research on transnational activities are presented by the author.

Sebastian Kurtenbach discusses the connection between transnationalism and segregation. Therefore, he conceptualizes two different types of transnational social space: sending places and arrival areas. With such a holistic view on transnationalism, he is able to underlie the similarities, dissimilarities and connections between social segregated neighborhoods in differed nations.

Banu Çıtlak explores the educational pathways of children in urban neighborhoods under conditions of social segregation. In her contribution, she describes the structural and historical conditions which brought up disadvantaged neighborhoods in the cities of the Ruhr Area in Germany and how these neighborhoods provide unequal educational chances for children.

Nora Jehles analyzes the early childhood education (EDEC) and care institutions in Europe with an emphasis on social inequality and migration. Furthermore, the influence of the legal framework is discussed to explain the development of differences in participation in ECEC. The analysis of PISA data shows that immigrant students and students with low educated parents attend less to ECEC than native students or those with higher educated parents. The results show that the reforms of the system of ECEC influence the participation in general, even though the results are inconsistent.

As family life has undergone massive change in the last few decades, the contribution of *Barbara Fulda* aims at documenting the current state of partnership formation in European countries. She studies national patterns of when couples move in a common household or marry. After clarifying the concept of „transition to adulthood she reviews the literature on both transitions and tests these findings at the German case using the pairfam dataset.

Meglena Zlatkova and Stoyka Penkova present their research in the family life and migration, discussing the cultural inheritance and migration on the two sides of Bulgarian-Turkish border. They analyze different strategies of crossing the border of the families with dual citizenship. Resulting from the particularities of this form of liminality, there appears a wide range of life and biographical strategies (educational, social, and economic) of the children of out-migrants whereby the 'new young', i.e. the 'inheritors' of Turks from Bulgaria migrated to Turkey, exercise their everyday social interactions 'across' the border. The closer look into the forms of crossing one border actually gives the opportunity to contemplate the multiple dimensions of the lives and worlds of the young mobile people of Europe who, with the support of their families, develop strategies for investing in social capital and in inheriting cultural models from different countries.

The main thesis of *Rosita Lybuenva* is that the socialist authority exercised biopolitical control primarily through a new role of women and the mobilization of childhood. She uses archival materials i.e. official documents of the socialist institutions for her analysis to identify target points of the biopolitical dispositive which order and construct identities. Therefore, she uses Foucault's analysis of the dispositive as a theoretical framework. The study also draws on the theoretical preconditions of the historical sociology of socialism developed by the Bulgarian sociological school.

Svetlana Antova analyses one of the main problems that result from the labour mobility abroad in from Bulgaria after 1989, emphasizing on the problem of distance-parenting and children left behind and explores reasons why the separations of families to be preferred instead of going abroad together or of staying at home and what are the consequences of it. In the chapter, presenting her anthropological research, she states that the separated families develop and maintain new forms of trans-nationalized ties and relations. Leading transnational, multi-sited life means that the exchanges and interactions across borders are a regular and sustained part of migrants' realities and activities and family' roles and relations are changing.

Aneliya Avdzhieva discusses Roma women's labour mobility in Bulgaria and abroad, mainly in Europe and Turkey and focuses on the individual mobile labour strategies, tackling the role of the family in constructing these strategies and realizing mobility. She analyses the social consequences within the individual's interplay level, family relationships, and local community's connections, based on her field anthropological research. Her main consideration is that the traditional model of family labour division is starting to be changed and the mobility abroad of women and men and crossing the national and symbolic boundaries and borders changes the roles and positions in the family and the community.

Svetoslava Mancheva's approach of the anthropology of childhood looks at *child* as social actor who has a specific position from the point of view of the *"us – them"* dichotomy. She explores the processes of crossing social and cultural boundaries between Roma and non-Roma children. The chapter discusses how the sport and various collective activities represent universal body practices and techniques are used by youngsters as means of socialization in and out of their community. Her research is based on several neighborhoods, towns and villages in Bulgaria, inhabited by Romani people.

Banu Çıtlak focuses on parents' integration within the neighborhood and school context in ethnic diverse, low income neighborhoods in Germany. She explores the influence of individual and contextual characteristics for the local integration of families with adolescents. Her findings predict higher risks of marginalization for single-parent families. In order to include all parents, her results call for more ambitious community and school interventions in secondary schools, located in disadvantaged neighborhoods.

Maren Hilke takes a closer look on segregation in a cross-cultural perspective from a methodological point of view. Today, poverty is also a spatial phenomenon in the big cities all over the world. An increasing polarization between poor and rich parts of the cities appears. This has consequences for the living conditions and development of children in the poor parts of the cities. This contribution analyzes the existence of similarities of children´ experiences in social segregated neighborhoods. The contribution shows how differences in the childhood can be analyzed in cross-cultural designs. Therefore, it is suggested to integrate children as experts of their own social environment into the research process.

Ina Schäfer focuses on the conditions of growing up in disadvantaged neighborhoods. Her focus is on neighborhood effects which affect juveniles through segregation in a disadvantaged environment. Additionally, the development of opportunities with social work is important. She uses two methods in her analysis. First, the method reflexive photography and second interviews were conducted with community leaders. This considers the point of view of the youth and the impact of social work to create new opportunities and limit negative neighborhood effects.

This book represents a collaborative project between the "Center for Interdisciplinary Regional Research" (ZEFIR) at Ruhr-University of Bochum, the University of Applied Sciences Dortmund in Germany and the University of Plovdiv Paisii Hilendarski in Bulgaria. The Editors are grateful to all contributors.

References

Pries, L. (2001). New Transnational Social Spaces. In L. Pries (Ed.), *New Transnational Social Spaces. International migration and transnational companies in the early twenty-first century*, New York City: Routledge Taylor & Francis Group, pp. 3–36.

Studying transnationalism

On the empirical assessment and the overarching connections between diverse transnational activities

Sascha Riedel

1 The Problem

New patterns of migratory movements are nowadays influencing families in large parts of Europe. Migration represents a considerable tension for social ties even when only one family member migrates. Additionally, women are nowadays as likely to migrate to another country as first family members as men are (Schapiro et al. 2013: 48). Thus, today's transnational families face more complex situations than in the past. These changes of international mobility and their social implications are observable in all immigration countries of the world. Today's migratory movements challenge classical concepts of labor or forced migration theories. One of the most influential competing concepts in migration literature constitutes the idea of transnationalism[1]. According to this concept, immigrants pursue activities and forge cultures that are not limited to one particular national context. Thus, transnationalism is of extraordinary importance for the integration process of immigrants, e.g. regarding investments and socioeconomic integration (Itzigsohn/Saucedo 2002; Ley 2013; Marcelli/Lowell 2005; Snel et al. 2006; Tsuda 2012). However, as the phenomenon's definition is extremely wide, a uniform understanding of transnational activities and their empirical assessment is complicated. Therefore, existing empirical research on transnationalism tends to be rath-

---

[1] The terms of *transnationalism* and *transnationality* are used interchangeably in the remainder of this contribution. Further, *transmigrants*, *transnationals*, and *transnational immigrants* refer to an identical group of individuals.

er scattered and disconnected. This study engages in developing a more holistic framework for empirical research on transnationalism.

This contribution begins with presenting the theoretical foundation and current state of research on transnational activities and behaviors. Particularly, this first section reviews the empirical literature on transnationalism and presents different assessments of transnational behaviors. Subsequently, two distinct strategies of research are abstracted: one *focused* and one *comprehensive* strategy. This chapter also discusses each strategy's strengths and weaknesses. The final section discusses this contribution's implications for further research in the area of transnational activities.

2 Variety of research on transnationalism

Transnationalism surfaced in scientific discussion in the last decade of the twentieth century. In its most distilled version the definition of the term "transnational" indicates reference to more than one nation state. In the context of migration research, most common reference points are made up of immigrants' countries of origin and the receiving society. Yet, other setups are viable as well. For example, individuals may engage in more than two countries. A Spanish immigrant who resides in Belgium and travels frequently to France for business may at the same time maintain close social ties to relatives and friends in Spain, where he[2] periodically visits. Consistently, transnational immigrants are characterized by a "plethora of connections spanning home and host *societies*" (Waldinger/Fitzgerald 2004: 1177, emphasis added). Besides these arrangements spanning more than two nation states, individuals may also exclusively engage in countries other than their country of origin. For example, a Slovakian immigrant may live in Bulgaria and cross the border to Romania frequently, without ever returning to his country of origin. Hence, this transnational setup excludes his country of origin. The arrangement presents the prototypical transnationalist, who extends his way of living "*beyond* loyalties that connect to any specific place of origin or ethnic or national group" (Waldinger/Fitzgerald 2004: 1178, emphasis in original). Yet, most commonly, transnationalism is defined as "a set of cross-border relations and practices that connect migrants with their societies of origin" (Guarnizo 2003: 670). This contribution takes an individual micro-perspective. Therefore, it excludes transnational relations on the national, subnational, and supranational level, for example,

---

2   In the remainder of this study the term of *immigrant* shall refer to both male and female individuals.

between corporations or between political actors. Thus, this study focuses strictly on the individual perspective of immigrants. Transnationalism shall represent "a pattern of migration in which persons, although they move across international borders, settle and establish ongoing social relations in a new state, maintain ongoing social connections within the polity from which they originated" (Glick Schiller/Fouron 1999: 344).

The existing empirical research covers a wide array of topics and methodological approaches. The subsequent section subdivides the research area in *economic*, *political*, *social*, and *cultural and religious* transnational practices (Levitt/Jaworsky 2007) and presents corresponding studies and findings. The chosen areas necessarily represent an arbitrary selection of transnational activities. However, it tries to cover both transnationalism from above (global capital, media, and political institutions) and from below (local, grassroots activity) (Levitt/Jaworsky 2007: 132). Restricting the selection to the presented, prominent arenas of transnational activities ensures the readability of this contribution. Additionally, the subsequent section emphasizes the empirical operationalization of transnational behaviors.

2.1 Economics

Economic transnationalism largely refers to immigrant ventures regularly spanning more than one nation state. For example, this definition targets transnational entrepreneurs, according to a study of Portes and colleagues (2002: 284). There are those who travel abroad at least twice a year for business. Furthermore, transnational entrepreneurs consider the success of their firm to rely on regular contact with foreign countries, for example the country of origin. The findings indicate that 5% of all immigrants within the *Comparative Immigrant Enterprise Project* (CIEP) data are transnational entrepreneurs. This group, however, accounts for 58% of all self-employed immigrants within the sample (Portes et al. 2002: 285). Higher levels of education, years of US residency and size of social networks positively influence the probability to engage in transnational enterprises. Additionally, males engage more often in transnational entrepreneurship than females and Colombians – in comparison with Dominican and Salvadoran immigrants who are less likely to do so (Portes et al. 2002: 290). Furthermore, immigrant-owned transnational firms have a significantly larger number of employees and higher annual sales than non-transnational immigrant businesses (Wang/Liu 2015: 354ff.). Thus, transnational engagement constitutes a profitable strategy for immigrant entrepreneurs.

Another common area studies immigrant remittances to their country of origin. Although not all studies in this area are linked to the literature of transnationalism, monetary remittances are usually considered to "represent long-distance social ties of solidarity, reciprocity, and obligation that bind migrants to their kin and friends" (Guarnizo 2003: 671). In this regard, higher amounts of remittances characterize more transnational immigrants. A considerable stock of studies was able to produce the following insights. Studying foreign born Mexicans residing in Los Angeles County, Marcelli and Lowell (2005: 89) were able to show that immigrants who finished their education outside of the US are more likely to send money to Mexico. Additionally, a shorter period of residence in Los Angeles and context-characteristics, such as the population density in the place of residence and a rural home country context, significantly increase the likelihood of remitting money. Finally, participation in the receiving country's community in terms of visiting at least one community meeting renders monetary remittances more likely (Marcelli/Lowell 2005: 89). Relying on representative data of private households in Moldova, Siegel and Lücke (2013: 127) investigated 1139 bilateral relationships between migrant and recipient households. Their research focuses on the transfer channels used to remit money, which are grouped in formal, informal, and personal channels. Bank transfers and the use of post offices represent formal services for remitting money. Informal services rely on train conductors or minibus operators to convey money across borders, while personal transfers are operated by the immigrants themselves or relatives and friends. The findings indicate that formal services of remitting money are preferred by highly educated immigrants and by those who value speed, convenience, and security of their services (Siegel/Lücke 2013: 136). Additionally, illegal residency and/or a shorter stay increase the likelihood of using informal services. In general, the presented findings indicate that highly educated immigrants send higher amounts of money to the country of origin and prefer formal transfer channels. Furthermore, the time of residence is a meaningful predictor of immigrants' amount of remittances.

A third vein of research on economic transnationalism studies direct investment, for example-in homeownership. In this regard, two differing lines of argument are possible. First, transnational individuals, as an expression of their transnationality may invest in properties in more than one country. Thus, depending on individual financial resources transmigrants accommodate to two or more countries. In this regard, the investment strategy mirrors a long-term adaptation to not a single, but multiple societal contexts (Mazzucato 2005: 7). Secondly transnational immigrants due to their individual indetermination and as a sign of their "refusal of fixity" (Vertovec 1999: 451) may avoid homeownership altogether. As they do not have long-term plans of residing anywhere permanently, the avoidance of large-scale investments constitutes a rational strategy for transmigrants. The lines of argument, therefore, differ in their predictions on the investment in properties and homeownership. Whereas the first expects transnationals to invest in residential property in at least two countries, the second assumes them to avoid capital-intensive and long-term investment altogether. Commonly, empirical studies investigate the second approach by explaining homeownership in the receiving country with transnational relations across borders (Kuuire et al. 2015; Vono-de-Vilhena/Bayona-Carrasco 2012). For example, using data of the *Longitudinal Study of Immigrants in Canada* (LSIC) Kuuire and colleagues (2015) could substantiate that both engagement in the transfer of remittances and the amount of remittances significantly decrease the probability of immigrants' homeownership in Canada. These effects operate independently of family income and level of education. Comparable findings could be obtained for immigrants in Spain (Vono-de-Vilhena/Bayona-Carrasco 2012). Applying discrete-time logistic models on longitudinal data of the National Immigrant Survey in Spain, the authors were able to show that remitting money to the home country significantly decreases the probability of investing in homeownership in the country of residence. Furthermore, home-owning immigrants are characterized by high educational levels and the intention to reside in Spain for the next five years (Vono-de-Vilhena/Bayona-Carrasco 2012: 109ff.). Investment in more than one country has been studied as well. Relying on nine life history interviews with Caribbean informants based in Birmingham and London, Joseph (2010) was able to show that investments in the home country and the UK are highly interrelated. On the one hand a certain share of respondents felt unsure whether they should establish multiple residencies or whether they should return to the Caribbean permanently. In this regard, selling UK property was perceived as a burning of bridges, as it would diminish the chances of returning. On the other hand, those respondents who already established multiple residencies dismissed the idea of returning to the home country for good. As those who have accumulated sufficient financial resources for homeownership in two contexts, they actively decided to engage in transnational lifestyle. The presented findings indicate that higher levels of education and higher financial resources consistently increase the probability of engaging in economic transnational behaviors. The distinct subfields of this research area are highly interrelated, most notably remittances and homeownership. In general, economic transnationalism is commonly measured by the amount of remittances, the frequency of business-related, cross-border contacts, and monetary investment in one or more countries.

2.2 Culture and Religion

The most modest form of *cultural* transnationalism refers to (fluent) bilingualism or multinational consumption behaviors. Yet, these measures do not distinctively discriminate between transmigrants and traditional immigrants as arguably both groups prefer the native language at home and speak the host language outside (Portes & Hao 1998; Portes & Schauffler 1994). In addition, a cosmopolitan and multicultural stance to consumption, as for example with regard to cuisine, art, and fashion, is neither a distinct feature of transnationals nor of individuals with migratory experience. In order to discuss cultural transnationalism, the inherently problematic term of *culture* requires elaboration first. Culture – usually in contrast to nature – refers to man-made concepts, such as values, beliefs, customs, and rituals (Lazear 1999: 96). In terms of cultural identity, it may relate to a "sort of collective 'one true self' (…), which people with a shared history and ancestry hold in common" (Hall 1990: 223). This definition strongly resembles the common notion of an ethnic group, whose members are interrelated by the belief of a common origin (Weber 2006: 367). Consistently, ethnic groups are frequently defined in cultural terms, they refer to "a segment of a larger society whose members are thought, by themselves and/or others, to have a common origin and to share important segments of a common culture and who, in addition, participate in shared activities in which the common origin and culture are significant ingredients" (Yinger 1976: 200). Studies on cultural and religious transnationalism relate to both bodily geographic and ideational behaviors. The former relate to activities that indicate an actual cross-border movement (Snel et al. 2006: 286). In contrast, the latter behaviors may be performed without physically crossing a border. Bodily geographic cultural transnationalism frequently relates to practices for which immigrants travel to their original community on a regular schedule, for example celebrations of saints. Research on internationally dispersed Hindu families was able to show that these gather for weddings in a certain place, such as Lisbon (Lourenço/Cachado 2012: 59). Thus, although internal family networks span national borders, their members reunite for significant cultural and religious occasions. In this regard, cultural transnational activities are measured by cross-border mobility, and are performed for distinct cultural or religious reasons. This measurement, however, requires the corresponding studies to survey the reason of cross-border trips, besides their frequency and length. Comparable findings could be obtained for migratory movements between the United States and Todos Santos Cuchumatán, Guatemala (Burrell 2005). For the *corrida de caballos*, which is a celebration including horse races, individuals that immigrated to the US return to the home town in order to engage in this cultural festivity. In this regard, the returned community members actively relate to their current place of residence, for example by wearing a "Stars-and-Stripes bandanna" and a "full-sized U.S. flag" (Burrell 2005: 14). Despite their strong connection to the home country, as indicated by the return visits to it, these immigrants strongly relate to the receiving country as well. This leads to another phenomenon, which is commonly subsumed under the term of cultural transnationalism: dual and hybrid identities. On this point, transnationalism as a "type of consciousness" (Vertovec 1999: 447) implies that transnationals feel linked to both countries of origin and host country. However, the majority of immigrants may eventually establish hybrid forms of identification. These include a "refusal of fixity" (Vertovec 1999: 451) as well as a "strong local element" (Vathi 2013: 909). Furthermore, the denial of a binary identification might be a strategy of coping with the individual's feeling that full citizenship in either context might not be achievable. By examining Pakistani Muslim immigrants in Norway, Erdal (2013: 992) was able to portray the strains, which adherence to Muslim faith poses in secular societies. Yet, transmigrants' experiences influence existing cultural activities and modify their inherent meaning. The practice of Alevi in France, Germany, and the Netherlands exemplify the revitalization of cultural practices that exert a repercussive effect on the country of origin's society, for example Turkey, where the cultural habits of Alevi had been largely suppressed in the past. The preceding examples additionally demonstrate the blurred line between cultural and religious transnational behaviors. Religious transnational organizations connect individuals residing in different countries. Thus, they have to accommodate individual needs in diverse societal contexts. Moreover, individuals adjust their religious faiths to their ways of living, and religious organizations also adapt to problems accompanying the increasing transnational activities of immigrants. In this regard, Nagel (2010, 2014) highlights the relevance of diaspora communities in religious transformation processes. For example, transnational online forums distribute religious fatwas dealing with the specific challenges of migrants' lives (Nagel 2014: 25). These often try to balance the restrictive rules of religion and immigrants' everyday needs. Thus, new hybrid beliefs emerge and religious practices are influenced by intermixing aspects of sending and receiving societies' contexts. Finally, religion spans a transnational field on its own, connecting individuals on a global scale. In this regard, empirical findings could show that for example British Pakistanis tend to return to a more basal practice of Islam in order to avoid strains between host's and country of origin's cultural and societal expectations (Jacobson 1997). In this respect, religion establishes membership as well as functional guidelines working on a transnational scale. In general, cultural and religious transnationalism is a highly ambiguous concept. Most empirical studies operationalize it by hybrid identities and engagement in cultural practices and celebrations in multiple nation states. Again, the distinction between bodily geographic and ideational activities may mediate the interrelation with other dimensions of transnational behavior.

2.3 Social ties

Changes in *social* life, for example referring to friendship ties and family relations, are commonly subsumed under the term of social transnationalism. Social ties usually constitute the key characteristic of transnationalism, as defined as "social action at a distance" (Boccagni 2012: 120). Transnationalism without a social dimension is inconceivable. However, with regard to the term "transnational ties", very diverse measures exist in the literature. Most researchers do not distinguish between social transnationalism and transnationalism in general. Thus, they utilize visits to the nation of origin, remittances, participation in home country organizations, or interest in home country politics as social transnationalism (Alcántara et al. 2015: 743; Gershon & Pantoja 2014: 333). In order to distinguish social issues from other dimensions, several studies focus on family life (Domínguez/Lubitow 2008; Lourenço/Cachado 2012; Nguyen-Akbar 2014; Olwig 2003; Peter 2010; Schans 2009; Schapiro et al. 2013). Transnational families are defined as families whose nuclear members are distributed across different national contexts. Additionally, most studies try to assess the intensity of the relationships between these members. The ethnographic work of Nguyen-Akbar (2014) on Viet Kieu (overseas Vietnamese) is based upon 70 interviews. She describes the obligations and burdens that overseas Vietnamese perceive towards their families in Vietnam. Furthermore, tensions and the ambivalent relationship between commonly wealthy Viet Kieu who return to Vietnam and their rural relatives are discussed. Particularly, the considerable lifestyle differences contribute to the described strains of family life (Nguyen-Akbar 2014: 190ff.). Comparably, Lourenço and Cachado (2012) depict transnational Hindu-Gujarati families that originated in the Indian State of Gujarat, then mostly migrated to Mozambique and finally settled in Portugal, predominantly in Lisbon. Additionally, certain families engage in a third wave of migration to the UK, mostly Leicester, Manchester, Reading, and Birmingham. Thus, many Hindu-Gujaratis represent so called *"triple* migrants" (Lourenço/Cachado 2012: 58, emphasis in original). Due to the allocation of family members across diverse nation states, new modes of family organization occur. Particularly, gatherings such as religious festivities and weddings in the Lisbon metropolitan area mobilize dispersed family members from India, Mozambique, and the UK. Finally, Schapiro and colleagues (2013) summarize the effects of transnational family formation on children. Their literature review identifies two central mechanisms of influence: separation and reunification. Studies on separation investigate children's – often negative – feelings, for example anger and distress. Feelings and effects are strongly mediated by third variables, such as the age and gender of the child and the migrating parent. In this regard, research could show that Latin American boys experience greater strains than girls when their fathers had migrated. Additionally, cultural factors may mediate children's reactions to their parents' migratory decisions. Whereas Filipino adolescents describe negative feelings, neutral or positive expressions were obtained from Jamaican and Mexican children (Schapiro et al. 2013: 56). However, future research needs to identify the causal mechanisms of these differences. Besides parental migration, children may leave the home country as well, for example for educational purposes. Besides separation the eventual reunification causes tensions as well. The effects strongly depend upon timing, gender, and pre-migration conditions. Again, the consequences of reunification vary widely for transnational families. These include children expressing pride for the sacrifices their parents had made as well as struggles in accommodating to the new family life, including loss of trust among family members (Schapiro et al. 2013: 58). Hence, transnational family structures strongly influence adolescents' private life. Social transnationalism, however, may also relate to friendship networks that span across international borders. In some cases, these contacts may be conveniently maintained, as countries share a border. Thus crossing the border poses fewer problems than in cases where home and receiving country are more remote to each other. For example, members of the German minority in Poland commonly sustain ties with relatives and friends in Germany, thus living "truly 'transnational lives'" (Jasiewicz 2012: 412, emphasis in original). Although the circumstances are more difficult, Ghanaian immigrants in Amsterdam engage in transnational friendship networks as well (Mazzucato 2008, 2010). In any case, social transnationalism of this kind is usually defined by contact to close friends that live abroad. However, measuring social networks of this kind is complicated. A common survey item reads: *Do you have regular contact with friends or acquaintances abroad?* on which the respondents answer in a dichotomous yes/no manner (for example GSOEP, see Holst et al. 2010: 23). This measurement instrument is problematic for two reasons. First, it does not include information about the network size, which is highly important in appraising the extent of social relations. Second, the item's wording and its simplistic answer categories do not allow for statements about the intensity of cross-national relationships. Interpretation of regularity of contact remains in the subjective realm and thus complicates the inter-individual reliability of the responses. Utilizing the aforementioned item, Holst and colleagues (2010: 16) were able to document a positive effect of transnational friends on the amount of remittances of female immigrants in Germany. A different stance on the measurement of transnational ties was chosen by Kraemer (2014), who conducted participant-observation with 30 core participants and their extended offline and online social networks. The online part of the study investigated individual activities on "Facebook, Skype, blogs, Twitter, and other instant messaging services" (Kraemer 2014: 60). The findings indicate that offline and online contacts and networks reciprocally reinforce each other. Thus social media contacts complement existing transnational (offline) relations (Kraemer 2014: 73). However, as participants do not know all online friends in person, averaging 60% of their Facebook friends, these connections partly represent ideational ties (Kraemer 2014: 65). Ideational transnational contacts are defined as social ties to individuals in multiple nation states that may be maintained without ever physically crossing borders. The presented findings on social transnationalism underpinned the crucial role of recent developments in mass communication in facilitating long-lasting social contact across international borders. The measurements are mostly restricted to ongoing contacts with relatives and friends living in a different nation state to the current residence. However, all presented measurement instruments fail to reliably assess the intensity of contact. Some immigrants may maintain contacts only via email, while others may visit friends and relatives several times per year. Yet, both cases are covered under regular contact with friends and acquaintances abroad. The gradual differences between these, however, may be highly relevant for explaining the impact of social transnational ties on other transnational activities of immigrants.

2.4 Political activism

The *political* arena of transnationalism is one of the most regarded in academia and public. It builds an original constituting factor of the phenomenon (Agarwala 2012; Glick Schiller et al. 1995; Guarnizo 1994; Guarnizo et al. 2003). A substantial corpus of studies investigates large-scale political linkages across borders. Policies (Erkkilä 2014) as well as institutions and actors (Holmes 2014; Niederhafner 2014, Østergaard-Nielsen 2011) may outreach international borders. This contribution, however, focuses on the individual level. In this regard, political transnationals are commonly defined as active members of political parties and civic organizations in both their home and receiving country. Hence, they frequently speak out on societal issues in both countries of reference. Furthermore, transnational strategies may empower people to overcome and criticize restrictions they suffer in a single nation state. Social activism on climate change (Hadden 2014), gender equality (Hughes et al. 2015), and LGBTQ politics (Binnie/Klesse 2013) represent prevalent fields of research. However, these studies commonly do not measure transnational interrelations, but a priori assume certain organizations – usually NGOs – represent transnational actors. In this regard, these studies restrict their analyses to ideational transnational ties. Individuals who engage in transnational organizations share common interests, ideas, and goals that go beyond single nation states. However, their members may pursue these common goals without ever leaving their home countries. Other studies focus on active engagement in political and civic organizations in multiple nation states. For example, Guarnizo and colleagues (2003: 1223) distinguish between transnational electoral and nonelectoral participation. The former term is operationalized by membership in a home country political party, monetary contributions to these parties, and participation in home country electoral campaigns and rallies. In contrast, nonelectoral participation refers to membership in civic hometown associations, the provision of money for home country community projects, and membership in charity organizations that engage in the country of origin (Guarnizo et al. 2003: 1227). The authors define transmigrants as a "new class of immigrants, economic entrepreneurs or political activists who conduct cross-border activities on a *regular* basis" (Guarnizo et al. 2003: 1213, emphasis in original). All items are surveyed on three-point scales with the answer categories: never, occasionally, and regularly. Their data comprise immigrants from Colombia, El Salvador and the Dominican Republic who reside in the U.S. In multivariate analyses the authors apply negative binomial regression models on these indicators of transnational political activities. In this regard, the dependent variable counts the number of regularly conducted activities. The findings indicate that high human capital and larger social networks increase political transnationalism. In addition, age is related to transnational activities in a reverse U-shape functional form. Transnationalism increases up to a certain age and then continuously decreases in old age. Finally, the number of years of residence in the US positively influences immigrants' transnational participation. Further research studied transnational linkages of Chinese citizens via cyber-space. Zhang and Nyíri (2014) coined the term "netizens" for Chinese Internet users, who are spread worldwide and engage in political campaigning and support for China. Through shared interests, these netizens constitute a transnational space that spans China and countries such as Australia, France, Germany, and the US. The authors present ample examples of cooperation between mainland and overseas Chinese, such as in criticizing European one-sided media coverage on the Tibetan Uprising Day (Zhang/Nyíri 2014: 117f.). These transnational netizens distinguish themselves from earlier generations of citizens as they "actively seek information from various sources" and highly value "independent thinking and creative self-expression"

(Zhang/Nyíri 2014: 126f.). In contrast, Boccagni (2011) focused on the attempts of the Ecuadorian government in fostering transnational activities of Ecuadorian immigrants. Most notably, the government tries to "enhance channels for migrants' savings and, potentially, investments back home" (Boccagni 2011: 321). Thus the acknowledgement of a political transnational space may perpetuate and fortify economic transnational activities. The potentials of mobilizing ethnic communities worldwide have been recognized by political leaders as well. As a result, politicians of sending countries host electoral events in countries of arrival, while at the same time leaders of the host countries try to activate the potential constituency for elections on lower – such as local – levels. For example, the political representation of the Salvadoran diaspora is reflected in its denotation as 'Departamento 15' besides the fourteen departments of El Salvador itself (Rodríguez 2005). The presented studies indicate that political transnationalism may best be surveyed by participation in political and civic organizations and events that span international borders. However, several studies delimit the scope of the phenomenon to ideational interactions between mainland and diaspora citizens. In order to study political transnationalism in a strict sense, active individual engagement across international borders represents a more reliable indicator.

3 Two distinct strategies of studying transnational activities

The literature review exposed that transnationalism refers to very diverse aspects of individuals' lives. Note that the four chosen fields represent an arbitrary (yet necessary) choice. Thus, by including even more areas, the complexity of research on transnationalism would have increased significantly. However, the presented studies on economic, cultural and religious, social, and political transnational activities featured two distinct characteristics in their operational definitions of transnationalism: First, transnational activities of interest have to be conducted on a regular schedule. Remitting money once or travelling to a country twice does not establish a transnational phenomenon. Second, transnationalism is regarded as an enduring phenomenon. Therefore, activities associated with it should not gradually vanish in the course of time. The exact period of time remains unspecified, yet it may be argued that transnational lifestyles establish in a lifelong manner, thus covering the whole adulthood of individuals. Hence, *regular* and *persistent* cross-border activities (of any kind) are considered the *core* of transnationalism, connecting most of the different arenas of research on this issue (Portes et al. 1999: 219). However, as Waldinger and Fitzgerald (2004: 1178) pointed out, this definition "makes freedom of movement the point of departure, as if this were not a world divided by states". This assumption is inherently problematic. For example, European immigrants are considerably less restricted in travelling within Europe than third-country members. Thus empirical studies need to account for these restrictions and cover irregular and illegal migration more reliably.

The presented studies, however, diverged significantly with regard to the approaches of researching transnationalism. Two distinct research strategies can be identified: a *focused* and a *comprehensive* strategy. As the literature review has shown, transnational activities relate to a great diversity of behaviors. Therefore, researchers that apply a *focused* strategy delimit their analyses to distinct transnational activities. This is also reflected in the chosen wording, relating to distinct dimensions rather than to transnationalism in general, such as transnational activism (Agarwala 2012; Binnie & Klesse 2013), transnational entrepreneurship (Bagwell 2015; Portes et al. 2002), and transnational families (Lourenço/Cachado 2012; Nguyen-Akbar 2014; Schans 2009). Focused studies facilitate in-depth understanding of immigrants' engagement in certain transnational behaviors. In addition, they avoid overcomplicating issues by restricting their research to distinct areas of transnationalism. Yet, little is known about the interrelation of different transnational dimensions. As *focused* studies, by definition, are restricted to certain areas of transnational behaviors, they do not permit insight into the overall interconnections of such. Thus, *comprehensive* studies are needed. These conjointly cover different areas of transnational activities and aim at either revealing their interrelations or at formulating general statements about transnationalism. However, *comprehensive* studies are systematically underrepresented in research on transnational activities. Among the presented studies, few tried to present a holistic picture of transnationalism (see Mau et al. 2008; Snel et al. 2006). Consistently, "neither transnational*ism* as a condition of being, nor *transmigrants*, as a distinctive class of people, is commonly found" (Waldinger 2008: 3, emphasis in original). According to a strict perspective in favor of focused research, studies on the overall interlinkages of transnational activities are neither necessary nor meaningful. This contribution, however, disagrees with this view for two reasons.

First, most empirical research is based upon restricted samples, such as Latin American immigrants (Waldinger 2008)[3] or former guest workers (Constant/Zimmermann 2012). Thus research on other groups or national contexts may end up with considerably diverging insights. Additionally, at least some, if not all, transnational activities may relate to each other. For example, existing research could

---

3   Immigrants from Mexico, Cuba, Colombia, El Salvador, and the Dominican Republic residing in the U.S. constitute approximately 80 % of Waldinger's (2008) sample.

show that political and social-cultural activities in the country of origin predict identification with compatriots (Snel et al. 2006). Thus, political and cultural transnationalism seem to be positively related to each other. In contrast, professional economic activities in the home country do not influence immigrants' identities (Snel et al. 2006: 298). Moreover, empirical research on the European Union seems promising. Existing research was able to substantiate that due to free movement of EU nationals, these are more mobile than immigrants, which face more rigid restrictions in crossing borders (Constant/Zimmermann 2012). Transnational behaviors of any kind are therefore more prevalent among Europeans within Europe than among third country members.

Second, it seems reasonable to separate bodily geographic from other forms of transnational behaviors. In this regard, empirical and theoretical research needs to identify the common causes underlying transnational activities. Despite the huge stock of empirical studies, sociologists know astonishingly little about the causal determinants of transnational engagement. Commonly family members in the home country, high educational levels, and sufficient financial resources are utilized in order to explain behaviors that span borders, yet the underlying causal mechanisms need elaboration. Their identification should facilitate sounder understanding of transnational activities. In this regard, besides more rigorous empirical studies, theoretical research is needed as well.

For these reasons a more holistic approach to research on immigrant transnationalism constitutes an auspicious strategy. Particularly, empirical studies should utilize more sophisticated statistical tools, such as latent structure modelling, to establish common ground of transnational activities. In this regard, cluster analysis, confirmatory factor analysis, latent class analysis, structural equation modelling, and factor mixture analyses could strongly enrich the research agenda (Clark et al. 2013). These models allow the identifying and testing of latent structures underlying distinct observable items. The huge advantage of these models comes from their capability in identifying common and unobservable factors, which may influence various observable indicator variables. Thus, by utilizing these models, future studies may include differing transnational activities, for example social ties, return visits, identities and alike, and investigate to what extent these are determined by a common latent predisposition (such as transnationalism). Therefore, latent structure modelling constitutes a promising set of techniques, which have not yet been utilized in research on transnationalism. Instead, most studies arbitrarily select a distinct transnational behavior and regress it on a set of predictor variables. However, as theoretically derived knowledge on the predictors of transnational activities is scarce, this approach is problematic. Cross-sectional regression analysis yields biased results when relevant predictor-variables are omitted. When omitted variables correlate with the observed variables of a regression model – particularly with the dependent variable – unobserved heterogeneity poses a serious threat to the reliability of the obtained results. Hence, existing findings are not overwhelmingly trustworthy with regard to the inference of causal effects. In order to tackle this ambiguity, future research needs to engage in the identification of a coherent set of predictors of transnational behaviors. Furthermore, empirical studies need to make use of the advantages of longitudinal data analysis. In order to infer causal effects these are superior to cross-sectional methods which are still most commonly applied in the study of transnational activities (Guarnizo et al. 2003; Portes et al. 2002; Waldinger 2008).

Additionally, as regularity and persistence constitute the common ground of diverse transnational activities, future research could aim at these two characteristics for empirically assessing transnationalism. In this regard, however, studies would have to distinguish between bodily geographic and ideational activities. The term *ideational* refers to behaviors, which may be conducted without physically crossing borders, such as watching foreign television or communicating to residents of foreign countries via social media. Therefore, four types of activities may be distinguished, which future research needs to separately investigate. Table 1 displays the four types.

Table 1 Types of transnational activities

	Regular and persistent	Non-regular and/or non-persistent
Bodily geographic	Strict	Recreational
Ideational	Symbolic	Latent

In line with existing research, this presented typology applies a *strict* understanding of transnational activities, whenever an individual engages in activities which are conducted regularly and persistently in a bodily geographic manner across nation states. For example, an immigrant who regularly visits another country for business-related reasons represents the type of *strict* transnational activities. In another example, an Italian immigrant, who lives in Greece and regularly travels to Denmark in order to meet business clients, fits in this category as well. In contrast, *symbolic* transnational activities are restricted to the ideational level. However, individuals conduct *symbolic* actions regularly and persistently. As these actions can be conducted without crossing a border, they usually involve lower costs than *strict* transnational engagement. Identifying in a hybrid manner and with consumption of cultural commodities, such as arts and cuisine, which are directed towards multiple nation states belongs in this category. As such, a Dutch immigrant in Poland, who persistently identifies as Dutch-Polish and who regularly watches Dutch and Polish TV programs, engages in *symbolic* transnational activities. *Recreational* transnational engagement refers to bodily geographic activities, which individuals conduct either non-regularly or non-persistently or both. A Spanish immigrant who lives in France and who occasionally visits his family in the home country engages in a *recreational* transnational activity. The last type of activities refers to non-regular and/or non-persistent ideational behaviors. This type may be labeled as *latent* transnational activities. Individuals engaging in these kinds of behaviors conduct low-cost, cross-border activities. Among others, informing oneself about a specific event in the home country represents a *latent* transnational behavior. A Turkish immigrant living in Belgium who does not follow Turkish media, but keeps particularly informed about the Soma mine disaster in 2014, engages in a *latent* transnational activity. *Latent* transnational activities presuppose the lowest level of engagement. However, activities that belong to this category may constitute a starting point for other, more demanding types of conduct.

4 Conclusion

This contribution reviewed parts of the empirical literature on transnational activities. It did so with a specific focus on the measurement of transnationalism. Although it provided no exhaustive review, the contribution highlighted the great diversity of areas, phenomena, and variables, which are researched under the term transnational activities. According to the presented studies, this contribution subsequently distinguished two research strategies: a *focused* and a *comprehensive* strategy. As the majority of studies obey a focused approach, this contribution argued in favor of future engagement in comprehensive research projects. Particularly, the interrelations of different transnational areas constitute considerable blind spots. Thus, despite their obvious problems, *comprehensive* studies are needed in order to gain more holistic insights into transnational behaviors.

Furthermore, a typology of four kinds of transnational behaviors was proposed. Future research may utilize this typology and extend it. However, the corresponding studies need to specify how regularity and persistence of activities would be assessed. Following that, researchers need to identify the causal predictors of the distinct cross-border behaviors. These will most likely differ across the four presented types. The conceptual distinction between different types of activities helps disentangling confounding effects and variables. Particularly, it provides researchers with a heuristic technique to identify the specific kind of transnational behavior one aims to study. However, the presented typology has the following limitations. First and foremost, the defining characteristics of regularity and persistence need further elaboration. No particular timing has been proposed that defines a regular or persistent activity. Specifically, the timing may differ according to the particular activity of interest. For example, traveling to another country once a year may constitute a regular schedule, while reading a foreign newspaper once a year may not. Accordingly, the presented types can only be distinguished as long as agreement on regularity and persistence is achieved. For example, a Russian immigrant in Finland who travels to Russia once in ten years may be classified as *recreational* transnational. However, how many visits are necessary for the exact same individual in order to engage in a *strict* transnational activity? Both one and five visits in ten years may represent a coherent answer to this question. Thus, the limits of every category and type need to be adjusted according to the specific research question. However, the presented typology may provide guidance in this process. Furthermore, future studies need to intensify efforts to establish a common inventory of cross-border activities referring to the different types of activities. Subsequently, the improved and unified measurements would contribute to cumulative research that may unify the existing scattered insights into transnational activities. A better understanding not only serves social sciences, but also informs political and societal stakeholders about what measures need to be taken to improve societal service and immigrants' integration. In this regard, the presented typology specifies at least four distinct target populations that need to be approached separately.

References

Agarwala, R. (2012). The State and Labor in Transnational Activism: The Case of India. Journal of Industrial Relations 54(4), pp. 443–458.

Alcántara, C., Molina, K. M. & Kawachi, I. (2015). Transnational, Social, and Neighborhood Ties and Smoking Among Latino Immigrants: Does Gender Matter? American Journal of Public Health 105(4), pp. 741–749.

Bagwell, S. (2015). Transnational Entrepreneurship amongst Vietnamese Businesses in London. Journal of Ethnic and Migration Studies 41(2), pp. 329–349.

Binnie, J. & Klesse, C. (2013). 'Like a Bomb in the Gasoline Station': East–West Migration and Transnational Activism around Lesbian, Gay, Bisexual, Transgender and Queer Politics in Poland. Journal of Ethnic and Migration Studies 39(7), pp. 1107–1124.

Boccagni, P. (2011). Migrants' social protection as a transnational process: public policies and emigrant initiative in the case of Ecuador. International Journal of Social Welfare 20(3), pp. 318–325.

Boccagni, P. (2012). Rethinking transnational studies: Transnational ties and the transnationalism of everyday life. European Journal of Social Theory 15(1), pp. 117–132.

Burrell, J. L. (2005). Migration and the Transnationalization of Fiesta Customs in Todos Santos Cuchumatan, Guatemala. Latin American Perspectives 32(5), pp. 12–32.

Clark, S. L. et al. (2013). Models and Strategies for Factor Mixture Analysis: An Example Concerning the Structure Underlying Psychological Disorders. Structural Equation Modeling: A Multidisciplinary Journal 20(4), pp. 681-703.

Constant, A. F. & Zimmermann, K. F. (2012). The Dynamics of Repeat Migration: A Markov Chain Analysis. International Migration Review 46(2), pp. 362–388.

Domínguez, S. & Lubitow, A. (2008). Transnational Ties, Poverty, and Identity: Latin American Immigrant Women in Public Housing. Family Relations 57(4), pp. 419–430.

Erdal, M.B. (2013). Migrant Transnationalism and Multi-Layered Integration: Norwegian-Pakistani Migrants' Own Reflections. Journal of Ethnic and Migration Studies 39(6), pp. 983–999.

Erkkilä, T. (2014). Global University Rankings, Transnational Policy Discourse and Higher Education in Europe. European Journal of Education 49(1), pp. 91–101.

Gershon, A. A. & Pantoja, A. D. (2014). Pessimists, Optimists, and Skeptics: The Consequences of Transnational Ties for Latino Immigrant Naturalization. Social Science Quarterly 95(2), 328–342.

Glick Schiller, N., Basch, L. & Szanton Blanc, C. (1995). From Immigrant to Transmigrant: Theorizing Transnational Migration. Anthropological Quarterly 68(1), pp. 48–63.

Glick Schiller, N. & Fouron, G. E. (1999). Terrains of blood and nation: Haitian transnational social fields. Ethnic and Racial Studies 22(2), pp. 340–366.

Guarnizo, L. E. (1994). Los Dominicanyorks: The Making of a Binational Society. The ANNALS of the American Academy of Political and Social Science 533(1), pp. 70–86.

Guarnizo, L. E. (2003). The Economics of Transnational Living. International Migration Review 37(3), 666–699.

Guarnizo, L. E., Portes, Alejandro & Haller, William (2003). Assimilation and Transnationalism: Determinants of Transnational Political Action among Contemporary Migrants. American Journal of Sociology 108(6), pp. 1211–1248.

Hadden, J. (2014). Explaining Variation in Transnational Climate Change Activism: The Role of Inter-Movement Spillover. Global Environmental Politics 14(2), pp. 7–25.

Hall, S. (1990). Cultural Identity and Diaspora, in Rutherford, Jonathan (ed.): Identity: Community, culture, difference. London: Lawrence & Wishart, pp. 222–237.

Holmes, P. (2014). The Politics of Law and the Laws of Politics: The Political Paradoxes of Transnational Constitutionalism. Indiana Journal of Global Legal Studies 21(2), pp. 553–583.

Holst, E., Schäfer, A. & Schrooten, M. (2010). Gender, Transnational Networks and Remittances: Evidence from Germany. SOEPpapers on Multidisciplinary Panel Data Research (296), pp. 1–25.

Hughes, M. M., Krook, M. L. & Paxton, P. (2015). Transnational Women's Activism and the Global Diffusion of Gender Quotas. International Studies Quarterly 59(2), pp. 357–372.

Itzigsohn, J. & Saucedo, S. G. (2002). Immigrant Incorporation and Sociocultural Transnationalism. International Migration Review 36(3), pp. 766–798.

Jacobson, J. (1997). Religion and ethnicity: Dual and alternative sources of identity among young British Pakistanis. Ethnic and Racial Studies 20(2), pp. 238–256.

Jasiewicz, J. (2012). Transnational ties and ethnic activism: The case of Poland. International Sociology 27(3), 403–421.
Joseph, R. (2010). Housing wealth leakage, return migration and transnational housing markets: Experiences of UK based African Caribbean home owners, in Doling, J., Elsinga, Marja & Ronald, Richard (ed.): Home ownership: Getting in, getting from, getting out. Part III. Amsterdam, the Netherlands: IOS Press. (Housing and urban policy studies, 34), pp. 79–95.
Kraemer, J. (2014). Friend or Freund: Social Media and Transnational Connections in Berlin. Human–Computer Interaction 29(1), pp. 53–77.
Kuuire, V. Z., et al. (2015). Impact of Remittance Behaviour on Immigrant Homeownership Trajectories: An Analysis of the Longitudinal Survey of Immigrants in Canada from 2001 to 2005. Social Indicators Research.
Lazear, E. P. (1999). Culture and Language. Journal of Political Economy 107(6), pp. 95–126.
Levitt, P. & Jaworsky, B. N. (2007). Transnational Migration Studies: Past Developments and Future Trends. Annu. Rev. Sociol. 33(1), pp. 129–156.
Ley, D. (2013). Does Transnationalism Trump Immigrant Integration? Evidence from Canada's Links with East Asia. Journal of Ethnic and Migration Studies 39(6), pp. 921–938.
Lourenço, I. & Cachado, R. (2012). Hindu transnational families: transformation and continuity in diaspora families. Journal of Comparative Family Studies 43(1), pp. 53–70.
Marcelli, E. A. & Lowell, B. L. (2005). Transnational Twist: Pecuniary Remittances and the Socioeconomic Integration of Authorized and Unauthorized Mexican Immigrants in Los Angeles County. International Migration Review 39(1), pp. 69–102.
Mau, S., Mewes, J. & Zimmermann, A. (2008). Cosmopolitan attitudes through transnational social practices? Global Networks 8(1), pp. 1–24.
Mazzucato, V. (2005). Ghanaian migrants' double engagement: A transnational view of development and integration policies. Global Migration Perspectives 48, pp. 1–17.
Mazzucato, V. (2008). Simultaneity and networks in transnational migration: lessons learned from a simultaneous matched sample methodology, in DeWind, Josh & Holdaway, Jennifer (ed.) Migration and development within and across borders: Research and policy perspectives on internal and international migration. Geneva, Switzerland, New York: International Organization for Migration; Social Science Research Council, pp. 69–100.
Mazzucato, V. (2010). Reverse remittances in the migration-development nexus: two-way flows between Ghana and the Netherlands. Population, Space and Place 17, pp. 454–468.
Nagel, A.K. (2010). Vom Paradigma zum Pragma: Religion und Migration in relationaler Perspektive. Sociologia Internationalis 48(2), pp. 221–246.
Nagel, A.K. (2014). Religiöse Netzwerke: Die zivilgesellschaftlichen Potentiale religiöser Migrantengemeinden, in Nagel, Alexander-Kenneth (ed.) Religiöse Netzwerke: Die zivilgesellschaftlichen Potentiale religiöser Migrantengemeinden. Bielefeld: transcript. (Kultur und soziale Praxis), pp. 11–36.
Nguyen-Akbar, M. (2014). The Tensions of Diasporic 'Return' Migration: How Class and Money Create Distance in the Vietnamese Transnational Family. Journal of Contemporary Ethnography 43(2), pp. 176–201.
Niederhafner, S. (2013). Comparing functions of transnational city networks in Europe and Asia. Asia Europe Journal 11(4), pp. 377–396.

Olwig, K. F. (2003). "Transnational" Socio-Cultural Systems and Ethnographic Research: Views from an Extended Field Site. International Migration Review 37(3), pp. 787–811.

Østergaard-N., Eva (2011). Codevelopment and citizenship: the nexus between policies on local migrant incorporation and migrant transnational practices in Spain. Ethnic and Racial Studies 34(1), pp. 20–39.

Peter, K. B. (2010). Transnational Family Ties, Remittance Motives, and Social Death among Congolese Migrants: A Socio-Anthropological Analysis. Comparative Family Studies 41(2), pp. 225–243.

Portes, A., Guarnizo, L. E. & Landolt, P. (1999). The study of transnationalism: pitfalls and promise of an emergent research field. Ethnic and Racial Studies 22(2), pp. 217–237.

Portes, A., Haller, W. & Guarnizo, L. E. (2002). Transnational Entrepreneurs: An alternative form of immigrant economic adaption. American Sociological Review 67(2), pp. 278–298.

Portes, A. & Hao, L. (1998). E Pluribus Unum: Bilingualism and Loss of Language in the Second Generation. Sociology of Education 71(4), pp. 269–294.

Portes, A. & Schauffler, R. (1994). Language and the Second Generation: Bilingualism Yesterday and Today. International Migration Review 28(4), pp. 640–661.

Rodríguez, A. P. (2005). "Departamento 15": Cultural Narratives of Salvadoran Transnational Migration. Latino Studies 3(1), pp. 19–41.

Schans, D. (2009). Transnational family ties of immigrants in the Netherlands. Ethnic and Racial Studies 32(7), pp. 1164–1182.

Schapiro, N. et al. (2013) Separation and reunification: the experiences of adolescents living in transnational families. Current problems in pediatric and adolescent health care 43(3), pp. 48–68.

Siegel, M. & Lücke, M. (2013). Migrant transnationalism and the choice of transfer channels for remittances: the case of Moldova. Global Networks 13(1), pp. 120–141.

Snel, E., Engbersen, G. & Leerkes, A. (2006). Transnational involvement and social integration. Global Networks 6(3), pp. 285–308.

Tsuda, T. (2012). Whatever Happened to Simultaneity? Transnational Migration Theory and Dual Engagement in Sending and Receiving Countries. Journal of Ethnic and Migration Studies 38(4), pp. 631–649.

Vathi, Z. (2013). Transnational Orientation, Cosmopolitanism and Integration among Albanian-Origin Teenagers in Tuscany. Journal of Ethnic and Migration Studies 39(6), pp. 903–919.

Vertovec, S. (1999). Conceiving and researching transnationalism. Ethnic and Racial Studies 22(2), pp. 447–462.

Vono-de-Vilhena, D. & Bayona-Carrasco, J. (2012). Transition towards homeownership among foreign-born immigrants in Spain from a life-course approach. Population, Space and Place 18(1), pp. 100–115.

Waldinger, R. (2008). Between "Here" and "There": Immigrant Cross-Border Activities and Loyalties. International Migration Review 42(1), pp. 3–29.

Waldinger, R. & Fitzgerald, D. (2004). Transnationalism in Question. American Journal of Sociology 109(5), pp. 1177–1195.

Wang, Q. & Liu, C. Y. (2015). Transnational activities of immigrant-owned firms and their performances in the USA. Small Business Economics 44(2), pp. 345–359.

Weber, M. (2006). Wirtschaft und Gesellschaft. Paderborn: Voltmedia.

Yinger, M. (1976). Ethnicity in Complex Societies: Structural, Cultural, and Characterological Factors, in Coser, Lewis A. & Larsen, Otto N. (ed.) *The uses of controversy in sociology*. New York, NY: The Free Press, pp. 197–218.

Spatial Transnationalism: An analytical approach[1]

Sebastian Kurtenbach

1 Introduction

With the increase in intra-European mobility, formal nation-determined boundaries are in effect being replaced by boundaries determined by the actions of individuals. It has become normal for people who live in different European countries, or commute be-tween them, not to regard a national boundary as a means of defining or constraining them. Europeanization has an impact not only on nations' economics, but also on individuals' everyday lives in Euro-pean countries. Greater mobility and more possibilities for work, as well as economic differences between the member states of the Eu-ropean Union, have led to a new diversity of family types. These family structures, which include the transnational family, are the fo-cus of other contributions to this book. The goal of this chapter is to explore and explain the link between neighborhoods and transnation-alism with respect to neighborhoods' function as sending or receiv-ing places.

This contribution, based on Glick Schiller's (2012) claim that cities are important nodes of transnationalism, addresses the gap between the locality, or neighborhood, and the transnational actions of its res-idents. The chapter elaborates and substantiates spatial concepts in the discussion about transnationalism in order to develop an ap-proach for further empirical research. Of central interest are mi-gra-tion movements under conditions of poverty. The main question ad-dressed is: What characteristics do transnational neighborhoods have?

---

[1] I like to thank Prof. Dr. Martina Löw and Dr. Karol Kurnicki for their comments which helped to improve the contribution and give an outlook on further research.

In the first part of the chapter, the state of research concerning trans-national social spaces is discussed. In the second part, the attributes of transnational neighborhoods are illustrated and analyzed through a comparison of two types of transnational neighborhood. Finally, conclusions are drawn in answer to the main question, and a pro-gram for further research is outlined.

2 Transnationalism and transnational social spaces

Research on transnational social spaces forms part of the greater dis-cussion about transnationalism itself. In the body of urban sociologi-cal literature, the topic of transnationalism is largely absent. To con-nect transnationalism with social space, a brief summary of the na-ture and meaning of transnationalism is given. Afterwards, the state of research concerning transnational social spaces is discussed.

2.1 Transnationalism

Transnationalism is a relatively new concept in the research of migra-tion and can be understood as the social processes migrants use to link the social spaces of their countries of origin and settlement, in-dependent of the geographical distance between them (Glick Schiller et al. 1992: 1). It is not the intention here to give an overview of the history of the concept, which has already been done by Waldinger (2013) and Dunn (2005). Transnationalism is not a new pheno-menon, but rather a new perspective on migration: "back-and-forth movements by immigrants have always existed" (Portes et al. 1999: 217). In the past, regular exchanges between migrants and their rela-tives and other contacts at their place of origin were usual, but not as easily conducted as they are nowadays. It may be helpful to distin-guish between different types of migrants in order to make this new perspective on mi-gration clear. A useful typology of migrants, which is shown in Figure 1, has been developed by Pries (2001b: 55).

The first type, emigrant/immigrant, is the classical migrant, who moves from one nation to another. The destination country is consid-ered the new home country. The stay in the destination region is ex-pected to be permanent. In contrast, the second type, the return mi-grant, stays for a relatively short time in the destination country, of-ten only for as long as there is available work. In Germany, for ex-ample, guest workers were considered return migrants. Diaspora migrants constitute the third type of migrant. The migrants' reasons for staying abroad may be that there is political discrimination in their country of origin or there may be better job opportunities in the des-tination country. Such migrants are strongly oriented towards their place of origin and may engage in political activism. Some African minorities in Europe constitute examples of this type of migrant. Transmigrants constitute the fourth type of migrant. The characteris-tic feature of this group is that its members commute between two or more countries. Transmigrants' identities are not primarily bound to a single nation and the lengths of their stays vary considerably. The availability of technologies, such as Skype or mobile phones with low user costs for international communication, can facilitate the in-cidence of transnational workers.

	Relation to region of origin	Relation to region of arrival	Main impulse for moving	Time horizon of migration
Emigrant/ immigrant	Roots, ancestry, departure, farewell	Integration, New homeland	Economic, Sociocultural	Long-term, Unlimited
Return migrant	Continuous point of life reference	Maintain difference to host country	Economic, Political	Short-term, Limited
Diaspora migrant	(At least symbolic) Reference to the motherland	Maintain difference, Space of suffering or of mission	Religious, Political, Organizational	Medium-term, Limited
Trans-migrant	Ambiguous Mixture	Ambiguous Mixture	Economic, Organizational	Not determined, Sequential

Figure 1 Different types of migrants

Despite the clear distinctions between the different types of migra-tion, defining transnationalism poses a serious challenge. The re-search literature still lacks an unambiguous definition of the concept (Gowricharn 2009: 1621; Riedel 2016). The most important identifi-ers of transnationalism are that migrants commute between two or more countries (Pries 2004; Schimmer and van Tubergen 2014; Schunck 2011); that they communicate with people in different na-tions (Benítez 2012; Dekker 2015; Mamhud 2014; Riain 2015); and that they send goods or money to relatives who remain in the mi-grants' places of origin (Fokkema 2013; Pfau and Giang 2009). Fur-thermore, transnationals are sometimes involved in political initia-tives in other countries (Faist 2000; Morales and Pilati 2014; Tintori 2011) and create complex identities (Haller Landolt 2005; Park 2007). The preceding characteristics are by no means exhaustive. However, a key component of transnationalism is that the migrant is linked to a context, such as a neighborhood, in another nation.

Two main positions on what factors produce transnationalism are evident in the literature, which gives rise to two views of its creation.

- As a process from above: Transnationalism is created through developments at the macro-level, such as social inequality, the state of the global economy, or political issues. The effects of these influences trickle down from the macro-context to have an impact on the individual and make it possible for them to become a transnational as a response.
- As a process from below: Transnationalism is a lifestyle that is created through a combination of necessities and possibilities, such as informal or nontraditional jobs, international remittances, or social connectivity. In this view transnationalism emerges from individual decisions and actions (Guarnizo and Smith 1998).

Because transnationalism is not defined in terms of national borders, the traditional conceptual orientation towards national borders for the study of migration has been criticized for succumbing to methodo-logical nationalism. Critics argue that methodological nationalism contains inbuilt assumptions that bias it towards a context of nationa-lism for framing research, and which in turn render it unsuitable for any meaningful analysis of transnationalism. For the transnational, social relationships are not limited by national borders, and new kinds of social boundaries are created as a transnational's social net-works are spread over different countries (Wimmer and Glick Schil-ler 2002). To avoid the criticisms of methodological nationalism, transnational studies are frequently conducted using social network analysis as a methodological framework (Bernadi 2011; Ives et al. 2014; Wijers 2014).

In short, new methodological strategies are called for to study trans-nationalism. "The need to develop an adequate and satisfactory methodology for transnational research has not only to be identified but also substantiated" (Pries and Seeliger 2012: 235). The response to such a demand is given by examples of alternative methodologies that employ a more relational view (Amelina and Faist 2012). In con-trast, there are still many publications that do not conform to this perspective, such as the Mexican Migration Project (2016), which utilizes quantitative surveys that assume Mexico to be the home of migrants who reside full time in the United States.

Transnationalism is not only a new perspective on migration, it is also a new consideration in the discussion about migrant integration. A transnational's biographical project requires a narrative that in-cludes different national identities, common role models, and refer-ence to places. Thus neighborhoods, as places of migration, become the primary sites of interest in a transnational's life, a life determined by non-traditional contexts and the temporality of a stay.

2.2 Transnational social spaces

Transnationalism is a key concept in understanding new boundaries and the links between people in different locations, independent of national borders. Since the so-called "spatial turn," it is accepted that place has a particular social meaning. Place matters for transnational-ism and is discussed as transnational social spaces (Glick Schiller 2012). Spaces are more than geographical units; they are social units as well. "We understand transnational spaces as configurations of social practices, artifacts and symbol systems that span different ge-ographic spaces in at least two nation-states without constituting a new 'deterritorialized' nation-state or being the prolongation of one of these states" (Pries 2001: 18). In this perspective, the social struc-ture of a neighborhood, the opportunities (through artifacts) that it provides, and the symbols it contains, such as a shared language, construct an accessible social space.

Faist (1998) points out that transnational social spaces develop in two steps. "In a first phase they are a by-product of international migration" (Faist 1998: 215) and are established through migrants commuting between places (there may be more than two places). In this stage, migrant knowledge about the local places is collected, so-cial networks are created, and members of the community settle down. The second phase of development is marked by the growth of a transnational lifestyle within the space. Subsequently, Faist argues that "transnational social spaces are combinations of social and symbolic ties, positions in networks and organizations, and networks of organizations" (Faist 1998: 216). Such networks, which span individual organizations, need transnational nodes, similar to those that develop in the second stage of the creation of transnational social spaces.

It is assumed that a neighborhood becomes transnational if a relative-ly high proportion of the local population is bonded in transnational networks. These different transnational spaces can be connected through a network of networks, a transnational social field (Levitt and Glick Schiller 2004). All in all, transnational social spaces com-bine the local perspective on opportunities and symbols with the transnational biographies of a part of the local community.

3 Transnationalism and the city: The local-global

Transnational social spaces are useful because they provide a trans-national perspective to the initial activity of identifying links between neighborhoods as local units. Beginning with the definition of trans-national social spaces as "pluri-local frames of reference which struc-ture every practice, social position, biographical employment pro-jects, and human identities, and simultaneously exist above and be-yond the social context of national societies" (Pries 2001a: 23), transnationalism must be analyzed at the local level, the neighbor-hood. This consideration goes back to Burgess's model of the struc-ture of the city, shown in Figure 2.

I   Loop
II   Zone in Transition
III Zone of Working-Men's Homes
IV   Residential Zone
V   Commuters Zone

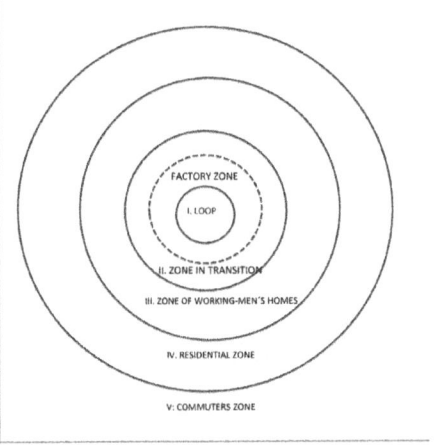

Figure 2 Theory of urban structure
Source: Burgess 1984 | 1925: 51

Burgess argues that a high proportion of first-generation migrants moved into Zone II, the zone in transition, that was located next to the central business district. In this zone, in segregated communities, first-generation migrants often lived next to other migrants from the same nation. In their classical study of the Polish community in Chi-cago in the early twentieth century, Thomas and Znaniecki (1996/1918) were able to show that migrants were highly connected to their place of origin. At that time, letters and newspapers were the common means of communication. The small-scale concentrations of migrants resulting from segregation, and individuals' transnational involvement through communication, suggest that spatial transna-tionalism was established in those days as well.

Glick Schiller (2012: 12) argues that cities have always been places where migrants lived in transnational networks. However, the link between transnationality and urban studies is often overlooked. "This classic scholarship of the city generally failed to address the histori-cal transborder social process that has given rise to urban life since the emergence of cities" (Glick Schiller 2012: 26). Simmel (2006/1903) also argued that cities are places where foreign impres-sions can be experienced. An explanation of the exchanges of peo-ple, ideas, and goods between places is therefore needed. Faist (1998: 217) describes the connections underlying transnationalism as a triadic relationship between the host state, the sending state, and the minority group. These connections are bound to the minority migrant groups, and these groups often live in segregated neighborhoods. "Cities are not themselves homogenous places. Neighborhood dif-ferences highlight, reflect and reproduce the uneven transnational processes of place-making within which cities are constantly rebuilt and reimagined" (Glick Schiller 2012: 29). This view of place-making as a transnational process is supported by a consideration of the effects of diasporas, on the one hand, and classical migration-flows, on the other.

In considering the neighborhood as a unit of analysis of the process of transnationalism, influences from above and below – which may inform social practices, artifacts, and symbols (Pries 2001a: 22) – are emphasized. However, the neighborhood perspective excludes the motives for migration, especially under conditions of poverty, such as hope for a better life. But because individuals create their own spaces and do not orient their actions towards national borders, dif-ferent types of transnational social spaces can be distinguished.

A simple and useful distinction can be made regarding places of origin and destination, which can be subnational (Faist 1998) or na-tional (Waldinger 2013). It is assumed that places of origin and des-tination become transnational through the circulation of people, goods, and ideas (Faist 1998: 220), each having a different profile. The main difference lies in the social pressures to migrate (the push factor) and the attractions of the receiving context (the pull factor). For people, these places of origin and destination become sending and receiving places. But there are also reverse flows of money, goods, and knowledge in exchange for individuals' time and work. In the remainder of this chapter, these two types of transnational neighborhoods – sending places and receiving places – will be dis-cussed in order to identify their similarities and differences.

3.1 Sending places

Neighborhoods within sending countries are affected by transnation-al linkages. They are influenced by such different macro-factors as demographic change, seg-regation, or poverty. The focus in this sec-tion is on the creation of spatial transnationalism due to conditions of poverty and the perceived absence of a better future in the sending place. Transnational spaces are created because individuals' needs, such as work, cannot be satisfied in the wider context of the home nation-state. In addition, the social boundaries of everyday life, such as social exclusion, increase the pressure on individuals to migrate.

Neighborhoods constitute the specific spatial contexts of a society. At the small-scale level, there are five characteristics of potentially transnational neighborhoods that are sending places. They are de-scribed in the rest of this section.

First, segregation, as a consequence of social inequality within the nation-state, is one factor in creating the conditions that lead to spatial transnationalism. Segre-gation results in distinct places that are social-ly homogeneous. Under conditions of poverty, for example, segre-gated places may be perceived as exclusion areas in which the inhab-itants feel especially discriminated against (Wacquant 2007).

A second characteristic of sending places is a low level of fluctuation in the neighborhood, because of such things as poor opportunities for work or lack of alternative habitations in the local housing mar-ket. This characteristic may result from discrimination or the imprac-ticality of moving to a more expensive part of the city. A low level of fluctuation reveals that the social structure of the neighbor-hood is immobile. The possibility of moving into another neighborhood within the same city is not open to residents of these poor neighbor-hoods (see, for example, Wacquant 2008).

The third characteristic of sending places is a group with contact to the diaspora abroad. This network marker is required to organize spatial transnationalism and works as a means of limiting the selec-tion of possible destinations. The group can consist of relatives or friends of members of the diaspora. The group members are them-selves members of a transnational community, even if they have nev-er left their hometown, by virtue of their migratory history. Relatives or friends of mem-bers of the diaspora abroad connect transmigrants with members of the diaspora in other countries (Bruneau 2010: 43). The main contribution of the group is to pre-select possible places of destination for transmigrants within the community and to spread often imperfect knowledge about these places.

Fourth, a better future, compared to living abroad, is denied collec-tively. Po-litical or economic factors, as well as the consequences of individual decisions, are among the major reasons that individuals do not view the future optimistically. The stresses caused by spatial dep-rivation and poverty make the individual's decision to leave one's hometown for work, and therefore become a transmigrant, a rational choice. Collectively, the absence of opportunities creates social pressure on those individuals who are eligible for jobs abroad, which increases the likelihood of emigration independent of any particular individual's willingness to migrate (Wacquant 2008).

The fifth characteristic is the availability of transnational opportuni-ties as anchor points for transnationals. Services, such as those for making remittances or for cheap international telephone calls, enable poor people to become transmigrants, although it is sometimes only a temporary part of their biography (Faist 1998: 21). The possibility of being able to receive economic remittances, such as goods and mon-ey (Braham and Boucher 1998; Young 2011), as well as social re-mittances, such as ideas and values (Levitt 2001: 11), is, for transna-tionals, an important feature of sending places. Thus, these services function as transmitters between family members who go abroad and their relatives who stay in their place of origin.

3.2 Places of destination: arrival areas

Transnational places of destination can be characterized by particular conditions. In many places, certain neighborhoods have always been entry ports to societies. In Burgess's model of the city, Zone II, the zone in transition, serves this purpose. In these neighborhoods, re-cent migrants find their first accommodations and jobs while living next to other migrants from the same region of origin. In Germany, some neighborhoods, for example, Nordstadt in Dortmund, became arrival areas for immigrants from Romania and Bulgaria after those two countries joined the European Union in 2007. The newcomers commuted so frequently between Nordstadt and their neighborhood of origin that the latter became colloquially known as Nordstadt.

Like sending places, arrival areas, a term that refers to transnational places of destination such as Nordstadt, exhibit five characteristics. They are described in the rest of this section.

First, segregation and a history of migration in the neighborhood is a marker of arrival areas. Newly arriving migrants are in contact with people from different countries and face few constraints in being assimilated into the neighborhood. Because of continuous in- and out-migration, the composition of the neighborhood is not stable. The local population is experienced in integrating newcomers, partly because a high proportion of them are migrants themselves. Such neighborhoods are often characterized by relatively bad housing conditions and usually have a bad reputation (Slater and Anderson 2001).

High rates of fluctuation constitute the second characteristic of arri-val areas. The high mobility of the residents leads to weak communi-ty between neighbors, and migrants are drawn to people with the same language. Such spatial instability can also limit social support and inhibit community activity within the neighborhood.

Third, the diaspora – originally diasporic migrants who are already settled in the neighborhood – fulfills a function for newcomers. It represents a point of contact between the arrival area and the receiv-ing neighborhood for newcomers, and it is a node in a transnational network. Such nodes are often integrated into transnational opportu-nities, and members of the diaspora may often be shop owners, who will provide information about the society of the arrival area as well as information about jobs for newcomers (Organ 2001).

Fourth, newcomers and transmigrants find employment opportuni-ties in arrival areas. Those jobs are often semi-legal, precarious, and underpaid. They are nevertheless considered an improvement when compared to conditions in the country of origin. After a while, when they have increased their knowledge of the local job market, migrants try to get more formal and better-paid jobs. By integrating into the labor market, the transnational phase of migrancy may end and the individual may become a traditional migrant. Integration establishes inter-ethnic ties, which notably increase the socioeconomic status of the (trans-)migrant (Riedel 2015).

Fifth, transnational opportunities are relatively common in arrival areas. They are similar to those in sending neighborhoods. They meet the needs of transnationals by providing opportunities to remit or receive goods and money, ideas, and values. The opportunities can be both formal and informal. Formal opportunities can be found, for example, in shops or transnational organizations that use multi-language signs to address specific language groups. In contrast, net-works present informal opportunities. Both formal and informal op-portunities are social spaces of orientation for newcomers (Landry and Bourhis 1997).

3.3 Spatial transnationalism

The interplay between local symbols, spatial configuration, and so-cial practices produces transnationalism at the local level. The preced-ing discussion about the spatial characteristics of sending places and arrival areas highlighted the similarities and dissimilarities of transna-tional spaces. The context of origin, the context of destination and the different types of migrants themselves also need to be distinguished (see also Faist 1998: 222). With respect to this differentiation, spatial transnationalism is not wholly independent of either context because, for example, the employment opportunities may not be the same in the two types of transnational neighborhoods.

Existing research does not fully recognize the binding forces of the sending place. At first glance, it does not seem to make sense to commute between a sending neighborhood and an arrival area. Both mobility and remittances are costly, and family members may beco-me alienated from each other. Several explanations for this apparent paradox have been proposed in the literature. Erdal (2012) studied the practices of Pakistanis who worked in the United Kingdom and bought houses in their region of origin, even though they could only return for holidays. They did so for prestige and to maintain the au-tonomy of relatives in the sending place. Barglowski et al. (2015) observe that family relations are a core factor in becoming transnati-onal, for caregiving, for example.

The preceding examples show the unbalanced relationship between the arrival area and the sending place, and how its restrictions are overcome through migration. One neighborhood, the sending place, is characterized by the collective negation of a better future; the other, the receiving place – also segregated – is a symbol of hope and a better life. The specific similarities and dissimilarities between the two places link them together. Table 1 compares the characteristics of sending places and arrival areas.

Table 1 Characteristics of sending places and arrival areas

Sending Place	Arrival Area
Highly segregated	Highly segregated
Low rates of fluctuation	High rates of fluctuation
People with knowledge about possible destinations and connections to the diaspora	(Linguistic) diaspora
Denied the prospect of jobs in the neighborhood	Jobs available for low skilled newcom-ers (semi-legal, precarious, underpaid)
Transnational opportunities	Transnational opportunities

The five pairs of characteristics of the sending and receiving places must all coalesce to ensure the correct identification of a neighbor-hood as transnational. Thus, one condition for considering a neigh-borhood transnational is that both the sending place and the arrival area are segregated neighborhoods. Segregation in the sending place refers to discrimination and exclusion. In the arrival area, segregation serves to protect migrants, permitting them to meet with other migrants and to speak what is, in their destination nation, a foreign lan-guage. A second similarity between sending place and receiving place relates to people who are embedded in a transnational network with migration-related knowledge of the arrival area. In both the re-ceiving and the sending contexts, such people could be relatives or friends of members of the diaspora. Additionally, people who speak the same language as the transmigrant may provide the same services as, and perform similar social functions to, members of the diaspora. Either way, the opportunities provided serve as anchor points in the transnational connection.

The other pairs of characteristics highlight the dissimilarities between the two types of transnational neighborhood. Sending places are very stable neighborhoods with low levels of fluctuation, and arrival areas are unstable and provide a destination for more than one migrant group. However, both are nodes in a network of transnationally linked places and a part of a transnational social space. The ethnic mix in arrival areas is usually extremely diverse (Vertovec 2006), whereas sending places are usually ethnically homogeneous. A pes-simistic perspective on the future and especially the poor job market work together as a push factor in the sending place. In contrast, jobs are available, or there can be at least the hope of finding a job, in the arrival area.

The interactions between the factors described by the five pairs of character-istics produce the specific context, the configuration, and the artifacts of a neighborhood to match the definition of a social space (Pries 2011). Spatial transnationalism is constituted by the relation-ships between several social contexts, such as economic and social remittances. Neighborhoods are defined by the transnational activi-ties of their inhabitants and their specific characteristics, such as the concentration of opportunities.

4 Conclusion

This chapter is intended to elaborate and substantiate spatial ap-proaches to transnationalism, with the goal of providing an adequate basis for further empirical research. Starting with the argument of Glick Schiller (2012), that cities are important nodes of transnational-ism, the chapter shows how the gap between urban studies and transnationalism can be bridged. Building upon Pries (2001) and Faist (1998), characteristics of the city and characteristics of transna-tionalism are linked to identify transnational neighborhoods, through discussions of transnational migrants and transnational social spaces. The chapter shows that on the one hand there are sending places, characterized by segregation, low rates of fluctuation, low expecta-tions of the availability of work, inhabitants with specific transna-tional knowledge about places of origin, and transnational opportuni-ties. On the other hand, there are arrival areas, to which transmi-grants move. These places are similarly characterized by segregation and transnational opportunities. Additionally, a (linguistic) diaspora with connections to the region of origin is located there. However, high rates of fluctuation and more job opportunities for unskilled workers distinguish arrival areas from sending places.

Further research is needed to empirically assess the value of this conceptualization. This chapter shows that the local level, as the con-text of daily experience, must play a key role in research on transna-tionalism. The openness of arrival areas and the binding forces of sending places represent necessary preconditions for transnational relationships.

References

Amelina, A. & Faist, T. (2012). De-naturalizing the national in research methodologies: key concepts of trans-national studies in migration. Ethnic and Racial Studies, 35(10), pp. 1707–1724.
Barglowski, K., Łukasz K., & Paulina Ś. (2015). Caregiving in Polish–German TransnationalSocial Space: Circulating Narratives and Intersecting Heterogeneities. Population, Space and Place 21, pp. 257–269.
Barham, B., & Stephen B. (1998). Migration, remittances, and inequality: estimating the net effects of migra-tion on income distribution. Journal of Development Economics 55, pp. 307–331.
Benítez, J.L.(2012). Salvadoran Transnational Families: ICT and Communication Practices in the Network Society. Journal of Ethnic and Migration Studies 38, pp. 1439–1449.
Bernardi, L. (2011). A mixed-methods social networks study design for research on transnational families. Jour-nal of Marriage and Family 73, pp. 788–803.
Bruneau, M. (2010). Diasporas, transnational spaces and communities. In Diaspora and Transnationalism. Con-cepts, Theories and Methods, Hrsg. Raineer Bauböck und Thomas Faist, Amsterdam: Amsterdam University Press, pp. 35–49.
Burgess, E. W. (1925|1984). The Growth of the City. In The City – Suggestions for Investigation of Human Behavior in the Urban Enviroment, Hrsg. Robert E. Park und Ernest W. Burgess, Chicago/ London: The Uni-versity of Chicago Press, pp. 47–62.
Dekker, R., Engbersen, G. & Marije F. (2015). The Use of Online Media in Migration Networks. Population, Space and Place.
Dunn, D. M. (2005). A Paradigm of Transnationalism for Migration Studies. New Zealand Population Reviews 31, pp. 15–31.
Erdal, M.B. (2012). A place to stay in Pakistan: Why migrants build houses in their country of origin. Popula-tion, Space and Place 18, pp. 629–641.
Faist, T. (1998). Transnational social spaces out of international migration: evolution, significance and future prospects. European Journal of Sociology 39, pp. 213-247.

Faist, T. (2000). The Bridging Function of Social Capital: Transnational Social Spaces. In The Volume and Dynamics of International Migration and Transnational Social Spaces, Oxford: Oxford University Press, pp. 195–241.

Fokkema, T., Cela, E. & Ambrosetti, E. (2013). Giving from the Heart or from the Ego? Motives behind Re-mittances of the Second Generation in Europe. International Migration Review 47, pp. 539–572.

Glick Schiller, N. (2012). Transnationality, Migrants and Cities: A Comparative Approach in Beyond Methodo-logical Transnationalism. Research Methodologies for Cross-Border Studies, Hrsg. Anna Amelina, Devrimsel D. NErgiz, Thomas Faist, und Nina Glick Schiller, New York City: Routledge Taylor & Francis Group, pp. 23–40.

Glick Schiller, N. & Fouron, G.E. (1999). Terrains of blood and nation: Haitian transnational social fields. Ethnic and Racial Studies, 22 (2), pp. 340-366.

Gowricharn, R. (2009). Changing forms of transnationalism. Ethnic and Racial Studies 32 (9), pp. 1619–1638.

Guarnizo, L.E. & Smith, M.P. (1998). The Locations of Transnationalism. In Transnationalism from Below,. Luis Eduardo Guarnizo und Michael Peter Smith (eds.), New Brunswick: Transaction Publishers, pp. 3–31.

Ives, N., Jill H., Walsh, C.A. & Este, D. (2014). Transnational elements of newcomer women's housing inse-curity: remittances and social networks. Transnational Social Review 4 (2-3), pp. 152–167.

Landry, R. & Bourhis, R. Y. (1997). Linguistic Landscape and Ethnolinguistic Vitality: An Empirical Study. Journal of Language and Social Psychology, 16(1), pp. 23–49.

Levitt, P. (2001). The Transnational Villager. Berkeley, Los Angeles, London: University of California Press.

Levitt, P. & Glick Schiller, N. (2004). A Transnational Social Field. International Migration Review 38 (3), pp. 1002–1039.

Mexican Migration Project. (2016). http://mmp.opr.princeton.edu/home-en.aspx; last seen: 02/26/2016.

Morales, L. & Pilati, K. (2014). The political transnationalism of Ecuadorians in Barcelona, Madrid and Milan: The role of individual resources, organizational engagement and the political context. Global Networks 14 (1), pp. 80–102.

Organ, C. (2001). Communication and Identity. Turkish Migrants in Amsterdam and Their Use of Media. Lan-ham/Boulder/New York/Oxford: Lexington Books.

Park, K. (2007). Constructing transnational identities without leaving home: Korean immigrant women's cogni-tive border-crossing. Sociological Forum 22, pp. 200–218.

Pfau, W.D., & Thanh Giang, L. (2009). Determinants and impacts of international remittances on household welfare in Vietnam. International social science journal 60, pp. 431–43.

Portes, A., Guarnizo, L. E. & Landolt, P. (1999). The study of transnationalism: pitfalls and promise of an emergent research field. Ethnic and Racial Studies 22 (2), pp. 217–237.

Pries, L. (2001a). New Transnational Social Spaces. In New Transnational Social Spaces. International migra-tion and transnational companies in the early twenty-first century, Ludger Pries (eds.), New York City: Routledge Taylor & Francis Group, pp. 3–36.

Pries, L. (2001b). The disruption of social and geographical space. International Sociology 16 (1), pp. 55–74.

Pries, Ludger 2004. Determining the Causes and Durability of Transnational Labour Migration between Mexico and the United States: Some Empirical Findings. International Migration 42(2), 3–39.
Pries, L. & Seeliger, M. (2012). Transnational Social Spaces: Between Methodological Nationalism and Cos-mo-Globalism. In Beyond Methodological Transnationalism. Resarch Methodologies for Cross-Border Studies, Hrsg. Anna Amelia, Cevrimsel D. Nergiz, Thomas Faist, und Nina Glick Schiller, New York City: Routledge Taylor & Francis Group, pp. 219–238.
Riain, R. & King, C. (2015). Emotional streaming and transconnectivity: Skype and emotion practices in transnational families in Ireland. Global Networks 15 (2), pp. 256–273.
Riedel, S. (2016). The Problems of Assessing Transnational Mobility: Identifying Latent Groups of Immigrants in Germany Using Factor Mixture Analysis. Social Indicators Research, 53(9), pp. 1689–1699.
Riedel, S. (2015). The Interrelation of Immigrants' Interethnic Ties and Socioeconomic Status in Germany. An Autoregressive Panel Analysis. European Journal of Population, 31(3), pp. 287–307.
Schimmer, P. & van Tubergen, F. (2014). Transnationalism and Ethnic Identification among Adolescent Chil-dren of Immigrants in the Netherlands, Germany, England, and Sweden. International Migration Review 48(3), pp. 680–709.
Schunck, R. (2011). Immigrant Integration, Transnational Activities and the Life Course, In: Wingens, Matthi-as, Windzio, Michael, Valk, Helga de & Aybek, Can (Eds..): A Life-Course Perspective on Migration and Inte-gration: Springer Netherlands, pp. 259–282.
Slater, T. & Anderson, N. (2011). The reputational ghetto: Territorial stigmatisation in St Paul's, Bristol. Transactions of the Institute of British Geographers, 37(4), pp. 530–546.
Tintori, G. (2011). The Transnational Political Practices of "Latin American Italians". International Migration 49 (3), pp. 168–188.
Yang, D. (2011). Migrant Remittances. Journal of Economic Perspectives 25 (3), pp. 129–152.
Vertovec, S. (2006). The Emergence of Super-Diversity in Britain. Working Pa. Oxford: University of Oxford; Centre on Migration, Policy and Society.
Waldinger, R. (2013). Immigrant transnationalism. Current Sociology 61 (5-6), pp. 756–777.
Wacquant, L. (2008). Urban Outcasts: A Comparative Sociology of Advanced Marginality. Cambridge: Polity Press.
Wacquant, L. (2007). Territorial stigmatization in the age of advanced marginality. Thesis Eleven, 91 (1), pp. 66–77.
Wijers, G D.M. (2014). Navigating a river by its bends: A study on transnational social networks as resources for the transformation of Cambodia. Ethnic and Racial Studies 37 (9), pp. 1526–1545.
Wimmer, A., & Glick Schiller, N. (2002). Methodological nationalism and beyond: nation-state building, mi-gration and the social sciences. Global Networks 2 (4), pp. 301–334.

Spatial segregation and the unequal educational pathways of children in urban areas

Banu Çıtlak

1 Introduction

In the past decades' families have become increasingly diverse in Western Europe. Two determining factors, in particular, led to social structural changes. First, compared to other regions of the world, like Africa, the population in most European countries is decreasing. Even if the current levels of international migration to Europe are accurately projected, Europe's population will be shrinking by about 32 million between 2015 and 2050 (UN-Population Division 2015). The population under the age of 18 declines continually in Germany, whereby family households, including statistically at least one adult and one person below 18 years of age, make only around 20 percent of all private households today (Mikrozensus 2014). Together with the population-aging process, this shrinking challenges the health, pension and social welfare system in Germany, and despite these fiscal and political challenges, the structural changes in the household composition of the population gives reason to think about the position of families in an aging society under conditions of social inequality (Zinnecke 2001). Second, while women were the population group in Germany which shared the highest risk of living in poverty until the 1980´s, children have become the population group with the highest risk of living on welfare today. According to national data, the welfare rate of children below 15 years old, is now twice as high as the welfare rate of adults (9%), whereby representative studies calculate the poverty risk of children even as high as 24.2 percent (PASS 2013: 10). In addition, within the statistical group of "poor family households", the share of single parented and migrant households, as well as families with more than 3 children, increased during recent decades (Statistisches

Bundesamt 2011: 50). However, in Germany, and especially within the state (Bundesland) with the highest population density North Rhine-Westphalia, the population below 18 years old has a poverty risk of 23.6 percent; particularly children living in a single parent household share as high a risk of 45.7 percent. In order to explain the unequal educational opportunities of children from different social backgrounds adequately, it is useful to pay more attention to the differing educational conditions in low versus high SES urban neighborhoods.

In this paper, I will mainly focus on the influences of social and ethnic segregation in neighborhoods and local educational institutions by referring to quantitative data. First, I will shortly describe the historical processes which led to the patterns of segregation in the cities of the Ruhr Area today. Then I will provide more insight into the consequences of neighborhood segregation on children's educational pathways by using population and school data of a selected city (Mülheim an der Ruhr) in the Ruhr Area. In doing so, I will focus on differences of children's pre-school experiences, health status, and language abilities by school entrance in neighborhoods with different SES profiles. As a requirement of the German educational system, children are selected and channeled into an academic or a vocational educational track after primary school (4th grade). By using school data, I will finally elaborate on the chances of children taking the academic track, which offers different career opportunities later in life. However, because empirical studies repeatedly confirm the link between parental education and children's school success (for example, PISA, KIGG) through family resources on the micro level, the question of spatial resources in neighborhoods or local schools on the macro level is often overseen. Therefore, I will close with a discussion of the findings and suggest policy implications towards a more committed local policy line.

Continuing social and ethnic segregation processes have increased spatial segregation in urban areas of Germany. The Ruhr Area is a cluster of cities with industrial background, geographically placed within North Rhine-Westphalia. In almost all cities of the Ruhr Area, the spatial co-occurrence of ethnic diversity and social disadvantage constitutes poor neighborhoods, which can be described as areas of concentrated disadvantage (Bogumil et al. 2012: 27). Families are relatively overrepresented in these disadvantaged neighborhoods, which is primarily due to the conditions of housing shortage in urban areas and the restricted financial resources of families. Compared to other European countries, like the Netherlands, Norway, or Spain, the share of home ownership in Germany is rather low, housing costs being one of the most challenging financial risks for families in Germany (Kurz 2004: 22). As a consequence, high rents consume a considerable share of families' financial resources. Regarding the Bundesland and the city, rental costs can exceed even more than 40 percent of the households' income and therefore constitute a serious poverty risk. As a consequence, in 60 percent of German cities, families with an average income are not able to pay the rent without falling below the welfare line (Tophoven et al. 2013).

Besides social segregation, ethnic segregation has become a crucial neighborhood characteristic, whereby the existence of highly segregated neighborhoods was taken as a sign for social disintegration and marginalization of immigrant groups in politics and media. With respect to children's educational opportunities, meta-analysis of international research on neighborhood affects show that high rates of ethnic diversity and concentrated poverty are associated with low individual educational outcomes. Depending on the theoretical background, the correlation between neighborhood characteristics and children's school performance is explained by the mediating influence of the quality of local institutions as well as the educational climate in the neighborhood (Nieuwenhuis/Hoomeijer 2014). First, it has been argued that the *quality of local institutions,* like kindergarten and schools, provide differing environments and influence learning opportunities and thus the educational outcomes. The quality of local educational institutions depends primarily on the specifics of the national educational system. Unlike countries where private schooling is more common, most children in Germany attend public schools and only around ten percent attend a private school (Statistisches Bundesamt 2014). Both public and private schools are required to fulfil some minimum standards regarding the school environment by law (for example, number of children per class). Therefore, the infrastructural quality of schools and kindergartens in high and low SES neighborhoods differs relatively less in Germany. However, the considerable level of spatial segregation leads to concentrated effects in local schools and has been found to have an adverse impact on the quality of these learning environments. For example, the language abilities of children have been found to differ between low and high SES neighborhoods as well as between those with a higher versus lower level of ethnic diversity in local schools (Kristen 2005, 2006; Teltemann 2014). However, analysis using the data from the second wave of PISA could only reveal negative effects of neighborhood poverty on children's math scores, but not for immigrant concentration (Baumert et al. 2005), suggesting that the ethnic concentration of pupils affects predominantly the conditions of language acquisition.

Second, the *educational climate in the neighborhood* (for example, school drop outs, educational level of the residents) has been found to moderate children's educational affords and future perspectives as well as parents' state of knowledge and attitudes towards (higher) education. As expected, most neighborhood research which has been done on educational achievement so far calculates a close link between neighborhood poverty and poor educational climate (Nieuwenhuis/Hoomeijer 2014; Nieuwenhuis et al. 2013). Theoretically, it is assumed that adolescents in disadvantaged neighborhoods develop a destructive and thus limited perspective on their own future early on, resulting from a lack of positive role models in the surrounding environment (Esser 2006; Friedrichs et al. 2003; Häußermann 2001). Another theoretical explanation, which is concerned with strategies of identity development during adolescence, refers to the adverse effects of ethnic concentration in schools due to a higher risk of self-exclusion and stigmatization. In particular, under conditions of ethnically segregated schools, children from immigrant families feel forced to adopt and perform stereotyped expectations of the surrounding environment (such as ethnic community, peers). As a consequence, they get only restricted opportunities for self-exploration and individual identity development (Cooper et al. 2011, Scherr 2015).

2 Ethnic and social segregation in the Ruhr Area

As in other urban areas of Europe, cities in the Ruhr Area are segregated with respect to the demographic, ethnic, and socioeconomic situation of their residents (Kersting et al. 2009). In this context, cities are subdivided into administrative spatial units, which I will refer to as neighborhoods. Statistically, the socioeconomic characteristics of the population in each neighborhood are measured by the share of unemployed and the share of residents who are receiving welfare. Until recently ethnic segregation has been captured by the share of the population with foreign citizenship. This has been expanded lately by the variable "immigration background", which includes immigrants in the following generations also who are born and grow up in Germany. Finally, the demographic segregation refers to the fact that some neighborhoods in the cities are predominantly resided by an older population (share above 65 years of age), whereas others are characterized by a rather young population. Low income families, who are of interest in this paper, are predominantly resided in inner city neighborhoods, where the share of immigrants and the percentage of adults working are below the city average. A second type of area in which low income families live is geographically located outside of the town centre in former working class districts, near industrial facilities such as former factories or mining plants (Bogumil et al. 2012). Additionally, in some cities, there are also neighborhoods in the city centre, mostly placed near the central station which allows low cost housing as well as low paying jobs for recently arrived immigrants, and part time working opportunities for single parents (Kurtenbach 2014). Although family households are rather scarce in these neighborhoods, those who reside are predominantly low income families, immigrants, and single parents.

The current patterns of segregation seen in the cities of the Ruhr Area are, on the one hand, caused by demographic changes, aging, and a decreasing population, as well as processes of in and out migration. On the other hand, these patterns are a consequence of changes in the labor market which led to the impoverishment of former industrial workers throughout the last 40 years (Strohmeier 2002, Bogumil et al. 2012). Along with these structural changes, a significant part of former factory employees and miners lost their jobs. Most of them were too unskilled or too old to adapt to new jobs in other sectors of the labor market and therefore remained unemployed. Legislative changes to unemployment insurance in the last 20 years have further reduced the household income of the jobless in Germany. Consequentially, the unemployment rate within segregated neighborhoods of former industrial workers continually rose through the 80´s and 90´s of the last century. As a result of higher birth rates within the immigrant population in general, and due to new immigration processes, the percentage of immigrant families increased in this low income neighborhood's continuity. Also social segregation processes continued, whereby middle class families left the inner cities and settled down in the surrounding cities of the Ruhr Area. Consequentially, the former working class neighborhoods became more and more socially homogenised and ethnically diverse.

The changing requirements of the new labor market have also strongly affected the future prospects of children growing up in these disadvantaged neighborhoods. Until the late 80´s, working class children used to attend predominantly low qualifying secondary schools (Hauptschule or Realschule) and went on to vocational training or to work after finishing the mandatory years of schooling. After the transition processes on the labor market, a higher secondary school graduation (Abitur) with a university diploma has become the normal requirement for entrance in many sectors. Thus, the classic educational pathways of working class children don't work anymore. The local schools as well as working class parents were not sufficiently able to adapt to these transition processes. On the one hand, the German educational system was unable or unwilling (Gomolla/Radtke 2001) to cope with the changing requirements, and so local schools kept allocating predominantly social disadvantaged and minority children into the low qualifying schools. On the other hand, working class and minority parents were not familiar with the academic track and therefore could not calculate the future consequences of graduating from a lower qualifying school for their children, according to the new requirements of the labor market realistically. Consequentially, the social homogeneity of pupils within local secondary schools increased, both in higher and lower SES neighborhoods. Although homogeneity in middle class neighborhoods as well as in higher qualifying schools had never been noticed thus far, schools in disadvantaged neighborhoods had received a lot of public attention in the past; specially schools with disproportionally higher shares of students from immigrant families, placed in disadvantaged neighborhoods have been stigmatized as "problem schools" in media.

3 Local disparities in children's pathways through the educational institutions

Before starting primary school, all children in Germany are required to pass a school entrance test at around the age of six. The data collected in this exam provides insight into the early developmental stages of children. After assigning the individual data by postal codes to each neighborhood, it allows a comparison of the developmental stages of children in low and high SES neighborhoods. The school entrance test includes a standardised developmental screening assessing language ability in German, fine motor skills, and gross manual dexterity as well as the overall health conditions of each child. Results of regional cohort analysis for different cities in the Ruhr Area indicate that, compared to children from middle class neighborhoods, children in disadvantaged neighborhoods show developmental problems more often in all examined categories. These observed differences between the developmental stages of children from low and high SES neighborhoods are moderated by differing pre-school experiences in the home environment and also through unequal conditions within the local pre-school institutions. Concerning the home environment, research provides evidence for the mediating influences of parental education on children's learning opportunities. More specifically, higher educated parents have been found to provide a more stimulating home environment and to be more often engaged in activities, which allow preschool children to develop scholarly skills than lower educated parents do (Bradley 2002). In line with this, a cohort analysis of 3,960 pre-schoolers in the Ruhr Area revealed that children with parents who had less than 9 years of schooling – as well as those from immigrant families – were less likely to participate in extracurricular activities, had a less-stimulating literacy environment at home, and were more likely to watch TV for several hours a day (Leyendecker et al. 2014). Unequal learning conditions at home can be compensated through formal preschool education. Therefore, attendance of kindergarten is of crucial interest for children in Germany in general, and especially for socially disadvantaged children and minority children (see also Jehles in this book). In particular the language abilities of minority children can be improved through a full time (3 years) attendance of a kindergarten or even through starting earlier than 36 months of age (Caspar/Leyendecker 2011; Spieß et al. 1997). However, the local segregation processes lead to concentrated effects in kindergarten thus homogenizing the learning environments of children and making peer-learning processes more difficult than in pre-schools with an ethnic and socially diverse composition. In order to describe the influence of local segregation on the composition of children in local kindergartens, we need to consider both the composition of the neighborhood and the organization to which each kindergarten belongs. The scatterplot in figure 3 illustrates the social position (x-axis) and the ethnic diversity (y-axis) of the population in the neighborhood. The horizontal line represents the mean percentage of immigrants and the vertical line the mean percentage of the population below welfare in the city.

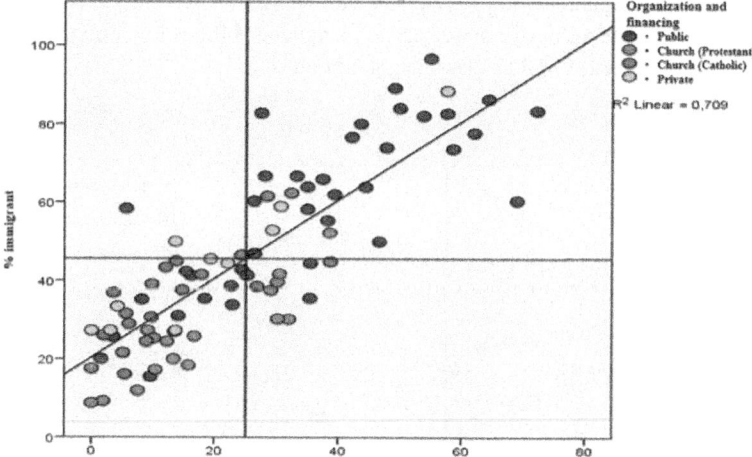

Figure 1 Ethnic and social segregation in kindergarten
Source: Amonn/Groos 2011

The linear regression line reveals a positive relation between the two population variables. It indicates that higher percentages of welfare dependency are correlated with a higher share of immigrant residents in neighborhoods. In addition to socioeconomic and ethnic concentration, figure 3 also illustrates the unequal distribution of immigrant children through each institution. As kindergarten in Germany is traditionally organized and founded either by church, local government, or by private associations, children are distributed unequally through these facilities depending on their religious and financial background. Children, particularly from

Muslim immigrant families, are excluded from the facilities of the Catholic church and therefore remain predominantly in public kindergarten. This leads to further concentration of children with less German language ability in public kindergartens. As a consequence, positive effects of kindergarten attendance on language acquisition before school entrance are rather low. In addition to the institutional concentration effects in the kindergarten, children from minority families and those who live in low income households participate less in extracurricular learning activities, such as sports classes, play groups, or artistic programs, both before and during kindergarten age (Çıtlak 2010; Leyendecker et al. 2014). Furthermore, families with restricted financial resources are not able to pay the costs of day care services for younger children (below 3 years of age) as well as extracurricular educational programs before and during school age (Schröder et al. 2015).

Primary school: As a consequence of unequal learning opportunities during pre-school age, more children from low SES neighborhoods enter primary school with developmental delays and restricted language abilities in German than children from better off middle class neighborhoods.

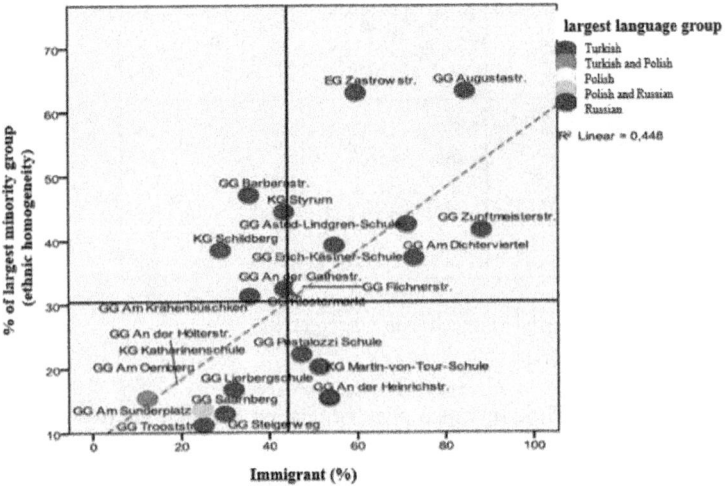

Figure 2 Ethnic composition of pupils in the primary schools in the city of Mülheim a.d.R.
Source: Amonn/Groos 2011

Local segregation affects the conditions and quality of the learning environments in primary schools which further reduces children's chances of improving their scholarly skills. The scatterplot in figure 4 shows the ethnic composition of children in primary schools. The horizontal axis represents the percentage of children from immigrant families and the vertical axis the share of children from the largest ethnic group in each school, Turkish, Polish, or Russian, respectively. The higher the share of pupils from immigrant families in the school, the more homogeneous the ethnic composition of the pupils becomes. While the composition of pupils from immigrant families in the primary schools which are placed in the lower left and right cell of the matrix are ethnically diverse, the ethnic composition in the schools above the horizontal mean line are more homogeneous. In addition to the socioeconomic segregation of the neighborhoods, the concentration of immigrant children and even those with the same ethnic background in school classes and kindergarten, provides children with only a limited chance to improve their verbal language abilities in German. However, language skills are of crucial importance in order to get a recommendation for the higher qualifying secondary schools.

Secondary school: After four years of primary schooling, children in Germany are selected and allocated into either a vocational track or an academic track, which goes through the Gymnasium. Thus the selection for Gymnasium predicts better job opportunities for the future and is therefore of crucial interest. Figure 3 illustrates the negative correlation between the welfare rate in the neighborhood and the percentage of children in each primary school of Mülheim a.d.R who were allocated to the Gymnasium.

Besides the linear relation, the figure also shows the noticeable gap between better off neighborhoods, in which no resident below 15 years is living on welfare and where all children are recommended for attending a Gymnasium (school 81), and poor neighborhoods, where the welfare rate under 15 years of age is above 50% and children's chances of getting a recommendation for a Gymnasium is around 20 % (school 11 and 24). Consequentially, the composition of students in the low and high qualifying secondary schools is more homogenous with respect to the socioeconomic and ethnic background than in the primary schools. In addition, once students are graduated from the lower qualifying secondary schools and transit to vocational training, they face discriminating processes in at least two ways. First, students with a lower school diploma need to compete against those with a Gymnasium diploma who decide to go through the vocational training after achieving the Gymnasium diploma. The latter is often preferred by employers. Second, especially young immigrants face discrimination while searching for a company where they can complete their vocational training. Research indicates that firms are excluding candidates from immigrant families in some sectors in order to meet costumer's expectations (Scherr et al. 2015). Thus, a share of students with a Hauptschule degree are facing trouble to finish their vocational training and transiting to the labor market. Another risk which is embedded in the national educational system is the likelihood of repeating classes and by doing so students can exceed the mandatory school age and exit the system without any qualifying school diploma. Consequentially, youth in disadvantaged neighborhoods have the highest risk of failing a sufficient labor marked integration and being unemployed.

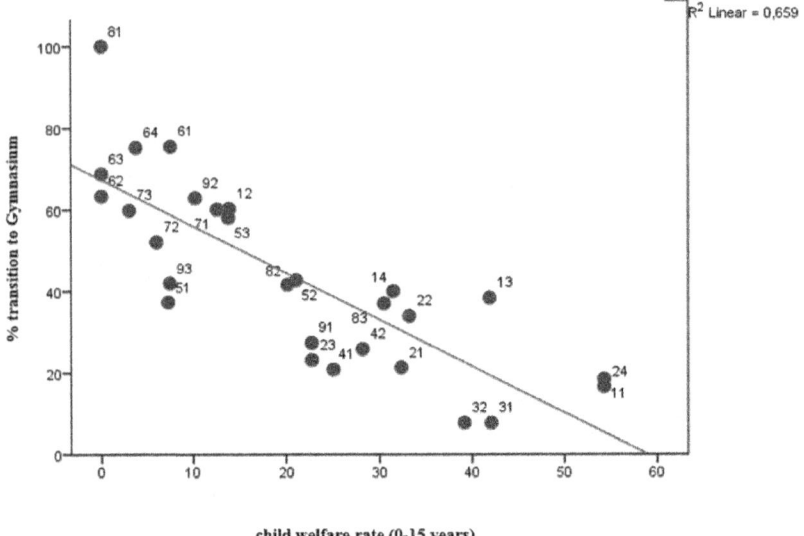

Figure 3 Share of 10 year olds transiting to the academic track by neighbourhood SES in year 2011/12.
Source: ZEFIR 2012, see also Bogumil et al. 2012, p. 72.

4 Conclusion and policy implications

During the last ten years the unequal opportunities of children in poor and ethnically diverse inner city neighborhoods has become a major theme in public policy debates in Germany. However, empirically, there are significant differences in language ability, the educational achievement, and health status of children and youth in poor and ethnically diverse neighborhoods within each city. Using the data of a city in the Ruhr area, I briefly sketched the pathways of children in high and low SES neighborhoods through the educational institutions. While the concentration of low income families is mainly caused by economic reasons (such as labor market and housing), the school segregation process is rather a political issue calling for elementary changes. The educational tracking system especially, as well as the circumstances of selection, has been criticized by authors in the context of individual prejudice and institutional discrimination (Gomolla/Radtke 2000; Scherr/Niermann 2012). The analysis presented in this paper cannot reveal individual prejudice or institutional discrimination but it predicts a higher risk for children in disadvantaged neighborhoods to be excluded from a more supporting pre-school environment and also from the chance to improve language ability during primary school. In addition, the obvious link between neighborhood SES and the unequal chances of children to transit to the Gymnasium illustrates that the allocation and selection after primary school is the major mechanism for the social reproduction of educational and social inequality.

Since a change of the national educational system is not conceivable, what could be an effective intervention for the disadvantages that children in poor and ethnically diverse neighborhoods face today? Three policies are of major interest in order to sufficiently answer this striking question. First, more interventions are needed in disadvantaged neighborhoods to improve the school related skills of pre-schoolers. The conditions in ethnically segregated kindergarten groups of the public providers are not sufficient to ensure that children from minority groups learn enough German to enter primary school without delays. Therefore, it is necessary to build smaller groups in local kindergarten and to ensure that children get the chance to interact not only with peers from the same language group. It is also important that kindergarten teachers are better trained in skills of second language acquisition than they are today. Also, extracurricular activities with pre-schoolers can enlarge children's learning environments. Minority children, as well as their parents, profit from these extracurricular learning programs, but currently participate in these significantly less than natives (Çıtlak 2010). Nevertheless, for any preschool intervention, it is important to include parents in order to inform and empower them. This is particularly necessary in the case of immigrant parents with less school experience and limited language capacity. The ways of reaching parents and children in ethnic communities and disadvantaged neighborhoods are thus far not exhausted. A very promising community based intervention in order to empower particularly mothers of young children in aspects of child development, school system, and access to social support systems are peer based programs like "community mothers". For this purpose, mothers of different ethnic backgrounds were educated first in the context of a short qualification program in order to then support community families through home visits, organized meetings, or family cafes (Stolzenberg et al. 2012). This program has been realised successfully in two inner city neighborhoods of Mülheim in the Ruhr area, too. However, even if the success of these programs has been proven, they still capture only a few disadvantaged neighborhoods and have usually a limited time frame. Thus, it is necessary to adopt these kinds of programs on a permanent basis in order to support the preschool education and wellbeing of children in disadvantaged urban neighborhoods. Second, because working class and immigrant youth are not familiar with the academic track through Gymnasium and higher education and lack a supportive social network to find a firm for vocational training, they are mostly in need of guidance during these transition periods. Individual coaching programs can help in overcoming these challenging situations during the last years of secondary school. Third, as a consequence of complementary interventions, the share of students from non-academic families rose during the last 20 years within the institutions of higher education in the Ruhr Area as well as in Germany in general. However, the transition to higher education is more challenging for working class students. Thus, the higher education system needs to anticipate these needs and provide preparation courses and additional sources for students from non-academic families. Finally, more research on the effects of spatial segregation is needed in order to gain more insight into the impact of concentrated poverty and ethnic diversity on the educational opportunities offered for children in disadvantaged neighborhoods. If the impact of these structural and contextual variable are overseen, individual characteristics like ethnic background, culture or being raised in a single parent family, receive more attention in public policy and the media. In order to avoid these misinterpretations which usually lead to stigmatization and discrimination of children and youth growing up in disadvantaged neighborhoods, it is necessary that future research sheds more light on the impact of structural conditions, such as the quality of learning in kindergarten and primary schools in these neighborhoods, than on the exploration of individual characteristics.

References

Amonn, J. & T. Groos (2011) `Die Entwicklung von Schulsozialindices und -profilen für die Grund- und weiterführenden Schulen der Stadt Mülheim an der Ruhr´ [The development of school profiles for the primary and secondary schools of the city of Mülheim an der Ruhr]. Präsentation at the ZEFIR wokshop on 2.11.2011. Bochum: Zentrum für interdisziplinäre Regionalforschung (ZEFIR)

Baumert, J. et al. (ed.) (2001) `PISA 2000: Basiskompetenzen von Schülerinnen und Schülern im internationalen Vergleich` Opladen: Leske + Budrich.
Bogumil, J., Heinze, R., Lehner, F. & Strohmeier, K.P. (2012) `Viel erreicht – wenig gewonnen. Ein realistischer Blick auf das Ruhrgebiet´ [Achived a lot but won less. A realistic view on the Ruhr Area] Essen: Klartext Verlag.
Bradley, R. H. (2002). `Environment and Parenting´, in Bornstein, M.H. (ed.), Handbook of Parenting: Biology and ecology of parenting, 2nd ed., Vol. 2. Mahwah, NJ: Erlbaum, pp. 281-314.
Caspar, U. & Leyendecker, B. (2011). `Deutsch als Zweitsprache. Die Sprachentwicklung türkischstämmiger Vorschulkinder in Deutschland´ [German as a second language. The language development of Turkish preschoolers in Germany]. Zeitschrift für Entwicklungspsychologie und Pädagogische Psychologie, 43 (3), pp. 118 – 132.
Çıtlak, B. (2010). `Bildung und Partizipation. Perspektiven und Voraussetzungen der Sozialisation türkeistämmiger Vorschulkinder im Ruhrgebiet´ [Education and participation. Socialization perspektives and requirements of turkish preschoolers in the Ruhr Area], in Hirsch, A.; Kurt, R. (ed.) Jugendkultur – Interkultur. Bildung neu verstehen, Wiesbaden: VS Verlag für Sozialwissenschaften, pp. 227 – 242.
Cooper, C. R. (2011). `Bridging Multiple Worlds: Cultures, Identities, and Pathways to College´. Oxford New York: University Press.
Esser, H. (2006). `Migration, Sprache und Integration´ [Migration, language and integration]. Arbeitsstelle interkulturelle Konflikte und gesellschaftliche Integration (AKI) (ed). AKI-Forschungsbilanz 4. Wissenschaftszentrum Berlin für Sozialforschung (WZB), January 2006: Berlin.
Friedrichs, J., Galster, G. & Musterd, S. (2003). `Neighborhood Effects on Social Opportunities: The European and American Research and Policy Context`, Housing Studies 18(6), pp. 797-806.
Gomolla, M. & Radtke, F.-O. (2000). `Mechanismen institutioneller Diskriminierung in der Schule´ [The mechanisms of institutional discrimination in school], in Gogolin, I.; Nauck, B. (ed.): Migration, gesellschaftliche Differenzierung und Bildung, Opladen: Leske + Budrich, pp. 321-341.
Häußermann, H. (2001). `Marginalisierung als Folge sozialräumlichen Wandels in der Großstadt´ [Marginalization as a consequence of spatial changes in large cities], in Gesemann, F. (ed.): Migration und Integration in Berlin, Opladen: Leske + Budrich, pp. 63–85.
Kersting, V., Meyer, C., Strohmeier, K.P. and T. Terpoorten (2009). `Die A40 – Der Sozialäquator des Ruhrgebiets´ [The A40 – the social line of the Ruhr Area], in Prossek, A. (ed.) Atlas der Metropole Ruhr, Köln, pp. 142-145.
Kurz, K. (2004). `Home ownership and social inequality in West-Germany´, in Kurz, K.; Blossfeld, H. (ed.) Home ownership and social Inequality in a comparative Perspective, Stanford: Stanford University Press, pp. 21-60.
Kurtenbach, S. (2014). `Ankunftsgebiete – Erklärungen für die räumliche Konzentration armutsgeprägter Zuwanderung´ [Arrival Areas – Explanations for the spatial concentration of poverty shaped migration], in Çıtlak, B.; Kurtenbach, S.; Gehne, D. (ed): Global Social Work: Regionale und lokale Herausforderungen der Armutszuwanderung aus Südosteuropa. ZEFIR Forschungsbericht, Nr. 8, Bochum.
Leyendecker, B., Çıtlak, B., Schräpler, J.-P. & A. Schölmerich (2014). `Diversität elterlicher Einstellungen und vorschulischer Lernerfahrungen – Ein Vergleich deutscher und zuge-

wanderter Familien aus der Türkei, Russland und Polen'. [Diversity of parental attitudes and early learning experiences – A comparison of German and immigrant families from Turkey, Russia, and Poland] Zeitschrift für Familienforschung [Journal of Family Research], No. 26(1), pp. 70-93.

Nieuwenhuis, J., Hooimeijer, P., van Ham, M. & W. Meeus (2013). `Neighborhood Effects on Migrant Youth's Educational Commitments: An Enquiry into Personality Differences'. IZA Discussion Paper, No. 7510, Juli 2013, Bonn: Institute for the Study of Labor (IZA).

Nieuwenhuis, J. & Hooimeijer, P. (2014). `The association between neighborhoods and educational achievement, a systematic review and meta-analysis'. OTB-Reseach Institute, Working Paper 2014-06, Delft: Delft University of Technology.

United Nations Department of Economic and Social Affairs/Population Division (2015). `World Population Prospects: The 2015 Revision, Key Findings and Advance Tables'. New York.

Scherr, A., Janz, C. & Müller, S. (2015). `Diskriminierung in der beruflichen Bildung: Wie migrantische Jugendliche bei der Lehrstellenvergabe benachteiligt werden' [Discrimination during vocational education. How immigrant youth are discriminated against on their way to vocational training] Wiesbaden: Springer VS.

Scherr, A. & Niermann, D. (2012). `Migration und Kultur im schulischen Kontext' [Migration and culture in the school context], in Bauer, U., Bittlingmayer, U., Scherr, A. (ed.): Handbuch Bildungs- und Erziehungssoziologie, Wiesbaden: Springer Fachmedien, pp. 863-882.

Schröder, C., Spieß, C. & Storck, J. (2015). `Private Bildungsausgaben für Kinder: Einkommensschwache Familien sind relativ stärker belastet' [Private costs of childrens' education. Low income families are put under relatively more pressure.] DIW-Wochenbericht, Vol. 32:8, pp.158-167.

Spieß, C., Büchel, F. & Wagner, G. (1997). `Bildungseffekte vorschulischer Kinderbetreuung – Eine repräsentative empirische Analyse auf der Grundlage des Sozio-oekonomischen Panels (SOEP)' [Educational effects of preschool education. A representative empirical analysis on the basis of the socioeconomic panel], Kölner Zeitschrift für Soziologie und Sozialpsychologie, No. 49: pp. 528-539.

Statistisches Bundesamt: Mikrozensus 2014

Statistisches Bundesamt: Private Schulen 2013

Stolzenberg, R., Berg, G. & U. Maschewsky-Schneider (2012). `Healthy upbringing of children through the empowerment of women in a disadvantaged neighbourhood: evaluation of a peer group project' Journal of public health, No. 20, pp. 181-192.

Strohmeier, K.P. (2002). `Bevölkerungsentwicklung und Sozialstruktur im Ruhrgebiet' [The development and social structure of the population in the Ruhr Area], Projekt Ruhr (ed.), September 2002: Essen.

Tophoven, S., Wenzig, C. & T. Lietzmann (2013). `Kinder und Familienarmut. Lebensumstände von Kindern in der Grundsicherung' [Children and family poverty. Life situation of children in welfare]. Institut für Arbeitsmarkt- und Berufsforschung, Nürnberg.

Teltemann, J. (2014). `Der Einfluss des Migrantenanteils an Schulen auf die Leseleistungen von Migranten – ein internationaler Vergleich' [Effects of the share of immigrants in schools on the reading performance of immigrant students – an international comparison], in Bicer, E.; Windzio, M.; Wingens, M. (ed.): Soziale Netzwerke, Sozialkapital und ethnische Grenzziehung im Schulkontext. Wiesbaden: Springer VS.

Zinnecke, J. (2001). 'Children in young and aging societies: The order of generations and models of childhood in comparative perspective', in Hofferth, S. L.; Owens, T.J. (ed.): Children at the Millenium: Where have we come from, where are we going? Oxford: Elsevier Science.

Development of participation in early childhood education and care in Europe in relation to social inequality and migration

Nora Jehles

1 Introduction

Institutions of Early Childhood Education and Care (ECEC) – also known as preschools – became a highly regarded instrument for employment, family, population and social policy in European countries. ECEC are formal, institutionalized opportunities for children from birth until the start of the school and they are the first elements in the educational system. The participation of families in ECEC should support the work-life balance, especially from women, and should promote gender equality (European Council 2002: 47). ECEC should raise the birth rate in European countries to decelerate the aging and shrinking of the European population. ECEC should be an essential foundation for successful lifelong learning, social integration, personal development and later employability especially for immigrant and socially deprived children (European Commission Early Childhood Education and Care 2011: 1). The following article focuses on the aims of integration and compensation of ECEC. For these aims, the findings – that immigrant children and children from socially deprived families are less likely to be successful in school and have poorer competencies in reading, writing and calculating than native children – are fundamental (Becker/Lauterbach 2010: 11; Quenzel/Hurrelmann 2010: 1; Müller/Ehmke, 2013: 270; Gebhardt et al. 2013: 297; Bos et al. 2003).

In all European countries, institutions of ECEC exist, but there is a variety in organization between the countries in some regards, for example in accessibility (European Commission et al. 2014: 33). On the one hand, there are countries where children have a legal entitlement to ECEC, and on the other hand, there are countries where ECEC is compulsory. A first question is if there are differences in participation in ECEC between the European Countries. With regard to the aims of ECEC integrating immigrant children and reducing social deprivation, the second question is whether the participation of these children in ECEC varies between the countries. To analyze the role of the legal framework on the participation in ECEC, the data of two different survey dates are compared and the role of the legal framework is discussed.

To answer the questions, the terms of immigrant background and social deprivation are defined and the international state of research about the effects of ECEC is summarized. Thus it is clarified that the participation in ECEC contributes to the integration of immigrant children and compensates social deprivation. In the empirical part of the article the PISA data was analyzed by descriptive methods with regard to the question of differences in participation in ECEC by immigrant background and social deprivation. The PISA data was used because it contains information about the participation in ECEC, immigrant background and the social deprivation of children for different European countries, for the years 2003 and 2012. Thereby the development in participation can be analyzed. Furthermore, the information about the legal framework from different publications was used to explain the development of differences in participation in ECEC. The article ends with a short summary of the findings and shows approaches for further research.

2   Research on the effect of ECEC

In the first step, the terms of immigrant background and the social deprivation were defined. In the second step, the state of research about the effects of ECEC especially with regard to immigrant and social deprived children is described. The empirical part analyses if these children participate in ECEC and if they can benefit from ECEC.

An immigrant background is mostly defined by the child's country of birth, their parents, or their nationality. These definitions neglect the heterogeneity of the people with immigrant background with regard to further characteristics such as the duration of stay in a new country, the country of origin, and the educational and economic background (Scarvaglieri/Zech 2013). These characteristics influence the need for integration of children. Different studies show that the country of origin influences language skills: German studies about language skills and success in school show that Russian students have better language skills than other immigrant students, when other factors like the educational background were controlled (Ditton/Aulinger 2011: 109; Becker/Biedinger 2006). These differences can be caused by several factors, but a main factor is the institutional arrangement of the educational system (Crul 2013).

Social deprivation has also been defined differently: Social deprivation of children can be defined by different dimensions; for example, the income of a family, and the education or the occupation of the parents. It is also known as low socio economic status (SES). There is not necessarily a causal relationship between the two dimensions, but they influence each other. For example, lower educated parents are more often unemployed and therefore they are more often dependent on social security benefits than higher educated people. The jobs for lower educated people are often paid worse than the jobs for people with higher education (Lampert/Schenk 2004: 57).

Furthermore, different studies show that immigrant background and social deprivation influence each other. Therefore, disparities between students with and without an immigrant background are based on the socially deprived conditions in which these children grow up. For example, their families have lower incomes, are less educated and are, more often than not, unemployed. Considering these factors, the depriving influence of the immigrant background still exists (Stanat 2008: 186).

Different international point out, that ECEC can have positive effects on the development of children, especially on cognitive attainment, sociability and concentration. Furthermore, children perform better in school in reading, mathematics, science and spelling, when they participated in ECEC. ECEC is especially effective for immigrant children and children from socially deprived families.

The first intervention study focused on the effects of the High/Scope Perry Preschool Program in Michigan, USA from 1962 until 1965. 123 three-years-old Africa Americans from families with a low socioeconomic status were selected. The socioeconomic status was measured by low scores from the parents' years of schooling, occupational status and the number of rooms per person in the household. The children were divided into two different groups: the first group participating in the High/Scope Perry Preschool Program (intervention group), and the other group not (control group). From October to May the children in the intervention group got 2.5 hours of education and care from the age of three or four until school. The staff-child-ratio was one teacher for five or six students. In addition, the teacher did a 1.5 hour home visit a week. The study shows positive effects of the Preschool program on "children's readiness for school and their subsequent educational success, economic success in early adulthood, and reduced number of criminal arrests throughout their lives" (Schweinhart, 2003: 2; Berrueta-Clement et al. 1984).

A second intervention study examined the effects of the Abecedarian Project in Orange County, North Carolina. For this project, 111 African American children born between 1972 and 1977 were selected. The children lived in socially deprived families, defined by low income, welfare payments and parental characteristics such as education, school history, intelligence and occupation. The children were divided into two groups: the first group attended full-time, high-quality educational intervention in a childcare setting, while the second group did not attend this intervention. The teacher-child-ratio varied between 1:3 for toddlers and 1:6 for older children. The intervention started in the first year of life until the age of five years and took place five days a week. In contrast to the High/Scope Perry Preschool Program, the children were educated for the full year. The study showed that children, who participated in the Abecedarian Project reached better results in math and reading in elementary and secondary school, had lower levels of grade retention and fewer placements in special education classes (Masse et al. 2002).

These programs showed a high effectiveness, but based on a small sample size and focused on very deprived children. Therefore, the studies only show the effect of daycare on deprived children, and not of children from non-deprived families. It could be criticized that the intervention programs had very specific conditions, like small groups or intensive supervision, and therefore results are not transferrable on ECEC in general (Besharov et al. 2011: 20). For some aspects of these programs, such as the visits at home or the very early start in the Abecedarian Project, these critics are still right. It must be mentioned that the programs are more than 40 years old and that participation in ECEC has changed. In the 1970s, participation in ECEC was less common, started later and was shorter. At that time, the programs – an education for 2.5 hours a day – were indeed a special condition, but today this is the minimum duration of ECEC a day. Also full-year participation in daycare became normal. In that fact, it could be assumed, that the results of these programs are today more transferable on ECEC in general, than in their time of origin.

With regard to the question of this article, the High/Scope Perry Preschool Program and the Abecedarian Project show that especially children from disadvantaged families profit from ECEC. Hence, it should be examined whether the children of European countries participate in ECEC in the same way and what impact the organization of ECEC has on the participation of these children.

Besides these intervention studies, there are a number of longitudinal studies which have examined the effects of regular attendance of ECEC with a large group of children. The Effective Provision of Pre-School Education study (EPPE) is the first European longitudinal study about the effects of the ECEC on children. Since 1997, 3,100 children in United Kingdom were examined between age three and seven. 2,800 of these children participated in ECEC and 300 children stayed at home (the "home group"). The results of EPPE show that participation in a high quality pre-school has a positive impact on the development of children at the beginning of school: "EPPE found that pre-school attendance improves all children´s development. Children with no pre-school experience (the 'home group') had poorer cognitive attainment, sociability and concentration when they started primary school" (Sylva et al. 2004: 3). The effect of ECEC is greatest when the participation starts between age two and three. Beyond these general results, EPPE examined the effect of ECEC on children at risk of special educational needs in a sub study called Early Years Transition and Special Educational Needs (EYT-SEN). Children at risk of special educational needs were defined by the characteristics of the child (first language is not English, large family size, low birth weight), the parents (low qualification and unemployment of the parents) and the home environment (Sylva et al. 2004: 49). The statistical analysis of the pre-school group and the home group shows that the home children were, more often than not, disadvantaged in their cognitive, social and behavioral development. Furthermore, the study shows that the risk of Special Educational Needs declines during participation in pre-school: At the start of the study, one-third of the children in the pre-school group were at risk of Special Educational Needs. At the end of pre-school this proportion was reduced to 21%. Moreover, EPPE shows that cognitive attainments were higher when the children started pre-school between two and three years old (Sylva et al. 2004: 51).

Another longitudinal is the Early Childhood Longitudinal Study, Kindergarten Class (ECLS-K), which focuses on the experiences of 21,260 children in kindergarten and through middle school in the United States. The information was collected in 1998-1999 during the last year of kindergarten, and in the first, third, fifth and eighth grade. In general, the results of ECLS-K show that "center care improves children's reading and math skills but also increases behavioral problems relative to parental care" (Loeb, 2007: 60). Furthermore, the poorest children (measured by family income) had the greatest academic returns regarding the skills of reading and math from early education and care experience. Differentiated by race (White, Black, and Hispanic) the results showed that the reading skills of Hispanics profited three times more than the skills of white students (Loeb, 2007: 61).

The greatest positive effects in reading and math are those of institutional care if it starts at the age of two and three. Both, an earlier, as well as a later education and care experience can negatively affect cognitive and behavioral development impact. These patterns are evident across income groups and race (Loeb, 2007: 63).

All in all, research shows that high-quality early education and care may have positive effects on the development of children, especially for socially disadvantaged children and those with an immigrant background. Furthermore, studies show that especially high quality ECEC influences children's development in a positive way. ECEC can influence the development of children, and thereby it is important that children participate in ECEC. Kaufmann differentiated in this context the three steps of effects: in the first step, an opportunity has to be on the horizon of the acting target group, in the second step, the children have to participate in ECEC, and in the third step the opportunity can influence the development of children (Kaufmann et al. 1980: 112). In relation to the question of the article, the three steps of effects mean that the parents have to perceive the opportunity of ECEC before their children can participate and before ECEC can influence the children's development in a positive way. Participation is a necessary condition for children to be able to profit from ECEC. Hence, it is important to answer the question of the article and describe the different conditions of the access to ECEC in European countries.

3 Empirical analysis about the participation in ECEC with regard to the legal framework

For the empirical analysis, different data was used. First, the PISA data was used to describe the differences in the participation in ECEC with regard to immigrant background and social deprivation in 2003 and 2012. Furthermore, for the information about the legal framework of ECEC, different sources were used.

3.1 PISA as a database about the participation in ECEC by immigrant background and social deprivation

The PISA survey is conducted to find out how successful different education systems are in to preparing young people for the demands of participation in society, adult life and lifelong learning. As a continuous, educational monitor, the PISA study is able to provide information about the strengths and weaknesses, as well as problems and challenges, of the education system (Sälzer/Prenzel 2013: 13). For this purpose, every three years, since 2000, 15-year-old pupils have been tested in their achievements in mathematics, science and reading. Furthermore, the students are asked in questionnaires about their activities for learning and leisure time as well as their origin and their participation in ECEC. The number of participating countries has risen steadily from 32 in 2000 to 65 in 2012.

For the following analyses, the PISA data from 2003 and 2012 were used because the information about participation in ECEC is available. In 2003, 117,427 students from European countries were tested and surveyed. In 2012, the number of students rose to 193,038. Selected countries participated in PISA in both years and had a sufficient number of cases. The data of Belgium and the United Kingdom are excluded from the analysis because the systems of early education in single regions are very heterogeneous. The following table shows the number of surveyed students in the selected countries.

Table 1 Number of participants in PISA, 2003 and 2012

State	State ID	2003	2012
Austria	AU	4,597	4,755
Czech Republic	CZ	6,320	5,327
Germany	DE	4,660	5,001
Denmark	DK	4,218	7,481
Spain	ES	10,791	25,313
Finland	FI	5,796	8,829
France	FR	4,300	4,613
Greece	EL	4,627	5,125
Hungary	HU	4,765	4,810
Ireland	IE	3,880	5,016
Italy	IT	11,639	31,073
Luxembourg	LU	3,923	5,258
Latvia	LV	4,627	4,306
Netherlands	NL	3,992	4,460
Poland	PL	4,383	4,607
Portugal	PT	4,608	5,722
Sweden	SE	4,624	4,736
	EU	117,427	193,038

Source: PISA 2003 and 2012, own calculations

To examine the question of participation in ECEC, immigrant background and parental education of both parents will be analyzed. Immigrant background is measured by the question of the birth of the student, as well as the birth country of parents'. The immigrant background is accordingly differentiated in "native", "first" and "second – generation". Students are natives when they and their parents were born in the country where they lived at the time of the study. Students of the first immigrant generation were born in another country from where they lived at the time of the study. Second generation immigrants were born in their current country of living, but at least one of their parents was born in a foreign country. In some countries, the number of surveyed children with an immigrant background is too small for a differentiated analysis of the first and second immigrant generation. Hence, the different immigrant generations will be combined and immigrant students will be compared to natives. In 2003, 106,979 students were natives (91.1%) and 7,895 students had an immigrant background (8.9%). In 2012, the proportion of immigrant students rose, while the proportion of native students declined: 169,385 of the questioned students were natives (87.7%) and 18,752 students were immigrants (12.3%). Despite this combination, the sample size of some countries is too small for an analysis, or the error probability is 5% or more. Therefore, the data of Finland, Hungary, Ireland, Latvia and Poland cannot be analyzed.

The educational background of the students will be recognized over the highest educational attainment of their parents, classified according to the International Standard Classification of Education (ISCED)[1]. The analysis of the educational level of parents is divided into two categories due to a low number of cases either without tertiary education, which means a university degree (ISCED 0 to 4), or with a university degree (ISCED 5 and 6). In 2003 the majority (62,432 53.2%) of the parents of the tested students did not have a university degree. The parents of 48,152 students had a university degree (41.0%). Almost 10 years later, in 2012, the differences between the number of educational degrees declined: more than half of the parents had a university degree (94,277 50.8%). Meanwhile, 91,290 students had parents without tertiary education (49.2%).

Participation in institutions for early childhood education is also recognized with the questionnaire. A distinction is made between "no use of ECEC", "use for less than one year" and "use for one year or more". In the first two categories, the number of cases in some countries is too small for a differentiated analysis. Hence, these two categories were summarized in the category "no use or less than one year". With regard to the state of research, this summarization is unproblematic because the EPPE shows that ECEC has positive effects on children when it starts between two and three years of age. While immigrant and educational background are recognized in all surveyed years, the participation in ECEC was detected only

---

1   ISCED 0: Early childhood education, ISCED 1: Primary Education, ISCED 2: Lower secondary education, ISCED 3: Upper secondary education, ISCED 4: Post-secondary non-tertiary education, ISCED 5: Short-cycle tertiary education, ISCED 6 and more: University degrees (Bachelor, master, doctoral level) (United Nations Educational, Scientific and Cultural Organization (UNESCO) 2012: 25 ff.)

in 2003 and 2012. Therefore, these two years were selected for the analysis of the evolution of the differences in participation.

3.2 Legal framework

For reaching the aims of integrating immigrant children and compensating depriving living conditions, European countries have different approaches. There are countries where children have a legal entitlement to ECEC, and countries where ECEC is compulsory. The following table shows the type of legal entitlements in the selected countries.

By comparing the results of participation in ECEC in 2003 and 2012 it must be mentioned that this data is based on the questioning of 15-year-old students. Hence, the data is retrospective and shows the participation of ECEC from 1993 and 2002. Therefore, the legal framework and the reforms between these years are relevant in interpreting the differences of participation in ECEC. The table shows reforms after 2003 because it is assumed that a country that introduces an obligation in 2014/2015 – Croatia, for example – did not have an entitlement before. If it is noted that a country reforms their obligation or legal entitlement, and enlarges the group of children in regard to age, both times and entitlements were listed. For example, Germany introduced a legal entitlement for children three to six years old in 1996 and reformed legal right in 2013, so that younger children also have a legal right.

The table shows that most of the analyzed countries have an obligation or a legal entitlement of ECEC. Most of the countries have a legal right (10 of 22), five countries have an obligation, and in three countries the municipalities have been obliged to guarantee places. Four countries have neither a legal right nor an obligation. With regard to the retrospective data of participation in ECEC, it must be mentioned that the legal entitlements were introduced after 2002 (grey countries), so that these entitlements did not influence participation in ECEC of the surveyed children in PISA 2003 and 2012.

Table 2 Type of entitlement and year of implementation in European countries

Country	Type of legal entitlement	Year of implementation	Aged covered
Austria	Obligation	2010	5
Czech Republic	No legal right	2005	5
Croatia	Obligation	2014/2015	1
Denmark	Municipalities have been obliged to guarantee places	2001	0,5
Estonia	Legal right	1999	1,5 – 7
Finland	Legal right	1996	3 – 7
Finland	Legal right	1990	0 – 3
France	Legal right	-	3
Germany	Legal right	1996	3 – 6
Germany	Legal right	2013	1 – 2
Greece	Obligation	2007/2008	5
Hungary	Obligation	2015	3
Ireland	Legal right	2000	4 – 6
Italy	No legal right or obligation		
Luxembourg	Obligation	2009	4 – 6
Latvia		2002	
Netherlands			
Norway		2009	
Poland		2009	
Portugal		2009	
Slovak Republic		2008	
Slovenia		2008	
Spain		-	
Sweden		1995	
Sweden		2003	

Sources: European Commission/ Education, Audiovisual and Culture Executive Agency (EACEA)/ Eurydice/ Eurostat 2014; Organization for Economic Co-Operation and Development (OECD) 2011; OECD 2013.

3.3 Results of participation in ECEC

In 2003, 76.6% of the 15-year-old students answered that they had attended ECEC for longer than one year. The data shows a wide spread in these proportions in the European countries between less than a third and more than 90%. The proportion of students who used a day care center for more than one year was the highest in

Hungary, the Netherlands and France. The lowest proportions of children who participate in ECEC for more than one year are in Ireland and Poland. These differences in the participation of ECEC show that the proportion of children who profit from ECEC varies between the European countries. There are different causes for the differences in participation, for example the legal framework and therefore the access to ECEC. The overview of the legal entitlements shows that at the beginning of the 1990s (the time, when the students who participated in PISA 2003, were in the ECEC-age), only the children in Finland had a legal right to an ECEC opportunity, but the participation rate in Finland is lower than in countries without a legal right. Thus there is no direct connection between the participation rate in ECEC and the legal entitlements.

The participation rate in 2012 shows the situation of ECEC at the beginning of the 2000s. Almost 80% of the 15-year-old students answered in 2012 that they had attended ECEC for longer than one year. Compared to 2003, the proportion of students who used ECEC for more than one year had risen: from 76.6% in 2003 to 79.6% in 2012. In Hungary, the Netherlands and France, the participation rates were especially high – about 90% or more. In contrast, this only applies to half of the students in Ireland, Croatia and Poland.

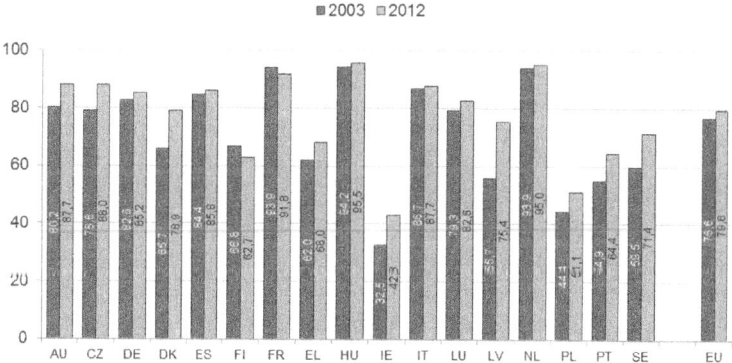

Figure 1 Proportion of students who participate in ECEC, 2003 and 2012, in %
Source: PISA 2003 and 2012, own calculations

Looking at the development of participation in each country, the analysis shows that the participation in some countries is above, and in other countries below, the European average. While in all European countries, the proportion of children who used a day care center for more than one year had risen by 3.0 percentage points (pp), there are 11.8 and 19.6 pp in Latvia, Denmark and Sweden. In all of these above-average countries, access to ECEC was reformed between 1993 and 2002. In Sweden (1995), Denmark (2001) and Latvia (2002), the municipalities have been obliged to guarantee places in pre-school education. Maybe the introduction of these obligations is an explanation for the exceptional increase in participation in ECEC. In other countries, the participation in ECEC has risen, too, but less than in Sweden, Denmark and Latvia. Some of these other countries reformed their system of ECEC and introduced a legal right, for example Estonia, Germany and Ireland. There are other countries though like Italy, the Netherlands or Spain, where participation rises, even though the system of ECEC was not reformed there. Thus, there is no direct connection between the rise of participation and the reforms of the ECEC system. In Finland and France, however, the proportion of students who participate in ECEC was reduced from 2003 to 2012. A reason for this decrease could be the reform of the services for families in the 1990s, when regulated home-based ECEC was supported (Konrad Adenauer Foundation 2004: 17). In Finland, a legal right to a place in ECEC for children until three years of age and older was already in existence at the beginning of the 1990s. In 1996, this legal right was expanded for children between the ages of three to and six. If there is a connection between the expenditure of the legal right and the reduction of the participation in ECEC, this should be analyzed.

3.4 Participation in ECEC by immigrant background

For 2012, the data of the participation in ECEC can be used from 14 European countries in terms of immigrant background. The results for Finland, Hungary, Ireland, Latvia and Poland could not be considered because the sample sizes are too small or not significant (error probability is 5% or more).

The data from 2012 shows that native students were more likely to attend ECEC for more than one year compared to immigrant students: on average, in the European countries 81.0% of the native students used ECEC for more than one year, while only 68.7% of the immigrant students do. The difference in participation rate was 12.4 pp. Immigrant children participate less in ECEC and – with regard to the state of research – profit less from the effects of ECEC, although their needs are greater. The map shows the difference in participation in ECEC in the European countries by immigrant background.

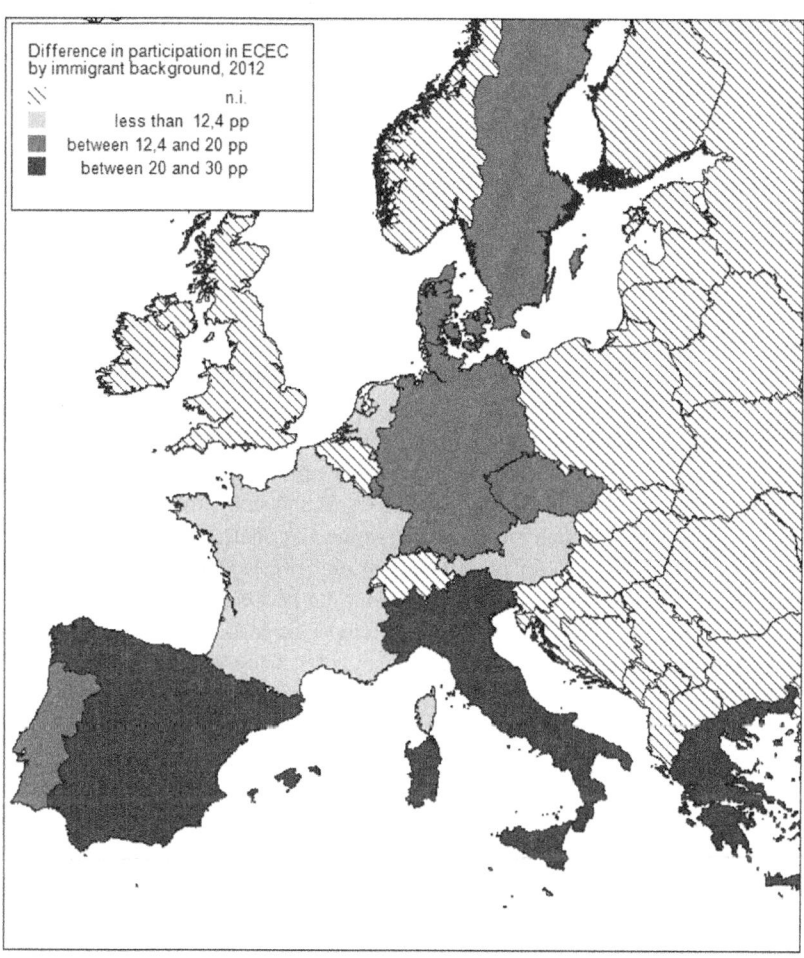

Figure 2 Proportion of students who participate in ECEC by immigrant background education, 2012, in %

Source: PISA 2012, own calculations

In France and the Netherlands, the difference in ECEC participation rates is less than in the European average. In these countries, immigrant children are better integrated in ECEC than in other countries. Regarding the legal framework, it must be noted that children in France have a legal right to a place in ECEC, while the children in the Netherlands do not. Thus, the results do not show a direct relation between a legal right and a below average difference in participation by the immigrant background. In Italy, Spain and Greece, the difference in ECEC participation rates of those with an immigrant background were the highest (20 pp). In any of these countries the children had a legal right or an obligation to ECEC, which could be a reason for this exceptional difference in the participation in ECEC by immigrant students. It can be summarized, that the difference in the participation in ECEC by those with immigrant background and with regard to the legal framework is inconsistent: in countries without a legal right or an obligation, the differences in participation by those with immigrant background are both above and below the European average. Thus, there is no direct influence between the legal framework and the difference in participation in ECEC by immigrant background. It should be discussed which other factors, such as the costs for ECEC, could explain the differences.

In 2003, 76.7% of the European students attended ECEC for more than one year. Thus the participation rate had risen by 3.1 pp in comparing the 2012 figures. Differentiated analysis by the immigrant background shows that this rise does not concern all students equally. On average, in the 12 countries, 77.4% of the native students attended ECEC for more than one year, while 69.0% of the immigrant students did. The difference in participation rate between native and immigrant students is 8.3 pp. That means that the difference in participation rate by the immigrant background in 2012 is higher than in 2003. Therefore, the participation in ECEC in general rises between 2003 and 2012, but the difference in participation by the immigrant background rose, too. With regard to the state of research these results suggest that the benefit of ECEC for immigrant students is reduced between 2003 and 2012.

In half of the examined countries, the difference between the participation of students with and without immigrant backgrounds from the year 2003 to 2012 has become larger: this especially applies for Italy (+8.6 pp), Czech Republic (+7.1 pp), Portugal (+7.0 pp) and Sweden (+6.9 pp). With regard to the legal framework, it must be mentioned that there were no reforms in Italy, Czech Republic and Portugal. In Sweden, the municipalities were obliged to provide a place in ECEC from 1995. This reform did not reduce the difference in participation in ECEC by immigrant children. Whether this reform has an influence on that difference should be analyzed in detail. On the other hand, the difference in the participation of students with and without an immigrant background in Austria, Spain and Germany declined by 11.7 to 6.0 pp. In Germany, a legal entitlement for children between three and six years old was introduced in 1996. Thus, the legal right in Germany could be an explanation for the declination in the difference of the participation in ECEC by immigrant students. In Austria and Spain, the legal framework of ECEC was not reformed in this period of time, thus there are other causes for the declination of the difference in ECEC by the immigrant background.

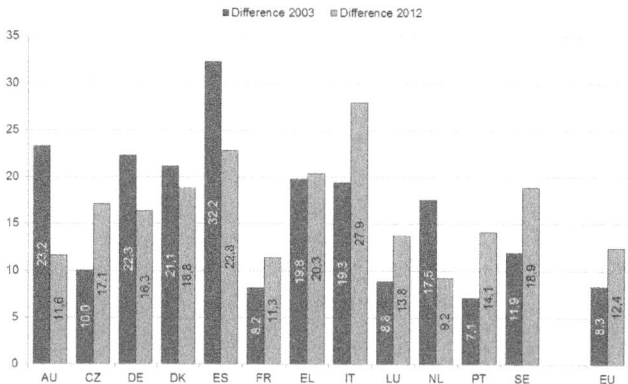

Figure 3 Difference in participation rates in ECEC by immigrant background, 2003 and 2012

Source: PISA 2003 and 2012, own calculations

3.5 Participation in ECEC by parental education

For the analysis of participation rates by parental education in 2012, the data from 11 countries can be used. The results for the other countries could not be considered because the sample sizes are too small or not significant (error of probability greater or equal to 5%).

On average, the difference in participation rates in ECEC between the students from families with and without tertiary education was 6.8 pp. While 83.5% of the students from more educated parents attend ECEC for more than one year, 76.8% of the students from less educated parents participate in ECEC for more than one year. The difference in the participation rate by education is less than by immigrant background. With regard to the state of research, these results indicate that students from less educated parents profit less from ECEC.

In all countries, students with less educated parents attended ECEC less than students with more educated parents. The highest differences in participation rate are in Poland with 33.5 pp, Latvia with 13.6 pp and Portugal with 12.7 pp. With regard to the legal framework, it must be noted that Latvia and Poland did not have a legal title or an obligation at the beginning of the 2000s, rather it was introduced later. In Latvia, the municipalities have been obliged to guarantee places in pre-school education since 2002. In what way this reform could influence participation is questionable. The lowest difference in participation rates are in Germany (3.7 pp), Austria (3.4 pp) and Spain (4.5 pp). While there were no legal entitlements or obligation in Austria and Spain at this time, in Germany children had a legal right to a place in ECEC since 1996. Thus, the legal right in Germany could be an explanation for the low difference in the participation in ECEC by students of less educated parents. It must be mentioned that, in Austria and Spain, the children did not have a legal right and the difference in participation by the parental education is as small as in Germany, thus there are other causes for the difference in participation in ECEC.

In 2003, the participation in ECEC can also be analyzed in 11 countries. 81.5% of children of parents with higher education have used at least one year, whereas this applies to 74.1% of children of parents with less education. The difference between the participation in ECEC after the education of the parents is 7.4 pp. Regarding the state of research, the results suggest that students from less educated parents profit less from ECEC than students from higher educated parents.

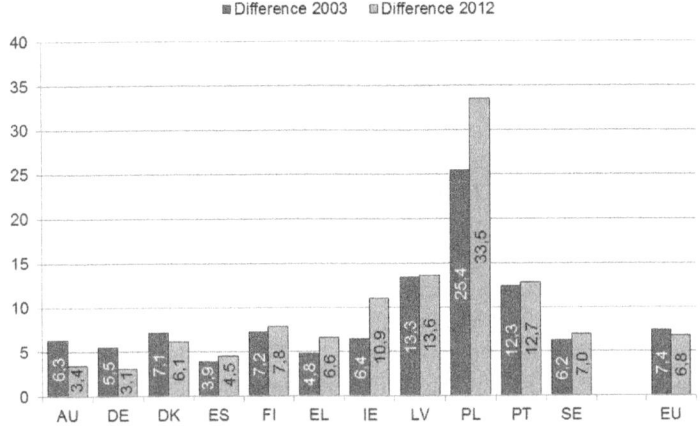

Figure 4 Difference in participation rates in ECEC by parental education, 2003 and 2012
Source: PISA 2003 and 2012, own calculations

Compared to 2012, the differences in participation by educational background are slightly decreased: from 7.4 pp in 2003 to a difference of 6.8 pp in 2012. Thus the participation of students by parental education is assimilated. In Austria, Germany and Denmark, the difference in participation in ECEC after the educational background fell by 2.9 to 1.0 pp. With regard to the reforms of the legal framework of

ECEC – Germany and Denmark, it can be mentioned that – these countries had introduced a legal right or an obligation for the municipalities to guarantee places in the period of time. It could be an indication that these reforms reduced the difference in participation in ECEC by parental education. In Austria, there were no reforms during this time, thus there are other causes for the declination of the difference in ECEC by parental education. In contrast, the difference in Poland and Ireland rose considerably. While there were no reforms in Poland during that time, Ireland introduced a legal right. How this reform increased the difference in participation should be analyzed in detail.

4 Conclusion

Both in 2003 and in 2012, most of the students participated in ECEC. Immigrant students and students with less educated parents attended ECEC less than native students or with higher educated parents. Regarding the state of research about the positive effects of ECEC, results suggest that the children with a higher need of ECEC attend less and therefore profit less. The comparison shows that the difference in attendance is higher when the students have an immigrant background. In relation to the results of national and international studies on the effects of ECEC, this means that especially the children for whom participation in ECEC could have the greatest effects in fact participate less. Thus, in terms of compensating and integrating effects from ECEC, there is still unused potential. In this way, the first question of the article can be approved. Compared to 2003, the results for 2012 shows that the differences between immigrant and native children have increased, while the difference in participation by the parental education has slightly decreased. While migration within and to Europe has increased, the integrating effect of early education and care declines. The results suggest that the system of ECEC did not affect the increasing number of migrants to the European countries in the past. In view of current increasing migration, it is necessary that children participate in and profit from ECEC.

Furthermore, the analysis shows different developments in participation rates between 2003 and 2012 in ECEC between the European countries (second question). With regard to the third question about the legal framework, it must be mentioned that the results are inconsistent: the highest increases in participation were in the countries where the system of ECEC was reformed (Latvia, Denmark and Sweden). The results indicate that the obligation of the municipalities to guarantee places in pre-school education supports the participation in ECEC. With regard to the countries with a lower rise in participation, the results are ambiguous because participation also rises in countries where a legal right was introduced, as much as in countries without reform and a legal right. Other reforms, like the support of home-based ECEC in France or the extension of the legal right in Sweden, reduced the participation in ECEC.

The analysis of participation in ECEC by the immigrant background shows differences between the countries in reaching the aim of integrating immigrant children. In terms of the legal framework, the results show that the difference in participation in ECEC by immigrant background rises noticeably in countries which did not reform the system of ECEC (Italy, Czech Republic, and Portugal) but it also rises in Sweden, where the municipalities were obliged to provide a place. This ambiguity appears in the countries where the difference in participation declined. While Germany reformed their system of ECEC by introducing a legal right and reduced the difference in participation in ECEC by immigrant background, Austria and Spain did not reform their system but also reduced the difference in participation.

In terms of the difference in participating in ECEC by parental education, the results are similarly ambiguous like the results for the immigrant background: on one hand, there are some countries, where the system of ECEC was reformed and the differences declined (Germany, Denmark), but other countries where the difference also declines (Austria) did not reform the system. On the other hand, the difference rises in countries without reform as well as in countries without reform.

These results show that reforms of the system of ECEC influence participation in general, even though the results are inconsistent. Regarding the aims of ECEC of integrating immigrant children and compensating social deprivation, the results are ambiguous. Hence, the reforms of ECEC and their effects on the participation should be analyzed in detail, for example with regard to the cost, long distances or further limitations of access. Furthermore, the analysis of other or newer data could enable findings about newer reforms on one hand, and about more countries on the other, especially that of Eastern European countries.

References

Becker, B & Biedinger, N. (2006). Ethnische Bildungsungleichheit zu Schulbeginn [Ethnic education inequality at the beginning of school]. Kölner Zeitschrift für Soziologie und Sozialpsychologie [Cologne Journal of sociology and socialpsychology]. 58 (4), 660–684.

Becker, R. & Lauterbach, W. (2010). Bildung als Privileg – Ursachen, Mechanismen, Prozesse und Wirkungen dauerhafter Bildungsungleichheit [Education as a privilege – Causes, mechanisms and effects of permanent educational inequality], in Rolf Becker/ Wolfgang Lauterbach (ed.): Bildung als Privileg – Erklärungen und Befunde zu den Ursachen der Bildungsungleichheit [Education as a privilege – Explanations and findings of educational inequality], Wiesbaden: VS Verlag für Sozialwissenschaft.

Berrueta-Clement J. R. et al. (1984). Changed Lives – The Effects of the Perry Preschool Program on Youths Through Age 19, Ypsilanti: High/Scope Educational research foundation.

Besharow, D. J., Germans, P., Higney, C. A.& Call, D. M. (2011). Assessments of Twenty-Six Early Childhood Evaluation – The High/Scope Perry Preschool Project. Maryland: School of public policy.

Bos, Wet al. (2003). First results IGLU – student performances at the end of the fourth grade in an international comparison. Münster: Waxmann.

Crul, M. (2013). Snakes and Ladders in Educational Systems: Access to Higher Education for Second-Generation Turks in Europe, in Journal of Ethnic and Migration Studies.

Ditton, H., & Aulinger, J. (2011). Schuleffekte und institutionelle Diskriminierung – eine kritische Auseinandersetzung mit Mythen und Legenden in der Schulforschung [Schooleffects and institutional discrimination – a critical discussion with myth and legends in schoolresearch], in Rolf Becker (ed.) Integration durch Bildung [Integration by education]. Wiesbaden: VS Verlag für Sozialwissenschaft, pp. 95 – 119.

European Commission/ Education, Audiovisual and Culture Executive Agency (EACEA)/ Eurydice/ Eurostat (2014) Key Data on early childhood education and care in Europe. 2014 Edition. Eurydice and Eurostat Report. Available at: http://eacea.ec.europa.eu/education/Eurydice/key_data_en.php (accessed 15 March 2016).

European Commission Early Childhood Education and Care (2011). Early Childhood Education and Care: Providing all our children with the best start for the world of tomorrow.

European Council (2002). Presidency Conclusion – Barcelona European Council, 15th and 16th of March, 2002, Drucksache SN 100/1/02 REV 1. Available at: http://ec.europa.eu/invest-in-research/pdf/download_en/barcelona_european_council.pdf (accessed 15 March 2016).

Gebhardt, M. et al. (2013). Mathematische Kompetenz von Schülerinnen und Schülern mit Zuwanderungshintergrund [Mathematical competences of students with immigrant background], in Manfred Prenzel/ Christine Sälzer/ Eckhard Klieme/ Olaf Köller (ed.) PISA 2012 – Fortschritte und Herausforderungen in Deutschland [PISA 2012 – progress and challenges in Germany]. Münster: Waxmann, pp. 275 – 308.

Kaufmann, F.X., Herlth, A. & Strohmeier, Klaus Peter (1980). Sozialpolitik und familiale Sozialisation. Zur Wirkungsweise öffentlicher Sozialleistungen [Social policies and family socialisation], in: Schriftenreihe des Bundesministers für Jugend, Familie und Gesundheit [publication series of the ministry of youth, family and health], 76, Stuttgart: Kohlhammer.

Konrad Adenauer Foundation (2004) Familienpolitik und Kinderbetreuung – Frankreich Klassenbester [Family policy and childcare – France Top of the class]. Available at: http://www.kas.de/wf/doc/kas_4766-544-1-30.pdf (accessed 15 March 2016).

Lampert, S.A. (2004) Gesundheitliche Konsequenzen des Aufwachsens in Armut und sozialer Benachteiligung [Health consequences of growing up in poverty and social deprivation], in Monika Jungbauer-Gans/ Peter Kriwy (ed.) Soziale Benachteiligung und Gesundheit bei Kindern und Jugendlichen [Social deprivation of children and youth]. Wiesbaden: VS Verlag für Sozialwissenschaften.

Loeb, S. et al. (2007) How much is too much? The influence of preschool centers on children's social and cognitive development. Economics of Education Review. 26, 52-66.
Masse, L. & Barnett, S. W. (2002) A benefit – cost analysis of the Abecedarian early childhood intervention. New Brunswick, NJ: National Institute for Early Education Research.
Müller, K. & Ehmke, T. (2013). Soziale Herkunft als Bedingung der Kompetenzentwicklung [Social background as a requirement for the development of competences, in Manfred Prenzel/ Christine Sälzer/ Eckhard Klieme/ Olaf Köller (ed.) PISA 2012 – Fortschritte und Herausforderungen in Deutschland [PISA 2012 – progress and challenges in Germany], Münster: Waxmann, pp. 245 – 273.
Organisation for Economic Co-operation and Development (OECD) (2013). Strengthening Social Cohesion in Korea, OECD Publishing. Available at: http://dx.doi.org/10.1787/9789264188945-en (accessed 15 March 2016).
Organisation for Economic Co-operation and Development (OECD) (2011). Network on Early Childhood Education and Care's Survey for the Quality Toolbox and ECEC Portal. Available at: https://webgate.ec.europa.eu/fpfis/mwikis/eurydice/index.php/Countries Available at: June 2011 (accessed 15 March 2013).
Quenzel, G, & Hurrelmann, K. (2010). Bildungsverlierer: Neue soziale Ungleichheiten in der Wissensgesellschaft [Education losers: New inequalities in the knowledge society], in Gudrun Quenzel/ Klaus Hurrelmann (eds.) Bildungsverlierer – Neue Ungleichheiten [Education losers – New inequalities]. Wiesbaden: VS Verlag für Sozialwissenschaften.
Sälzer, C. & Prenzel, M. (2013.) PISA 2012 – eine Einführung in die aktuelle Studie [PISA 2012 – an Introducion in the latest study], in Manfred Prenzel/ Christine Sälzer/ Eckhard Klieme/ Olaf Köller (eds.) PISA 2012 – Fortschritte und Herausforderungen in Deutschland [PISA 2012 – progress and challenges], Münster: Waxmann.
Scarvaglieri, C. & Zech, C. (2013) „ganz normale Jugendliche, allerdings meist mit Migrationshintergrund". Eine funktional-semantische Analyse von „Migrationshintergrund" ["quite normal teenagers, but often with immigrant background" . A functional-semantic analysis of "immigrant background"]. Zeitschrift für Angewandte Linguistik (ZfAL) [Journal for applied lingustic]. 58 (1), pp. 201–227.
Schweinhart, L. J. (2003) Benefits, Costs and Explanation of the High/Scope Perry Preschool Program, Paper presented at the Meeting of the Society for Research in Child Development, Florida.
Stanat, P. & Edele, A. (2011) Migration und soziale Ungleichheit [Migration and social inequality], in Reinders, Heinz/ Ditton, Hartmut/ Gräsel, Cornelia/ Gniewosz (eds.) Empirische Bildungsforschung [Empirical educationresearch]. Wiesbaden: VS Verlag für Sozialwissenschaft, pp. 181 – 192.
Sylva, K. et al. (2004) The Effective Provision of Pre-School Education (EPPE) project: Findings from the early primary years. Available at: http://eppe.ioe.ac.uk/eppe/eppepdfs/RBTec1223sept0412.pdf (accessed 9 June 2013).
United Nations Educational, Scientific and Cultural Organization (UNESCO) Institute for Statistics (2012) International Standard Classification of Education ISCED 2011, Available at: http://www.uis.unesco.org/Education/Documents/isced-2011-en.pdf (accessed 26 November 2015).

Moving in together and marrying for the first time

A comparison between European countries

Barbara Elisabeth Fulda

1 Introduction

Family life has changed. While the standardized life courses of men and women during the "Golden Thirties" has been replaced by a magnitude of different lifestyles, politicians struggle with the development of adequate reactions. Meanwhile lifestyles continue to diversify.

In this contribution I aim at presenting patterns of partnership formation within Europe, and to show if and how lifestyles continue to diversify. More precisely, I will provide deeper insights into the current state of partnership formation in Germany. The German case is of special interest as its economy is particularly well-off within the European community while having comparably low fertility rates in the last few decades. Furthermore, it is characterized by a conservative welfare regime, indirectly strengthening family ties. Due to its characteristics of strong family ties and low fertility rates, it is especially interesting in comparison to Eastern European countries with the same characteristics. Its good economic situation makes it an especially interesting case.

Concerning partnership formation, I decided to investigate when couples move into a common household, or marry. Both events mark a phase in each individual's life, which perfectly exemplifies the process of family formation in a society. As life course events are interdependent and affect each other, moving in with a partner can be regarded as being pre-conditional for many other events such as getting married or having a first child.

In doing this, I will also provide a literature review on how the typical life course differs across European countries. After describing European marriage and cohabitation patterns, I invoke influential factors usually named to explain cross-national differences in the timing of both transitions within an individual's life course. Existing research not only suggests that there are divergent models of household formation within Europe but also hypothesizes that life course patterns are influenced by current structures. Therefore, social policy differences play a central role in the explanation of national differences in life course patterns. For example, the welfare regime of each country is said to influence the age of leaving home as it affects the strength of family ties through social policy measures. Global developments such as rising labor market insecurity and a prolonged course of education represent additional influential factors, which I will discuss below in greater detail.

I proceed in four steps. Firstly, I introduce the concept of transition to adulthood and clarify how I define it. Secondly, I review the literature on both events, and thirdly present the results of an in-depth quantitative analysis of the German case with a German family panel of a couple of families. In the final section, I point out the gaps in the literature and challenges for future research.

2 The concept of transition to adulthood

Adulthood is generally associated with events such as entering a first partnership, leaving the parental home, moving in with a partner or giving birth to a first child. Moving in with a partner and marrying are among the last events in the transitional period from youth to adulthood. The scheduling and timing of life events are often conceptualized as a linear and sequential process, defined by age-appropriate behavior in stages throughout the life course (Elder 1985). The transition to adulthood has therefore mostly been described through a series of such transition events. Usually, the transition process is regarded as complete when an individual has experienced the whole process (Buchmann & Kriesi 2011, 482). In this paper, I concentrate on partnership formation processes, that is moving into a common household with a partner and entering into marriage. However, the reader should bear in mind that these are parts of a whole transitory process in which events are interlinked. As life course events are interdependent and affect each other, moving in with a partner can be regarded as being pre-conditional for many other events such as marrying or having a first child. Naturally, this depends on the periodical social context and on how ideal life courses are understood within this context. As moving in with a partner for the first time and moving out of the parental home often occur simultaneously, I will also provide empirical evidence on the event of moving out of the parental home.

3 The current state of literature

Explanatory factors in literature, of when and why individuals start to cohabit or marry are located on three levels: first, individual level factors, such as a person's income and her level of education, influence an individual's propensity to experience an event. Social age norms structure the decision-making process as well (Liefbroer & Billari 2010). As individuals are situated in different societal contexts, the influence of factors on the individual level is moderated by social norms disseminated within a social context. Second, each birth cohort has experienced specific historical circumstances and events. This affects a cohort's propensity to move in early with a partner, which is called the cohort effect. Furthermore, birth cohorts are affected differently by periodic circumstances: older cohorts are less vulnerable in times of periodic economic downturns than younger cohorts as they have already passed the initial stages of their careers. Third, national level explanatory factors matter, as countries naturally differ with regard to institutional regulations such as forms of labor market regulations, their educational systems and welfare regimes. As I intend to present a nationally comparative study here, I will concentrate on the third factor and only refer to both other factors if they matter for the explanation of national patterns. This can, for example be the case where the social composition of the population, – its age pattern – is relevant for the explanation of national family formation patterns.

3.1 Macro-level factors and the transition to adulthood

Existing studies on when and why people start to move in with their partners suggest that the large differences in the transition to adulthood within Europe can be associated with the three welfare state clusters identified by Esping-Andersen (1990).[1] Differing welfare regimes can, for example, have influence on the strength of family ties if social policy measures allow the weakening of intergenerational bonds. Furthermore, economic uncertainty plays a differing role depending on the provisions of the welfare regime being offered such as in the case of unemployment (Blossfeld & Klijzing 2005a).

With respect to Esping-Andersen's (1990) welfare regime typology, the social democratic regime associated with Scandinavian countries is said to weaken family ties. Late home leaving in Southern Europe can, on the other hand, be explained by widespread strong reliance on the family (Buchmann & Kriesi 2011, 489). Nordic countries differ from southern countries in that the welfare state provides young people with the opportunity to live independently at a very young age, which could be a reason why so many northern Europeans leave the family home so early, cohabit earlier and also have children at a younger age. Cohabitation and non-marital birth is furthermore much more common in Nordic countries compared to Southern Europe (ibid.). We therefore encounter a North-South divide within Europe relating to weak versus strong family ties.

Eastern Europe plays a special role, as the policy regime changed radically in 1989 after the collapse of the Communist regime. This entailed a comparatively quick and groundbreaking change in partnership stability as well as in birth rates since 1990. Thereby partnership formation patterns in Eastern Europe became similar to those in other parts of Europe. Post-communist regimes are characterized by the formerly global responsibility of the state and thus a relatively weak role of the family. Following the collapse of the Communist regime in 1989, ages at first marriage and premarital cohabitation rates rose sharply and union formation was postponed to higher ages (Lesthaeghe 2011). In the following years cohabitation rates continued to rise, as did the age at union formation. Eastern Europe thus experienced a rapid and late 'second demographic transition', characterized by later marriages and increasing proportions of non-marital living arrangements (Lesthaeghe 2011), which other European countries had already gone through in preceding decades. Billari & Liefbroer (2010) now observed a universal pattern of transition to adulthood in Europe as a whole, which is characterized by late occurrence of events such as marriage or first cohabitation, while the timespan between the first and the last transition is quite long.[1]

In addition, the opportunities and constraints associated with each welfare regime affect social groups differently. The type of welfare regime apparently plays a role in explaining the differential impact of income and education on when individuals experience events such as cohabiting or marrying. In familial welfare systems such as those in Southern Europe, individual level differences in income are of higher importance than anywhere else in Europe, as only those with higher incomes can afford to leave their parental home. Therefore, more individuals move out at a higher age than when they enter the labor market. As events such as leaving the parental home are interlinked with other events such as cohabiting or marrying, this fact also has consequences for the number of other events such as the first birth rate of a country. In Nordic countries it is otherwise much easier for

---

1 Buchmann & Kriesi (2011) even distinguish between the four clusters of the social democratic welfare regime, the liberal welfare regime, the conservative welfare regime and the Southern European welfare regime. Scandinavian countries form part of the first cluster, the UK and Ireland part of the second, Austria, Germany and the Netherlands of the third and Southern Europe part of the fourth cluster.

the young to pursue autonomy and already cohabit during educational enrollment due to social policies.

Depending on the generosity of housing policies, individual resources also play a larger or smaller role in the decision to cohabit or marry. Individual income has a smaller effect in countries with generous housing policies (Mulder et al. 2002). Where the public housing sector is small, individuals leave their parental home at a higher age, which is a pre-condition for later cohabitation and marriage. If there is instead a higher stock of privately rented compared to privately owned accommodation, young people are thus able to leave home earlier.

To summarize, the once stark contrasts of family formation patterns between European countries now seem to have diminished and a new European pattern has emerged. It is characterized by late marriage and high cohabitation rates as well as late childbearing.

Certainly, short-term effects such as economic up and down swings are also influential on transition events to adulthood. An economic downturn goes along with greater difficulties in finding a secure job and generates uncertainty, thus potentially leading to postponed transition events related to family formation. If in addition the labor market is more flexible and the low age sector is large, moving in with a partner or marrying is often postponed to a higher age. In view of rising unmarried cohabitation rates, Blossfeld & Klijzing (2005b) refer to an increase in uncertainty as a consequence of economic globalization. Differences in national institutions do however buffer the effects of those changes leading to differences in unmarried cohabitation rates.

The different cultural imprint of countries, being among other factors due to their religious heritage, also accounts for cross national variation in transition rates. Kalmijn (2007) finds differences in cohabitation rates between once catholic and protestant countries, which roughly translates into a North-South divide of European countries. Hajnal (1965) however, proposed an East-West divide between the cities of Trieste in North-Eastern Italy and St. Petersburg in Western Russia, which is commonly known as the "Hajnal-line". Late marriage, with a substantial number of women married for the first time in their thirties and forties, and a significant proportion of individuals who never married, was the dominant family formation pattern to the west of this line. To the east of this line, marriage was universal and occurred rather early in life while the extended family was the dominant pattern. In the western part of the model, empirical evidence identifies greater heterogeneity and diversity in contemporary marriage behavior. In conformity with Hajnal's (1965) theory we still observe differences between Western and Eastern European countries concerning age at first marriage or first birth (Billari & Liefbroer 2010), which have however diminished tremendously over time.

Apart from national cultural imprint, regional normative models of life course also prove influential on the age at which individuals decide to move in with their partners. Lutz (2013) even states that objective factors only matter for the decision making process of individuals insofar as they perceive them through the lens of their normative expectations. He labels this process as "normative transformation". Regional norms can therefore also be assumed to have influence on an individual's decision making processes. Santarelli & Cottone (2009, 4) therefore argue that institutional characteristics of the (Italian) welfare state or labor market conditions are not sufficient for the explanation of age at which individuals leave home. They state, that strong differences still exist in the transition to adulthood between countries even though socioeconomic improvements spread everywhere across Europe. That is why they focus on a so called "familistic approach" and take into account the regional cultural background which shaped family relationships.[2] Eastern Europe is not homogeneous either, and so we encounter regionally differing patterns of family formation. Szoltysek (2008) shows for the Polish-Lithuanian Commonwealth of the eighteenth century, the existence of three distinct types of regional family and household formation patterns.

3.2 Micro-level factors and the transition to adulthood

Variation in the process of transition to adulthood at the macro level is not only influenced by cross national legislative or cultural differences. Analysis of the determinants of the timing and sequencing of events at the micro level, thus the social composition of the population can provide further insights into why nations differ. The educational composition of the population matters, for example, in the explanation of cohabitation rates, as it is in conformity to norms, because the parameters of acceptable behavior may be so wide.[2] Marini (1984, 239) dissuades from using those variables as she expects "little variation in some countries normatively expected to finish one's education before moving in together with a partner". Thus the expansion of the educational system in many European countries has – over recent decades – pushed up the median age of completing initial schooling across Europe. Moving in with a partner is therefore said to be significantly affected by the extended period of education and late entry into employment (Blossfeld

---

2   However, social norms are hard to measure and therefore oftentimes not included in datasets. Santarelli & Cottone (2009) therefore use proximity to parents as a measure of strong intergenerational ties. In case, social norms are included as variables in datasets.

& Klijzing 2005b). Other transitions normally occurring after the completion of initial schooling, such as tertiary education and entering the job market, are then postponed to a higher age. Buchmann & Kriesi (2011, 484) also observe that age variance in completing initial education differs substantially between countries. Furthermore, several studies find differences between social groups in their rates of cohabitation so that a it is more prevalent among the lower social strata especially in Central and Eastern Europe.

Within Western European countries, the proportion of people marrying and cohabiting seems to have reversed over the last few decades: Wiik (2011) demonstrates for Norway that marriage has become the nonstandard behavior while cohabitation has become the standard behavior. Cohabitation is no longer regarded as a prelude of a later marriage, and it has even become an alternative to marriage in Western and Northern Europe (Hiekel et al. 2014).[3] Konietzka (2010) shows that getting married as an opportunity to move out of the parental home has lost its relevance in Germany. Instead, more and more individuals move out to live alone and a high number of individuals move out of the parental home to directly cohabit with a partner (Mulder et al. 2002). That is why both events of moving out and cohabiting with a partner often occur at the same time. In Central and Eastern European countries cohabitation is however less widespread and marriage is still the norm (Hiekel et al. 2014). The word "still" symbolizes what is assumed in most of the literature: Western and Northern European states are forerunners with regard to change in lifestyles which other European states will sooner or later imitate (Billari & Liefbroer 2010).

While Northern and Southern Europe certainly form two distinctive patterns of when individuals leave their parents' home, and with regard to age at first marriage being much higher in the north (Billari & Liefbroer 2010), there also exist strong subregional differences with regard to the occurrence of certain life course events. East and West Germany, for example, differ with regard to marriage rates and cohabitation, with women's marriage rates in East Germany being much lower than in West Germany, while cohabitation rates are much higher in the East (Adler 2004). In the East, 76.1% of all couples in which the woman is under age 25 cohabit, compared with only 43.2% in the West. This data indicates that cohabiting couples in the East do not consider living together necessarily as a step toward marriage (Adler 2004). Cohabitation therefore seems to have become a substitution for marriage in this part of Germany or is no more strongly linked to marrying one's partner.[3] This observed reluctance to getting married in the East

---

3   Social norms play a central role as regards common views on which events are indispensable in an individual's life course and which sequence of events is regarded

is often suspected to have economic reasons. There prevails a high unemployment rate among women (about 19%) and men (18.9%), which leads to increasing job insecurity (real and perceived), and poor earnings prospects. Particularly promising is the idea that the "marriage penalty" for dual-earner couples in a unified tax code may play an important role in the decreased popularity of marriage in the East (Kreyenfeld & Konietzka 2008).

Entering cohabitation may represent a different option for actors differing by age, social class, cohort and ethnic group membership. Cohabitation is becoming more popular, particularly among those below age 30 in both parts of Germany (Konietzka 2010). In Scandinavia, individuals leave home much earlier as than in other parts of Europe, while Italians leave home the latest within the whole of Europe (Santarelli & Cottone 2009, 2). Thus in 1994 Italy had the highest percentage of people aged 30 to 34 in Europe still living with their parents (ibid.). The moment when Italians leave their parental home often coincides with marriage, unlike in the Northern European countries (ibid.). However, in the so called northern model, which includes Germany, individuals leave home early (Kalmijn 2007). The age of first marriage in Europe also differs by gender. In the rest of Western Europe, the average age at marriage differs by two years between men and women, while men marry about three to four years later than women in Italy and Greece (Iacovou 2002).

The age at which individuals experience certain events such as moving in with a partner or marrying is also dependent on their economic situation. If the proportion of young people in higher education and with adequate financial resources is higher, this may as well account for the lower average age of leaving home (Buchmann & Kriesi 2011, 494). Everything else being equal, the income-related composition of the young population may therefore partially explain cross national differences in the age of leaving home. Depending on their social class, implicitly related to their individual financial resources, couples from the working class in the USA seem to move in together sooner after the beginning of their relationship than couples from the middle class (Sassler & Miller 2011). This reflects the differing financial resources they are able to fall back on: working class members are far more likely to move in together as they lack the financial resources to delay cohabitation (ibid.). The authors furthermore reject the widespread thesis that cohabitation represents a "trial marriage" and state that many individuals enter into cohabitation out of financial necessity, that is, economic rationality (ibid.). This

---

as usual (Hiekel et al. 2014). Social norms again influence an individual's propensity to act in a certain way as Thornton et al. (2007) show by studying the example of the transition from cohabitation to marriage.

finding supports on the one hand the thesis that the increase of cohabiting couples versus married couples in Western societies was due to the growing economic role of women in society and decreasing financial resources of couples. On the other hand, it contradicts the view that it is mostly due to a change in values that marriage rates are decreasing while cohabitation rates are increasing (Van de Kaa 1987). Compared with women's economic position, men's economic position however is said to play a specific role in the development of marriage rates. Kalmijn (2011) shows that men choose to cohabit instead of marrying their partner if they are unemployed or have a temporary job. This signifies cohabitation as the "poor man's marriage". Thus he proves that Oppenheimer (1988) was right in claiming that men's insecure economic position at young ages leads to the postponement of marriage.

Women's employment is, according to Friedman & Becker (1993), linked to low marriage rates as women face higher opportunity costs if they specialize on the traditional role of women in a marriage. Furthermore, he assumes that divorce rates are positively correlated with a larger share of women in employment because ending a poor marriage is less costly for them (ibid.). Originating from the general expansion of higher education in the population since the 1970s in Western European societies, a similar argument was linked to women's higher education. Highly educated women have a higher probability of receiving a higher income and are thus economically more independent of marriage, which should lead to lower marriage rates. While Kalmijn (2007) finds evidence for the first hypothesis, the second hypothesis is however not confirmed in his cross national analysis on the development of marriage and divorce rates in the 1990s. Yet cohabitation seems to be positively correlated to higher levels of tertiary education in the population.

In conclusion, a variety of individual level factors, such as differences in the economic situation of young people as well as long term institutional and cultural factors, interact in bringing about cross country differences in the transition to adulthood. Alongside the individual economic position of individuals, employment and gender have an effect on the timing and prevalence of cohabitation and marriage in the population. Here, we observe that cohabitation rates are higher in Northern versus Southern Europe while cohabitation is often associated with marriage in Southern Europe. In general, men marry at a higher age than women and, more often than not cohabit if they belong to a lower social stratum. The effect of these individual level factors is however moderated by national idiosyncrasies such as differences in social policy regulations, rules of labor market regulation and the specific cultural imprint of nations. Here, we observe an East-West divide between European countries.

4 Moving in with and getting married in comparative perspective: German cases

To test the findings in the literature I will now turn to my empirical analyses. For this purpose, I will make use of the German Family Panel pairfam (Nauck et al. 2014) and study first coresidence and marriage in Germany. The German case is of interesting as it constitutes a low fertility country although being economically well positioned within Europe. At the same time it is oriented towards the family and to maintaining the family's social status as a conservative welfare regime. As status based benefits are channeled to family members through the head of the household, this regime strengthens family ties (Buchmann & Kriesi 2011). This makes Germany especially interesting in comparison to Eastern European countries, being characterized by strong family ties, low fertility, late marriage and rising cohabitation rates.

Pairfam is a longitudinal study carried out annually since 2008. The dataset covers the three birth cohorts 1971-73, 1981-83 and 1991-93. As its members were too young at the time of the interview to have experienced several cohabitations and marriages, the birth cohort 1991-93 is not included in the analysis. The initial sample in 2008 consisted of about 7,200 anchor persons, who reported to have a partner. Among these, I concentrate on cohabitation as well as marriage patterns of West-German interviewees since East and West Germany are regarded as distinct cases in the literature (see empirical evidence in section 3).

When posing the question of how to measure an event during the transition to adulthood it can first be shown how many individuals experience that event within a society (Nauck & Lois 2015). This informs us about the prevalence of a given transition in a society. Second, the timing of an event within an individual's life course, that is the age at which it occurs, tells us when an event is normally taking place in an individual's life course. In case the event occurs at a certain age in the majority of the population's life courses, the typical life course in a society is said to be highly institutionalized. Finally, sequencing represents the ordering of events in a trajectory (Buchmann & Kriesi 2011, 483), which can vary considerably between societies. Following this, I will concentrate on the question of whether individuals experienced an event and when they experienced it, that is, the timing of an event. For this purpose, I will show descriptive statistics below as well as the results of several event history analyses with the pairfam dataset. One final note before I proceed with my results: I am well aware that the effects of individual and national level factors have changed over time. However, I leave the study of past changes and resulting effects for future studies and focus on present determinants of getting married and moving in with a partner since 2008.

Comparing both cohorts with regard to the age at which their members cohabited for the first time, I find no significant differences: the youngest individuals start cohabiting at the age of 13 although the proportion that does so is very small (see figures 1 and 2). Furthermore, we are interested in the distribution of when most individuals embarked on their first cohabitation. It seems as if a larger share of individuals in the older birth cohort of 1971-1973 started a cohabiting at the age of 20, while in the younger cohort most individuals started cohabiting when they were 23. They therefore decided on cohabitation at a higher age than the older cohort.[4]

Compared to moving in with a partner, getting married seems to loose relevance for the younger birth cohort of 1981-1983. At the age of 30, about 30% of individuals in this cohort were married, while 45% were married at this age within the older cohort. This already becomes clear by comparing the height of bars in both graphs 3 and 4. Do we therefore observe a division of this youngest cohort into those who marry at a young age and those who do not marry at all? As the oldest individuals within the cohort of 1981-1983 only turned 33 at the last interview date in 2014, this question cannot yet be answered with the data. Regarding only those who got married in both cohorts, minimum age at first marriage does not seem to differ. The distribution of when most members of this cohort marry appears to be slightly different (see figures 3 and 4). Less members of the younger than the older cohort marries at an early age. However, the highest proportion of respondents in both cohorts got married when they were about 26 years old. In conclusion, comparing both cohorts getting married seems to lose relevance as a lower proportion of individuals still gets married. However, trends in cohabitation are similar among both cohorts, with the youngest adults cohabiting for the first time at the age of 13. Therefore, we do not observe much change here.

As the literature widely discusses the destandardization of life courses, which leads nowadays to a pluralization of lifestyles, I finally take a look at the stability of partnerships. Can we observe a high possibility that couples separate or divorce? To answer this question, I take a look at the hazards of divorce or separation, which I calculate in an event history analysis of the pairfam data. Thereby I analyze the duration of time until one or more events happen. Survival analysis is usually conducted to answering questions such as – what is the proportion of a population

---

4   Here I only regard those who cohabited with a partner. Among both cohorts there are no big differences in the number of individuals having cohabited until the age of 30. While 40.3% of all interviewed individuals in the birth cohort of 1981-83 had cohabited by the age of 30, in the older cohort about 48,2% had cohabited with a partner by this age.

which will survive past a certain time? – making it a suitable tool for the analysis of when events such as divorce or marriage happen. I first take a look at the chance that a cohabitation relationship is ended by presenting the hazards of ending that cohabitation in figure 4. Contrary to hypotheses in the literature, I do not find any evidence of a high chance that a cohabitation relationship is ended. Instead, the chance that a relationship is ended is very low and diminishes with increasing duration of the cohabitation. Furthermore, I observe two peaks in the curve after couples cohabited for one or two years, which means that the hazards of ending a cohabitation relationship are especially high in the first and at the beginning of the second year of cohabitation. Note that time is measured in months, so that 180 months signifies 15 years of cohabitation. Thereby I do not find evidence of diminishing partnership stability as postulated in the literature.[5]

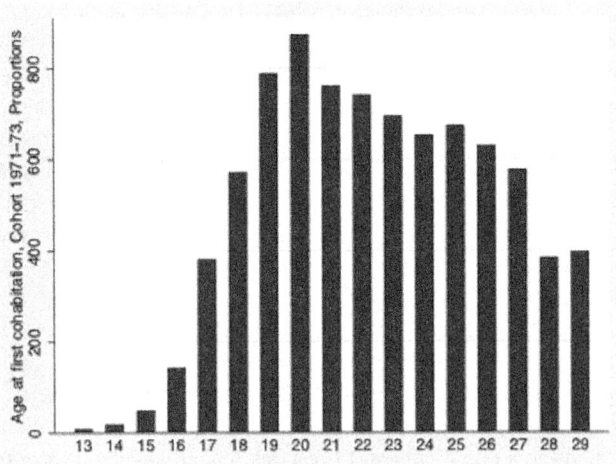

Figure 1 Proportions of the age at start of first cohabitation, birth cohort 1971-1973.
Source: pairfam, 2015, author's own calculations

---

5   Here, I concentrate on all cohabiting individuals in the dataset.

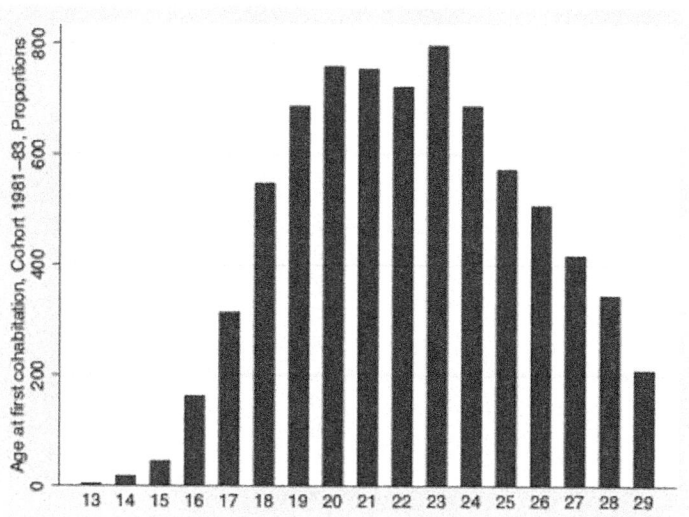

Figure 2 Proportions of the age at start of first cohabitation, birth cohort 1981-1983
Source: pairfam, 2015, author's own calculations

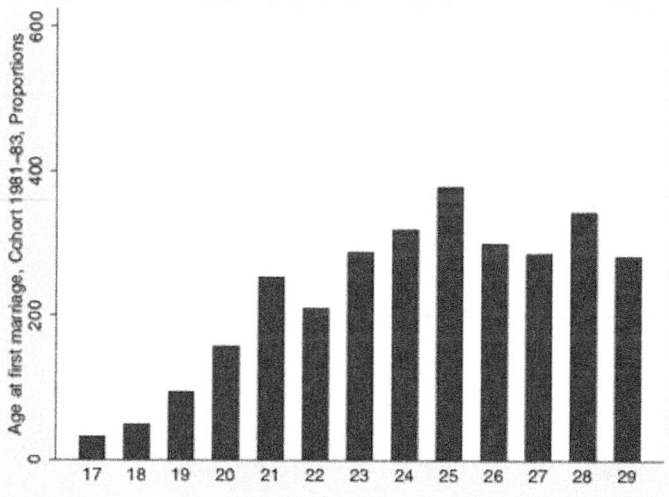

Figure 3
Source: pairfam, 2015, author's own calculations

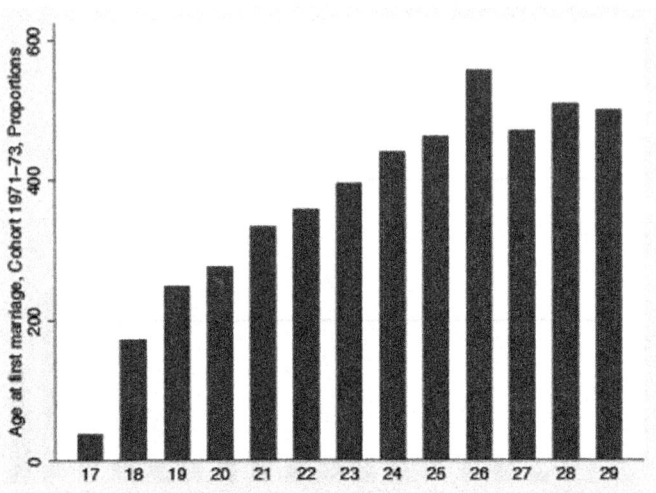

Figure 4
Source: pairfam, 2015, author's own calculations

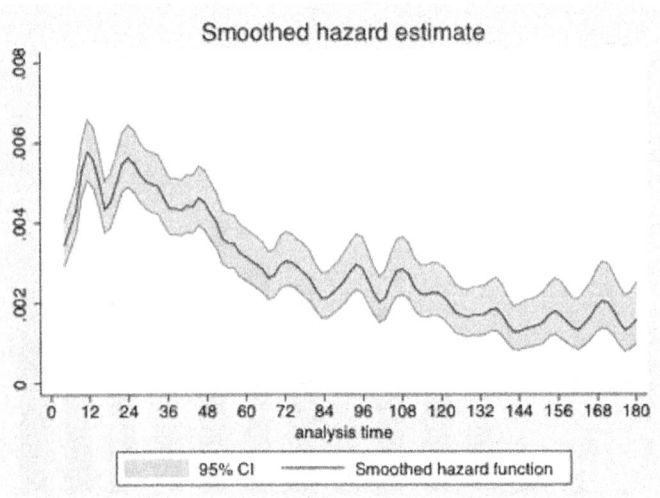

Figure 5 Hazards of ending a cohabitation relationship, cohort 1971-73
Source: pairfam, 2015, author's own calculations

I now turn to the study of the hazards that a first marriage is ended until the date of the last interview, thus when interviewees were between 39 and 43 years old. This is especially interesting as fewer and fewer people still get married. How stable are those marriages? Again, time was measured in months. Here we first observe that the hazards of divorce are constantly lower than the hazards of ending a cohabitation relationship. Second, the hazards of ending a marriage increase with increasing duration of the marriage, which is quite plausible. The hazards of ending a first marriage peak after a couple has been married for 4 years.

To summarize, I observed that the marriage rate of the younger cohort is lower than that of the older cohort, which supports the hypotheses of a continuing second demographic transition. Cohabitation rates are high in both cohorts verifying cohabitation as a quite common form of living. Age at first cohabitation is quite young at the age of 13, backing Billari & Liefbroer (2010) who observe even younger ages at the occurrence of transitory events such as cohabiting. The hypothesis in the literature of the flexibilization of partnerships can however not be supported by my findings as the chance of separation in cohabitation or marriage is quite low.[6]

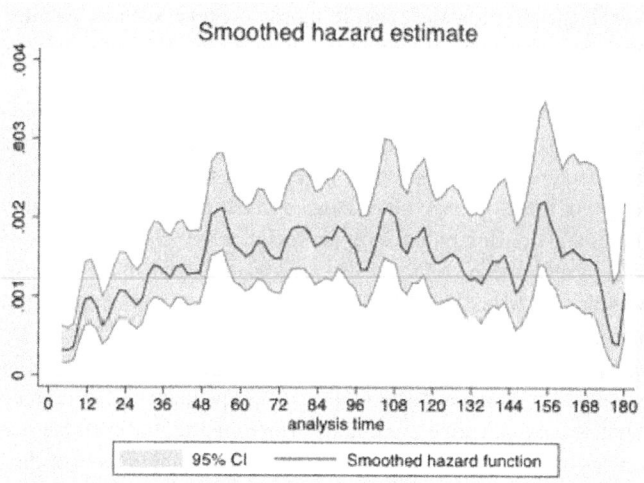

Figure 6 Hazards of divorce, cohort 1971-73
Source: pairfam, 2015, author's own calculations

---

6   Please keep in mind that this cohort did not yet reach an age at which divorce and remarriage rates can be interpreted for certain and so I refrain from drawing general conclusions.

5 Institutional differences or cultural influence? Why typical life courses in Western European countries still differ

Do we observe a common, new and stable pattern of transition to adulthood as Billari & Liefbroer (2010) postulate? My findings confirm the authors' findings as I show that cohabitation rates in the sample of the German Family panel are high and the chance that cohabitation is ended is quite low. Furthermore, couples in the younger cohort marry less than couples in the older cohort. Both findings indicate that cohabitation becomes more and more institutionalized while marriage less important. The chance that cohabitation is ended is furthermore quite low. This does, however, not support Billari's (2010) findings.

Evidence on the prevalence and timing of the event of moving in together or marrying in cross national comparison could, however, still be enlarged in two respects. Concerning the determinants of both transitions and their cross national comparison, more research on the interaction of macro level and micro level factors needs to be done. We therefore still lack research on how institutional differences relate to differences in the ordering of sequences within an individual's life course. Depending on the specific macro context, such as welfare regimes, educational systems and labor market regulations, the effect of micro level factors is different.

Bringing national level differences back in, the differential impact of macro level factors should also be examined in more depth: the relative weight of various macro level factors have not yet been tested for a wide range of European countries. We could, therefore, ask how changes in the timing of events are related to different national housing policies versus social policy measures.

Research is also needed on the consequences of change in the process of transition to adulthood. That is, to what extent do differences and changes in the timing and sequencing of events such as finishing one's education and leaving the parental home account for other societal differences and changes such as the decrease of marriage rates? By taking a closer look at interdependencies between events such as cohabitation and marriage, we could further answer, for example, whether cohabitation has become a prelude to marriage as suspected in most of the literature. To do this we should also forge new methodological paths such as using sequence and entropy analysis.

References

Adler, M. (2004). 'Child-free and unmarried: Changes in the life planning of young East German women', Journal of Marriage and Family 66(5), pp. 1170–1179.
Billari, F. C. & Liefbroer, A. C. (2010). 'Towards a new pattern of transition to adulthood?', Advances in Life Course Research 15(2-3), pp. 59–75.
Blossfeld, H.-P. & Klijzing, E. (2005a). Becoming an adult in uncertain times. A 14-country comparison of the losers of globalization, in H.P. Blossfeld, E. Klijzing, M. Mills & K. Kurz (2005). (eds), 'Globalization, Uncertainty and Youth in Society', Routledge, London/New York, pp. 423–441.
Blossfeld, H.-P. & Klijzing, E. (2005b). Globalization, Uncertainty and Youth in Society, Routledge, London/New York.
Buchmann, M. C. & Kriesi, I. (2011). 'Transition to Adulthood in Europe', Annual Review of Sociology 37(1), pp. 481–503.
Elder, G. H. J. (1985). Life course dynamics: trajectories and transitions 1968-1980, Cornell University Press, New York et al.
Esping-Andersen, G. (1990), The Three Worlds of Welfare Capitalism, Princeton University Press, Princeton.
Friedman, D. & Becker, G. S. (1993), A Treatise on the Family. Vol. 22, Harvard University Press, Cambridge et al.
Hajnal, J. (1965), European marriage patterns in perspective, in D. V. Glass & D. E. C. Eversley, eds, 'Population in History: Essays in Historical Demography', Aldine Publishing Company, Chicago, pp. 101–143.
Hiekel, N., Liefbroer, A. C. & Poortman, A. R. (2014), 'Understanding Diversity in the Meaning of Cohabitation Across Europe', European Journal of Population 30 (4), pp. 391–410.
Iacovou, M. (2002), 'Regional Differences in the Transition to Adulthood', The ANNALS of the American Academy of Political and Social Science 580 (1), pp. 40–69.
Kalmijn, M. (2007), 'Explaining cross-national differences in marriage, cohabitation, and divorce in Europe, 1990-2000', Population Studies 61(3), pp. 243–263.
Kalmijn, M. (2011), 'The Influence of Men's Income and Employment on Marriage and Cohabitation: Testing Oppenheimer's Theory in Europe', European journal of population = Revue europeenne de demographie 27(3), pp. 269–293.
Konietzka, D. (2010), Die Kopplung des Auszugs aus dem Elternhaus mit anderen Übergängen im frühen Erwachsenenalter, in 'Zeiten des Übergangs', pp. 205–236.
Kreyenfeld, M. & Konietzka, D. (2008), Wandel der Geburten- und Familienentwicklung in West- und Ostdeutschland, in N. F. Schneider, (eds.), 'Lehrbuch Moderne Familiensoziologie: Theorien, Methoden, empirische Befunde', UTB, chapter 7.
Lesthaeghe, R. (2011), The Second Demographic Transition: A Conceptual Map for the Understanding of Late Modern Demographic Developments in Fertility and Family Formation, in J. Ehmer, J. Ehrhardt & M. Kohli, (eds.), 'Historische Sozialforschung, Special Issue: Fertilität in der Geschichte des 20. Jahrhunderts: Trends, Theorien, Politik, Diskurse', vol. 36 no edn, Zentrum für historische Sozialforschung, Köln, pp. 179–218.
Liefbroer, A. C. & Billari, F. C. (2010), 'Bringing norms back. A theoretical and empirical discussion of their importance for understanding demographic behaviour', Population, Space and Place 16(4), pp. 287–305.

Lutz, W. (2013), 'Culture, Religion, and Fertility: A Global View', Genus 43(3), 15–35.
Marini, M. M. (1984), 'Age and Sequencing Norms in the Transition to Adulthood', Social Forces 63(1), pp. 229–244. URL: http://www.jstor.org/stable/2578867
Mulder, C., Clark, W. & Wagner, M. (2002), 'A comparative analisy of leaving home in the United States, the Netherlands and the West Germany', Demographic Research 7(17).
Nauck, B., Brüderl, J., Huinink, J. & Walper, S. (2014), 'The German Family Panel (pairfam)', GESIS Data Archive, Cologne ZA5678(Data file Version 5.0.0).
Nauck, B. & Lois, N. (2015), Forthcoming: Auszug aus dem Elternhaus in den Vereinigten Staaten, Taiwan und Deutschland, in J. Eckhard, I. Rapp & J. Stauder, (eds.), 'Soziale Bedingungen der privaten Lebensführung', Springer, Wiesbaden.
Oppenheimer, V. K. (1988), 'A Theory of Marriage Timing', American Journal of Sociology 94(3), 563.
Santarelli, E. & Cottone, F. (2009), 'Leaving home, family support and intergenerational ties in Italy: Some regional differences', Demographic Research 21, 1–22. URL: http://www.demographic-research.org/volumes/vol21/1/
Sassler, S. & Miller, A. J. (2011), 'Class Differences in Cohabitation Processes', Family Relations 60(2), 163–177.
Szoltysek, M. (2008), 'Three Kinds of Preindustrial Household Formation Systems in Eastern Europe: Challenge to Spatial Patterns of the European Family', The History of the Family 13(3), pp. 223–257.
Thornton, A., Axinn, W. G. & Xie, Y. (2007), Marriage and Cohabitation, University of Chicago Press, Chicago.
Van de Kaa, D. J. (1987), 'Europe's Second Demographic Transition.', Population Bulletin 42(1), pp. 1–59.
Wiik, K. A. (2011), 'Socioeconomic differentials in the transition to first cohabitation in Norway', International Review of Sociology 21(3), pp. 533–548.

Migration, family life and cultural inheritance

Perspectives from both sides of the Bulgarian-Turkish border

Meglena Zlatkova and Stoyka Penkova

1 Introduction

Yet again, the issue of borders in Europe gained prominence in 2015, not only for politicians and diplomats but also for people's everyday lives. This issue entered public discussions in relation to the new waves of moving people, called refugees, migrants – illegal, economic, labour and so on. One of the borders that became especially charged with significations and functions was the one between Bulgaria and Turkey. After over a century, with a long history of fluctuation and different phases of porosity or hardening, the former 'iron curtain' border is now an external border to the European Union separating spaces and people again. Our text focuses on this border and the forms of its crossing by a particular group of people and their descendants; people who have had different designations across time – migrants, re-settlers, and göçmen, Turks born in Bulgaria, who in different periods and for different (most often political) reasons had moved to settle in Turkey and who recently began 'coming back' to Bulgaria or started sending their children to study in the country. The change in the status and porosity of the border between the two states is related to the transformed political constellation of Europe after 2001. Throughout the twentieth century, there have been specific dynamics in defining the border between Bulgaria and Turkey, dependent on societal visions in the two neighbouring countries. The border frequently changed after the Balkan Wars 1912–1913 and was closed to people crossing freely after World War 2. Its status of "the forbidden and strictly guarded border," to a large extent synonymous with "the Iron Curtain" up to 1989, was linked to a number of regulated refugee and migration waves of people from both countries. The last wave of migration of Turks from Bulgaria to Turkey was in 1989 – 1990. The checkpoint procedures were liberalized in the 1990s. In 2001, Turkey waved the visa requirement for Bulgarian citizens and more than a million tourists from Bulgaria visited the neighboring country within the next three years. The status of the border and the regulations with regard to crossing it changed again in 2004 when Bulgaria became part of NATO, and once again in 2007 when the country joined the EU. In order to begin understanding the mobility which is the topic of discussion in this paper, two important factors warrant a mention – the granting of citizenship to Turks who were born in Bulgaria but live in Turkey and also to their descendants, and the lifting of the visa regime for Bulgarian citizens travelling to Turkey. The political framing of the border is still in place and the nation-state defines, in a top-down fashion this group of people as 'people with dual citizenship'. In our paper, we discuss the movements of these people and their interactions with institutions and other groups across the border, and their 'play' with identities, as a play with the status of being citizens of two countries. To this aim we employ the perspective of 'double play' along the lines proposed by Pierre Bourdieu (1998: 115). On the other hand, problematizing dual citizenship entails making visible the historical and cultural layers constituting the construction of identities and the interaction between the cultural models which mobile people master in the process of socialization in different countries. This is the reason why we focus on the particular manifestation of 'borderlines' in the uses of cultural and social capital in new social spaces; as one that can be inherited in Bourdieu's sense – in other words, through the strategies of families and their children. What is more, the emergence of new strategies for personal and group identification – for cultural contact and intercultural dialogue between 'the first generation' of migrants and their receiving communities – gradually articulates the necessity for the inception of strategies with which these will be passed on to their inheritors, 'the second generation'. The generational dynamic of strategies are influenced by the changes in both Turkish and in Bulgarian societies from the 1990's[1].

---

[1] The political changes in Turkey led to economic and social changes in the society. The level of education increased in general, the adaptation of migrants from Bulgaria was supported by the state policies. In observing this we should of course note the political will of the Turkish state in 1989-1990 as it recognized diplomas of education acquired in Bulgaria, offered job positions, ensured housing and in this way gave opportunities for a relatively high quality of life at the very beginning. On the other side of the border the political changes were directed towards a transition from socialist society to a democratic one. The efforts dramatically changed the social structure, economic and

This is one of the reasons why the issue of 'succession'[2] between the different generations of migrants, of the degrees to which social positions and biographic trajectories are 'perpetuated' through the concept of 'inheritance', acquired important dimensions. This 'receiving' and 'passing on' of inheritance – in our particular case of 'birth place', of 'father's home', and of 'mother tongue', with all their ambiguities – is not unproblematic. In the course of our field work, we encountered a number of contradictions in the process of mutual recognition of and significance attribution to different dimensions of inheritance. In this respect, we make use of the metaphor suggested by Pierre Bourdieu when describing various forms that may acquire the dimensions of "contradictions of inheritance" (Bourdieu 1999: 507-514). The conceptual framework offered by Bourdieu which includes the three nodes of 'field-capital-habitus' is the theoretical and methodological frame which corresponds most aptly to the analytical task at hand. It allows us to discuss the issue of migration and the inheriting of social positions of the 'first generation' from a more activist research perspective.

At first glance, the case in point might seem too local and specific but it poses, in fact, a number of questions of relevance to Europe on the move in 2015 when, on the one hand, cultural differences exist in shared space and, on the other, it is precisely cultural differences that spur the fear of not knowing others. This is why the presentation and the discussion of the case of the children of migrants who move freely between Bulgaria and Turkey and by extension across all European states as citizens of the European Union might give us an advanced perspective on the ways in which we think of migration in general.

2 Mobility and/or migration: methodological contexts

In discussing migration flows, the forms of citizenship and the effects of the increasing mobility among people, including those to and from Bulgaria, Ivaylo Dichev offers the view that "the fluctuation between here and there becomes the structure of contemporary life" (Dichev 2009: 64). When transition, migration and settlement in the new environment across the border have already happened, the return of the inheritors, and of the migrants themselves, is not a return to a symbol-

---

political systems of the state and provoked several waves of migrations outside Bulgaria. In this context of changing Europe after 1989 the last migrant wave of Turks from Bulgaria was the first large migration wave of Bulgarian citizens abroad.

2   One of the aspects of succession is also the reproduction of social position; upward or downward social mobility.

ic homeland, but to a place of birth – that is, 'the return' happens through national and territorial borders. This effect of crossing the boundary we define in terms of *mobility after migration*. In order to critically discuss this form of controversial inheritance, we have constructed an analytical model of 'cross-border return', taking into account the specific context of forms of return of young people – the second generation of migrants in the 'society of mobility', to use the vocabulary of Skot Lasch (Lasch 1990). This stipulated figure is a necessary condition which gives us the opportunity to analyze all *forms of border crossing* defined by the term 'mobility after migration'.

Even without resorting to defining our present as "the age of migration" (Castles/Miller 1993), we may claim that migrations pose a fundamental challenge to social sciences at the end of the 20th and the beginning of the 21st centuries. Post-1989, a process of reorganizing regional, national and transnational relations have been underway – which has accomplished and never seen before degree of transformations, intensifying conflicts between sociocultural localizations and globalizing processes. The increasing mobility – the endless impulses for migration, the dynamics of 'displacement' and 'replacement', the expanding circulations of cultural models and interpretations, goods and services, images, ideas, people, social knowledge and information in the "society of mobility" (Lasch 1990) and the "post-national constellations" (Habermas 2001) – these are the spreading and all infusing aspects of the contemporary social situation. These processes change in significant ways – the different interpretations of national and local enclaves – and evoke a critical perspective towards their social and cultural dimensions. Caught in the "turbulence of migration" (See Papastergiadis 2000), in order to problematize them we need to emphasize three core analytical aspects:

1. *mobility*
2. *borders*
3. *inheritance.*

Mobility understood in the context of migration as *spatial mobility* carries with it the idea of movement. What is important for such movement is that it entails both transfer of cultural models and interpretations and their contradictory clashing, as a result of which there appear strange assimilative combinations and hybrid forms, Different institutional models are carried over into other contexts, and a number of people find themselves in a cultural and social milieu which is different from the one in which they used to live up to that point. Seen from this perspective, mobility is a correlative to the (supposedly) stationary character of social reality and poses a challenge to the classical migration paradigms according to which the structures of social space are considered in *frozen* and *pre-given categories* – large social groups, stable group identities, established hierarchical positions etc. In this context, social mobility is thought of in terms of (re)producing social status and prestige which had been acquired as a result of occupying a certain static position within the frame of a particular defined (national) social space. But the 'turbulence of migration' rearranges mono dimensional models and necessitates the introduction of additional dimensions so as to establish correlations between and across them. The access to spatial and social mobility entails the acquisition of suitable skills for social positioning, attachment and survival, of certain resources and abilities related to gender, age, the body, imagination, adaptability, practical interests and motivations, but it also entails activating information networks and flows from the *accumulated and embodied social capital* (connections, relations, friendships, communities, etc.). Therefore, we will be interested first and foremost in exploring the relation between social and spatial mobility as a result of multi-dimensional factors and contradictions, individual solutions and strategic choices, personal dilemmas and (un)realized expectations related to social adaptation and survival in the situation of migration.

Next, that which becomes increasingly problematic is the degree of 'hardness' of borders in the situation of "humanity on the move" (see Bauman 2007). Social sciences and the humanities' engagement with 'border', 'space' and 'place' are more than obvious and have become increasingly necessary from the point of view of migration, mobility and (de)territorialization of the modern nation state. An essential characteristic of borders is their ambivalence. Borders are simultaneously instruments for exclusion and separation and zones for contacts, communication, gift exchanges and forms of exchange; they are internal and external, physical and symbolic, social and mental, subjective and objective. Borders include institutions, state policies, juridical coercion, control over human mobility and communication, but at the self-same moment they are also deeply rooted in collective identifications and everyday justifications for ascribing identity and belonging.

This already leads us to the third analytical node which forms the backbone of our study, namely that of cultural inheritance. Insofar as borders are something "unstable", subject to "constant negotiation" (Clifford 1997: 53), their instability is a prerequisite for the possibility of 'porosity' in the sense of identity and belonging. Therefore, in the next section of our analysis we will focus on explicating the ways in which the group of migrants we selected for this study instrumentalize their identity, belonging and cultural specificity in their everyday interactions through *the forms of family life* and *family strategies* with regard to the children – mostly related to education but also to professional careers, views on marriage, personal contacts and social networks, travels to and from Bulgaria and Turkey, among others (Zlatkova/Penkova 2012: 178).

3 Family and education: cultural inheritance and inheriting in the situation of mobility after migration

The main focus in presenting our field observations and findings from the interviews we conducted – as well as our work with focus groups, survey questionnaires and free format interviews – is on *educational mobility* from Turkey to Bulgaria and labour mobility of Turks from Bulgaria to Turkey, which is used more in the manner of a reference point than as a separate study. Studying abroad is one of the legitimate forms in the process of social initiation for contemporary young people, a status which ensures them an institutionally borderline position for several years. We have limited our case study in this text to students with dual citizenship only – Bulgarian and Turkish – who currently study in institutions of higher education in Bulgaria since the dimensions of the border here are not only *institutional* but also *symbolic*. For the second generation, the journey to study abroad is a symbolic return to the place of birth from the point of view of the family, because most of the families are still separated on the two sides of the border. These considerations, prompted by our preliminary research, gave us grounds to posit the hypothesis that the educational strategies on the part of young people with dual citizenship who have chosen to study in Bulgaria present a case of mobility after migration.

Educational strategies are a fundamental resource for 'inheriting' as well as for the transformations both of different types of capital and of the different spatial dimensions in which these types of capital bear a symbolic significance. They underpin similar forms of *'cross-border returns'* for the greater part of young people who are born in Bulgaria or in Turkey. The changes in the institutional reference to the border and to the change in the place of residence as part of life strategies related to education, career, marriage, etc. reveal a *specific form of 'liminality'* which is dual. The 'going to' Bulgaria or the 'return' to Turkey are returns of the relatives as foreigners, the choosing of a marriage partner on 'the other side of the border', the completion of education 'abroad', the pipe-dream of a peaceful retirement to the house in Bulgaria and so on and so forth.

This is the empirical context which prompted us to place our analytical emphasis on *family life in conditions of migration*. Without doubt, this gives us a very specific perspective on the family as a research category that entails explicating family strategies with regard to the children (that is, 'the inheritors') and their education, but also with regard to marriage, the preservation of the connection between generations and the realization of different forms of intergenerational mobility in the complex and intense situation of migration.

Why is this focus important to us when attempting to discuss global issues such as migration and mobility through local categories such as marriage, family, and family values?

On the one hand, the education of children in a Bulgarian university is connected – for some of the families – with finding a spouse through socialization in Bulgaria, which is indicative of a particular endogamy that is being followed rather consistently when choosing a husband or a wife from Bulgaria or from the Balkans. Another difference in the family structures of migrants from Bulgaria and those of locals noted in the study reference in the footnote is the extended family structure – two or three generations live in the same household. Still, there are quite a few cases in which with migration, especially to urban centers, this structure has changed to 'nuclear family'.

On the other hand, twenty-five years after the resettlement of the last large group of Bulgarian Turks to Turkey, a number of those who were then adults have by now retired and receive pensions from the retirement funds in both countries which allow them to have a relatively high living standard, especially if they live in Bulgaria. One of the measures of prosperity is the maintenance of two properties even after retirement and the return to Bulgaria for longer periods of time (half a year or nine months). This *specific intensification of mobility between Bulgaria and Turkey has some new aspects related to family strategies for mobility*. The older generation comes here with their grandchildren for the three-month-long summer holidays. The holiday visits to Bulgaria of the children born in Turkey before 2005 are different – their grandparents did not live in Bulgaria after they had resettled but they worked and reached retirement age in Turkey. This leads to encapsulating social contacts, especially in villages, within a social circle communicating almost entirely in Turkish. When it became smoother after 2000, this generation of 30-35 year olds we are describing in their coming to Bulgaria, connected with peers by communicating also in Bulgarian while the next generations to a large extent speak in Turkish only. The generation of 30-35 year-olds are now working parents who do not have time for their children and it is their already retired parents who make the connection with Bulgaria and gather the scattered cousins in inherited houses in Bulgarian villages.

First and foremost, however, education is a form of *inheriting cultural capital* which capitalizes on social positions and opens to 'inheritors' opportunities for personal investments in future social objects. This is the way in which the exchange of symbolic capital is being regulated between generations (first in the family and the domestic field, then in different educational institutions and particular social fields within which the successor falls). Therefore, education is a practical form within which a number of strategies for social investment are embodied. It is through them that the capital of social relations is being reproduced – during the first years of settlement and now; by the parents of the then active and now retirement generation, by the children of the then active and now active generation, by the born then and growing into maturity generation now. In the next paragraphs we will flesh out in further detail important analytical aspects, some of which we signposted above.

During the academic year of 2012/2013 Bulgarian universities admitted 1,657 foreign students, 1,173 of whom were from Turkey. In 2013/2014, there were 11,282 foreign students studying in HE institutions in Bulgaria and 3,982 of them were from Turkey. In 2014/2015, the high ratio of students from Turkey studying in Bulgarian universities is preserved and they make up 28.4 % of the overall constituency. There is a noticeable decrease in comparison with 2010/2011 when there were 1,400 more Turkish students studying in Bulgarian universities. In the overall number of students' form Turkey, we cannot establish precisely how many of them are children or grandchildren of migrants, since some of them have dual citizenship while others still have only Turkish citizenship. Our field observations conducted in the period 2009/2012 showed that even if the number of students from Turkey was increasing, the number of children of migrants among them was on the decrease. In other words, the more differences that occur in the generation gap from the generation of the early 1990s, the less priority that is placed on Bulgaria as a desired educational destination in comparison with other EU member states for which these students can apply using their Bulgarian passports. For those who still choose Bulgaria, their motivation includes factors such as it being the closest EU member state, the range of majors on offer, as well as the well-developed support network for socialization; there are a number of firms which offer services targeted specifically to accommodating and assisting students from Turkey.

In this respect, Bulgaria is one of the educational destinations for prospective students from Turkey who mostly choose medical and engineering science degrees. Since the choice of education relies on a decision made in most cases within the family, this category was also included in our study of the biographical choices young people make. To trace the degree of primary socialization within the family circle and the ways to subsequent secondary socialization, our study firstly aimed at describing the social environment and the forms of co-habitation of the young successors, and at the same time at outlining their sociodemographic characteristics. Along these lines, we focused our research on tracing the various living conditions and practices of cohabitation. We sought answers to questions related to the level, structure and distribution of income and consumption. We aimed at establishing parents' social status and prestige, and at registering their economic, cultural, educational and professional capital as functioning on both sides of the border, 'before' and 'now'.

The youngest generation, that of the children of out-migrants who come to Bulgaria in order to study in institutions of HE, have no traumatic experience in leaving the country. In other words, for them this step is more in the nature of 'coming to' than returning to. Cultural capital connected with Bulgaria and inherited from their parents is the memory of somebody else, the experience of somebody else or acquired during holiday visits with relatives and acquaintances. This generation does not have the linguistic nor cultural competence related to a context in which one has already lived. To ensure an easier and unproblematic adaptation in Bulgaria, there exists a number of firms and organizations which assist newly admitted students in finding housing and arranging the help necessary for their stay and for study documents. They also support them in creating a network of social contacts.

The interest towards institutions of HE is prompted by the attractive range of majors on offer, by the career possibilities after graduation (in medical or engineering professions), and also by the 50% discount in university fees which Bulgarian institutions of HE offer to students with dual citizenship. In some cases, avoiding mandatory military service in Turkey or escaping the 'ruling hand' of parents and the control of familiar social environment is also attractive. In such cases, the goal is to study 'at all cost' and it does not matter what exactly. Another motivational factor is that the education acquired in Bulgaria is thought of as a 'pass' to Europe.

4 Socio-demographic characteristics of Turkish students, children of Bulgarian re-settlers, studying in Bulgaria: social milieu, forms of cohabitation and social values

Our research aimed at establishing the ways in which 'the second generation' instrumentalized their identity and cultural particularities in everyday interactions. Our attention was focused on the range of living conditions and everyday practices of inhabiting space, as well as on the cultural, economic, educational and professional capital of this generation's parents on both sides of the Bulgarian-Turkish border, both *'before'* and *'after'*. In order to establish the degrees of *inherited cultural capital* we looked for social indicators such as the *education* and *occupation* of parents before and after migrating. The aim of our team was to explore whether there have been changes in the educational, professional and career development of the parents; whether the higher cultural capital accumulated as a result of the higher and better quality education in Bulgaria in the 1980s had aided the settlement in the new place; whether it has given better life chances; whether there has been a further development with regard to parents' educational and professional status; whether these considerations may have factored in the child's choice to pursue a higher degree, etc. Another important round of questions asked in our study was related to the personal plans and preferences of our respondents with regard to *important life choices and decisions*. The aim of our research probing was to establish patterns and tendencies with regard to the idea of *returning* to Turkey – continuing education or beginning a family, practicing the profession one is in the process of learning or looking for better career prospects (See Zlatkova/ Penkova 2011, 2012).

4.1 Socio-demographic characteristics

Among the Turkish students we interviewed[3], men make for the larger constituency (44% female vs. 56% male), and yet among the groups of respondents we could observe significant liberalization of views on marriage, family roles, gender equality and the right of women to make decisions concerning their educational and professional career paths. This to a great extent depended on the higher educational and cultural capital of the parents, a capital inherited by the children in one form or another. Different studies of immigration from Bulgaria to Turkey in and after 1989, cited by Cesur-Kılıçaslan and Terzioğlu. (Cesur-Kılıçaslan/Terzioğlu 2009) show that 72.56% of those migrants had completed their secondary education. This educational structure was different from the dominant educational structure in Turkish society, even more so if we consider that it was 85.5% of the women and 89.1% of the men who had then either high school or secondary vocational education. Cesur-Kılıçaslan et al. discuss this fact in relation to two aspects – on the one hand, the compulsory nature of school education in socialist Bulgaria and, on the other, the value ethnic Turks placed on education in Bulgaria. Among the parents of our respondents the majority are also those who have completed secondary or higher education. With parents in the lower education bracket, respondents often spoke about sacrifices and dramatic restructuring of family budgets so as to ensure resources for educating the children.

All the respondents are city dwellers whereby those living in regional centres are the majority – 44% followed by those living in big towns – 15% and in small

---

3 In the above-mentioned HE institutions we conducted questionnaire surveys with 55 students. Also, we conducted 20 semi-structured interviews and there were two focus groups.

towns – 12%. Only 9% of our respondents live in the capital. In itself, this aspect is indicative of the topological distribution of the accumulated *cultural capital* which is concentrated mostly in big cities. The participants in our study are *single* (100%) and they still live with their parents when they are in Turkey. All completed *secondary education* in their native towns.

The average family among the representatives of Bulgarian out-migrants to Turkey has 2.29 children. This indicates a preservation and reproduction of the nuclear idea of the family – parents and two children – while the informants' age is either noted at the time of leaving for Turkey or shortly afterwards. Our respondents were born between the years 1985 and 1991. In cases with three children, or four in only one case, we noticed a higher level of economic stability is stated. In those cases, our respondents identify themselves socially as 'middle class,' 'more or less rich' and even 'very rich'.

Therefore, alongside the more liberal attitudes of the community of Bulgarian out-migrants to Turkey, with regard to the opportunities they offer their descendants for advanced education and subsequent advancement in their careers, whereby the past educational, professional or cultural capital of the parents is either reproduced or enhanced (that is, there is a possibility of social mobility), we also observe reproduction of the *demographic behavior* among the young people – they postpone their marriages and they have fewer children. This runs in parallel to the increased aspirations for spatial mobility and higher education acquisition in other countries (Bulgaria is one of the desired destinations as an EU member state, see Zlatkova/Penkova 2011, 2012).

4.2 Social positions and social status

The family of our respondents migrated to Turkey between 1985 and 1989. Some of them were born in that period or were too young to have any real memories. Most of them were born in Turkey. The average period of their stay in Bulgaria is between 2005 and 2010. This period in practice overlaps with the period in which Bulgaria started negotiations with and eventually joined the EU. This is why the results we mentioned above in relation to Bulgarian education and Bulgarian universities should come as no surprise – the opportunity to have an EU diploma from a Bulgarian university increased the interest in studying in the country.

Overall, the scale of self-identification with regard to *social positions* gives us grounds to conclude that it is the children of middle class and upper middle class parents who can afford education in Bulgaria. The spread of the social positions occupied by our respondents is as follows: very rich (3%), rich (3%), more or less rich (12%), middle class (70%), more or less poor (15%). We see that even if not insignificant the percentage of those who would identify themselves as 'more or less poor', it is not significant in relation to the distribution of other social statuses and positions on the scale.

To summarize, our respondents are relatively well-positioned socially. Since their parents are in most cases well qualified, they became a part of the middle class and had the opportunity to upgrade their social status in the new 'place'. Contrary to the classical case of migration where one usually observes a lowering of the social status from 'before' migrating, here we encounter a different social phenomenon – *the opportunities for preserving and/or enhancing professional realization lead to vertical social mobility and to enhancing the social status 'after' migration.*

4.3 Social values and attitudes

For the purposes of our analytical focus it is undoubtedly also necessary to reflect on the social values and attitudes of the 'inheritors' of the first generation of migrants. As we observed above, the attitudes to *family life and marriage* but also *respect for parents and the value of family* remain significant markers which hold one's own identity and realize social investments. The investment in family values and morals very often means forming attachments with somebody who is 'one of us' or whom the parents 'like'. This observation is confirmed by a number of interviews and conversations we conducted. An owner of a firm specializing in legalizing citizenship documents of Bulgarian out-migrants in Kirdjali shared with us that there was a growing tendency – which might be called '*wedding tourism*' – among the children of Bulgarian out-migrants (as well as of local Turks from Turkey) who visit the town so as to 'get' a bride from Bulgaria. The wedding ceremonies are rather lavish, prolonged and double – they are organized both in Bulgaria and in Turkey. A similar tendency is observed in the responses to the standardized interviews. Young people's decision to start a life together or to marry their partner depends on their income, on whether they are employed, on their housing arrangements and health; on the other hand, however, their decision depends on the approval of parents and on their financial and moral support in the same measure. Irrespective of more liberal attitudes, marriage is still arranged by the parents, which is indicative of holding onto both values and patriarchal morals.

Along such lines, *respect for the parents* remains a significant and meaningful indicator which influences the life choices of the children[4]. Parents are not only regarded as the people who take care of you and secure your existential minimum, they are mostly regarded as those who share their life experience and wisdom with you and who command respect and must be honored. The responses measured on the scale of characteristics children should acquire at home reveal that obedience and respect for parents are two of the leading attitudes of young people. A 'good attitude' to parents is not simply stated and required, we may say that it has become an interiorized habit, and these dimensions can be traced on a number of different levels.

Therefore, we may summarize that good attitude, mutual help, respect and trust of others (mostly of significant others) are key in the formation of value systems and attitudes in our respondents. Since these are qualities acquired in the process of primary socialization at home, they have become habituated to such an extent that they are crucial in defining and forming identity and the sense of belonging. In parallel to these, our respondents state the importance of *'good manners'*[5]: the family is obviously the context in which the child is to be socialized in such a way as to behave well in society and achieve social success and prestige in the future. This is also a significant factor for the development of the future participant in social interactions. The Turkish students in Edirne also state that good manners are important. We suppose that social control, adequate behaviour – the cultural and symbolic capital – are a condition for legitimizing one's place in society, which is why children are taught such values from an early age. In this respect the two groups of this generation show no significant difference.

After the presentation of empirical data and initial research reflections, let us steer the discussion towards explicating the core educational strategies and biographic choices through which the 'successors' inherit social positions, capitals, prestige, that is, all that which allows them to 'endure in life' in the context of mobility after migration.

---

4   For the family values of Turkish families see also Kagitcibasi 2013.
5   A study of the acculturation of the first and the second generations of Turks in Germany was conducted by Banu Çıtlak et al. (Leyendecker, B., Schölmerich, A. and B. Çıtlak 2005, **Yalcinkaya, A., Çıtlak, B., Leyendecker, B. and R.L. Harwood 2006**).

4.4 Education and occupation – the inherited cultural capital

In order to establish the degrees of *inherited cultural capital* we looked for social indicators such as the *education* and *occupation* of parents before and after migrating. On the whole, the parents of our respondents are relatively highly educated. Higher educational capital is also linked to higher professional capital. The occupations are varied and range from bus driver, excavator driver in a private construction firm, economist, electrician, computer specialist, military, recipe specialist in sweets factories, cheese producer, kindergarten teacher, hospital nurse through to owners of shops, jewellery shops, or hotels and to positions of responsibility and top management in the social hierarchy (for instance Deputy mayor of Izmir).

Most of our respondents do not know what the occupation of their parents was in Bulgaria. That is understandable since this 'other' life of theirs is beyond their personal systems of relevance. What is worth noting though, is that whenever there is knowledge of the occupation of parents 'before', there is either evidence of economic prosperity and heightening of social status: the ex-construction worker has become a jeweller and the owner of a jewellery shop, the former bus driver is now an accountant in a bank with a degree, the field worker with junior high school education is now the owner of a hotel and his son describes him as a very rich man, and so on – or evidence of preservation of the social status in relation to the educational and professional, such as the specialist in recipes for sweets who worked in the same capacity in Bulgaria, and the accountant who was an accountant in Bulgaria, the building engineer and the general practitioner doctor who now has an impressive private practice, who also carry their cultural capital from Bulgaria. It is clear that they have succeeded in transferring their cultural capital to the foreign social environment and they have managed to reproduce it in the process of establishing their own social (but also economic, educational and cultural) position in Turkish society.

In other words: the testimony with regard to *'who-I-used-to-be-before'* is a meaningful biographical marker for *'who-I-am-now'* and *'who-I-will-be'* through which parents construct their own biographical trajectory and which – since it is important and significant – is 'shared' with their children as part of that life story and history. In cases when *'before'* does not contribute to a meaningful resource for recognition (collective or individual), it is repressed and 'forgotten' as a fact which is not worthy of attention from the point of view of life *'now'*.

Interesting observations emerge if we compare the responses from the members of this group to the responses from the '20's generation' – the children of out-migrants who study at the University of Thrace in Edirne. In this group too not all students know what their parents' jobs were in Bulgaria. Among the professions they identified are wrestler, builder, freelancer, worker, and driver. Here, there is a significant difference in terms of how the students position their mothers according to their social status indicated by occupation. The children of out-migrants tell us that in Bulgaria their mothers were either workers or housewives. Bearing in mind the fact that most of the respondents were yet to be born then, we can stipulate that the role of the father as a key economic source is especially important (even if not quite the same as in the dominant Turkish family). The children know the 'before' professions of their fathers, but do not necessarily know those of their mothers.

This is one of the differences in the perspectives of different generations. The parents of these students maintain that they have changed the established norms in Turkey, because they came from socialist Bulgaria where women were employed and had professions. In the new society, both parents alongside the oldest children and younger grandparents immediately start working which is a key factor in their economic advancement. Whether the responses in this section were prompted by the fact, that in the family they pay more attention to the occupation of the father in Bulgaria rather than to that of the mother, or that the children have already been socialized in the Turkish society and its respective values like everybody else, is yet to be established by further interviews. The difference in the responses of the children in their 20's and in their 30's is the knowledge they possess with regard to facts from the life of the family while they were in Bulgaria and the continuous comparison: "my mom and dad used to work in Bulgaria... we had a house and some land..., when we came here they started out as... Later, we bought an apartment, etc." (An interview with a female student in Medicine, 22 years old, Plovdiv)

On the other hand, the children who were born 'there' have already grown up and receive real inheritance 'here'. Even if the field has not yet provided evidence that their future plans will include material inheritance in the form of a business project, it is safe to say that inheritance may be used as a life project in which living and social investments have not only symbolic (cultural inheritance and inherited memory) dimensions but also economic and professional such as "when I retire, I will come back and figure out what to do", "one can set up a pastry shop", etc.[6]).

---

6   Answers from a group discussion with students in Medicine in Varna Medical University, Bulgaria.

4.5 After university – to return to Turkey, to stay in Bulgaria, or to go to somewhere else?

In this section of our study we focused on the personal plans and preferences of our respondents with regard to *important life choices and decisions*: to stay in Bulgaria or to return to Turkey; to continue one's education or to start a family; to begin your career in the field in which you studied or to look for better opportunities.

In terms of plans for a *return* to Turkey (50%) and to *stay* in Bulgaria after graduation (44%) the results are almost even when the question is phrased in a similar manner and offers specific choices which are enumerated. The motivation behind a decision to stay has various dimensions: in order to work in the field in which they currently study, or to start a family, or to start their own business. Another reason which obviously makes a subsequent stay in Bulgaria an attractive possibility is the fact of the country's EU membership. The European dimension, to which Turkey currently also aspires, is a reality for those who are also citizens of Bulgaria. It is not coincidental that in a number of interviews, and also on a range of levels of discussion – political, institutional, every day and social – the context of Bulgaria as a European country is seen as an opportunity for pursuing individual and/or collective desires and goals. In this context we will mention several strategies for border crossing employed by the 'successors' which allow them to use their 'inherited' and institutionally-upheld dual citizenship.

4.6 Strategies of playing with 'dual citizenship'

Bulgarian out-migrants to Turkey, who would like their children to be admitted to a good university, have developed particular strategies for 'double play' according to the existence of a dual status and dual citizenship. For instance, those Bulgarian out-migrants who migrated later, after 1989 (between 1990 and 1994), and who did not automatically get Turkish citizenship like the previous waves of migrants, have permanent residents' status and in recent years intentionally refrain from applying for citizenship. In this way their children sit exams in Turkey as foreigners. Their offspring, even if born in Turkey, are in practice Bulgarian citizens. It is until 2010 however that they could take advantage of this law and the entailing strategies for 'going around' the rule and playing with this double social position.

In Bulgaria, it is economically beneficial compared to studying in universities in Turkey. Moreover, prospective study at a Bulgarian university bears less cost for achieving something which anyway will not guarantee future employment, but will certainly carry social prestige with it. For example, in the words of parents who have supported their child through university, "Still, it is easy here, it's cheap and in the end you have a degree from an EU country... this is key." (Interview with a student in Kirdjali).

4.7 Strategies for 'double play' on behalf of the parents

Parents insist their child study in Bulgaria in the hope of him finding 'a bride' here. This can be illustrated by the following, in which one of our respondents shared: "His parents insisted he marry a Turkish woman in Bulgaria because we are smarter and hard-working, moreover he is a Bulgarian Turk... no Turkish woman will have him!" (Interview with a student in Kirjali)

4.8 Strategies for transforming economic into cultural capital

Acquiring a higher education certificate, as a material manifestation of cultural capital for those children of Bulgarian out-migrants who cannot meet the requirements for admission to Turkish universities, is possible only after parents pay for the preparatory language year at the University of Varna. The perception is that this very step already guarantees admission as students, even if with lower exam grades. The following is an excerpt from an interview with a lecturer at the University of Thrace in Edirne, born into a family of Bulgarian out-migrants from 1989 and a member of the '30's generation':

Well, possibly because Edirne is this kind of town and has this aim – people go to university or want to study at university because they want to find a job – this always matters. [...] I don't know whether you know, but it is quite expensive – about four thousand Euros and the whole fee, that is a lot of money. [...] So, in this branch which you visited today, where you met those students – they are the trickiest lot among the language departments. [...] The initial aim is that they study at university – this is very important. That they are some..., that they will get some diploma. (Interview with a teacher in Bulgarian language courses in Trakia University, Edirne, Turkey for students, admitted at the Medical University in Varna, Bulgaria) In this way we can register the transformation of one capital into another – economic into cultural, but also into social capital.

4.9 Strategies for mediated justification of the choice to migrate

This is evident where some parents 'showing off' their financial resources, which therefore secures the opportunity for their children to study abroad. "The local people [Turks in Bulgaria, authors' note] don't like them, because they come here to show off their affluence, show off money" (from an interview with a student in Kirdjali).

These are the ways in which we find manifestations of how education itself is a key strategy for transforming social, economic, etc., capital into cultural capital. This process is also what legitimizes the various types of 'cross-border returns' of the children of Bulgarian out-migrants to Turkey.

5 In lieu of conclusion

The basic conclusions – which certainly do not exhaust the diverse empirical data, the range of research reflections and possible analytical questions that the complex and very dynamic field on both sides of the Bulgarian-Turkish border offers – still give us an opportunity to approach the forms of family life and cultural inheritance in the situation of migration after mobility. We will attempt to render them in the next paragraphs in terms of a summary outline. The families from our study group, and their descendants, have good social positions with regard to the volume and structure of the *economic capital* they own possess. Even so, the education of children in Bulgaria requires significant economic resources. Our respondents declare moderate optimism and are relatively secure in their future and the plans they can make for the years of education ahead of them, as well as for their subsequent professional realization.

The second generation of migrants, that is the generation of 20-year-olds, who have 'dual citizenship' and who, in a situation of mobility after migration, come to study in Bulgaria, also need to adapt in the new environment which is not as unfamiliar to them as it is for their older brothers and sisters, that is for the 'generation of the 30-year-olds' when they migrated to Turkey.

The choice to stay in Bulgaria, citizens of which they are, is not coincidental and has its grounds for the group of Turkish students we researched, that is the children of Bulgarian re-settlers. This also means that this choice is not as dramatic and infused with emotions as the choice which their parents had to make twenty years ago when they were roughly the same age. In effect, for the 'generation of 20-year-olds', the important decision with regard to life and social realization is not necessarily linked to staying in Turkey. For them, like for most of their peers in 'the society of knowledge', spatial borders and limitations gradually begin to lose their materiality and real meaning, and are increasingly being perceived in terms of fluidity.

Family life, and attitudes to family remain a significant value which is important for the orientation within social relations and future life investments. Outside the family circle, it is difficult to form unconditional and unquestioned social networks. In that domain trust, is the priority under question and as such needs to be won and negotiated. A good attitude, mutual assistance, respect and trust towards others (especially towards significant others) are key in the formation of the value systems and attitudes of our respondents.

In conclusion, the study of various types of migration across the Bulgarian-Turkish border calls for an emphasis on the forms of crossing at the beginning of the twenty-first century, whose form then entails different ways of cross-border returns for the children of Bulgarian out-migrants; returns which are fostered by the particular ways of inhabiting the border – simultaneously 'on both sides of the Bulgarian-Turkish border'. Resulting from the particularities of this form of liminality, there appears a wide range of life and biographical strategies (educational, social, and economic) of the children of out-migrants whereby the 'new young', that is the 'inheritors' of Bulgarian out-migrants to Turkey, exercise their everyday social interactions 'across' the border. A closer look into the forms of crossing one border actually gives us the opportunity to contemplate the multiple dimensions of the lives and worlds of the young mobile people of Europe who, with the support of their families, develop strategies for investing in social capital and in inheriting cultural models from different countries. Finally, and to return to one of the most widely spread forms of family life for the Bulgarian out-migrants to Turkey, we end with the metaphor that the family of the mobile people of Europe at the beginning of the 21st century is an extended family, not only in temporal and generational terms, but also in spatial terms with its life in several countries and across several borders.

Translated by Milena Katsarska

References

Augé, M. (1994). Pour une anthropologie des mondes contemporains. Champs: Flamarion.
Barth, F. (1969). Ethnic Groups and Boundaries. The Social Organization of Cultural Difference. Oslo: Universitetsforlaget.

Bauman, Z. (2007). Humanity on the Move. In: Liquid Times: Living in an Age of Uncertainty. Cambridge: Polity, pp. 27–55.
Bauman, Z. (1998). Globalization: The Human Consequences. New York: Columbia University Press.
Berger P. & Luckmann, T. (1966). The Social Construction of Reality: A Treatise in the Sociology of Knowledge. New York: Doubleday.
Bourdieu, Pierre (1990). In Other Words: Essays toward a Reflective Sociology. Stanford: Stanford University Press.
Bourdieu, P. (1991). Language and Symbolic Power. London: Polity Press.
Bourdieu, P. (1993). La Misere du Monde. Editions du Seuil.
Bourdieu, P. (1998). Practical Reason. Stanford: Stanford University Press.
Bourdieu, P. (1999). The Weight of the World: Social Suffering in Contemporary Societies. London: Polity Press.
Bourdieu, P. (2004). Science of Science and Reflexivity. Chicago: University of Chicago Press.
Castles, S. &, Miller, M. J. (1993). The Age of Migration. In: International Population. Movements in the Modern World. Houndsmills: Macmillan.
Cesur-Kılıçaslan, S. & Terzioğlu, R. G. (2009). Families immigrating from Bulgaria to Turkey since 1978. In: Ethnologia Balkanica (13), pp. 43–58.
Clifford, J. (1997). Travel and Translation in the Late Twentieth Century. Cambridge, MA: Harvard University Press.
Elchinova, M. (2005). Alien by default: the identity of the Turks of Bulgaria at home and in immigration. In: Developing Cultural Identity in the Balkans: Convergence vs. Divergence, Detrez, R. & P. Plas (eds.). Brussels, P.I.E.: Peter Lang, pp. 67–110.
Elchinova, M. (2009). Migration studies in Bulgaria: scope, experiences and developments. In: Anthropological Journal of European Cultures, 18(2), pp. 69–86.
Ganeva-Raycheva, V. (2011). Migration, Memory, Heritage: the Example of the Thrace Bulgarians, Descendants of Refugees and Resettlers from Eastern Thrace. In: Bulgarian Folklore. Bulgaria – Slovenia: Research (Special Edition), pp. 48–66.
Habermas, J. (2001). The Postnational Constellation. Political Essays. Cambridge: Polity Press.
Kagitcibasi, C. (2013). Family, self, and human development across cultures: Theory and applications, second edition. New York and London: Taylor and Francis Croup.
Lash, S. (1990). Sociology of Postmodernism. London: Routledge.
Leyendecker, B., Schölmerich, A. & Çıtlak, C. (2005I. Similarities and Differences among First- and Second-Generation Turkish Migrant Mothers in Germany: The Acculturation Gap. In: M. H. Bornstein & L. R. Cote (Eds.), Acculturation and Parent-Child Relationships: Measurement and Development, Mahwah, NJ: Erlbaum, pp. S. 297-315.
Nora, P. (1989). Between Memory and History: Les Lieux de Mémoire. In: Representations, No. 26, Special Issue: Memory and Counter-Memory. (Spring). Available at http://www.timeandspace.lviv.ua/files/session/Nora_105.pdf [accessed: 31 October 2015.] , pp. 7-24.
Papastergiadis, N. (2000). The Turbulence of Migration: Globalization, Deterritorialization and Hybridity. Cambridge: Polity Press.
Parla, A. (2006). Longing, belonging, and locations of homeland among Turkish immigrants from Bulgaria. In: Journal of Southeastern Europe and Black Sea Studies, vol. 6 (4), pp. 543–557.

Schuetz, A. (1944). The Stranger: An Essay in Social Psychology. In: American Journal of Sociology, Vol. 49, No. 6 (May). Available at https://www.jstor.org/stable/2771547?seq=1#page_scan_tab_contents [accessed: 31 October 2015.] , pp. 499–507

Vukov, N. (2011). Border making and cross-border dynamics along the tripod-shaped border between Bulgaria, Turkey, and Greece in Eastern Thrace. Paper from the International Conference Remaking Borders, EastBordNet Project/ IS0803, Catania/Italy, pp. 20–22.

Yalcinkaya, A., Çıtlak, B., Leyendecker, B. & Robin H. (2006). Exploring the concept of Respect among Turkish and Puerto Rican migrant mothers. In: New Directions for Child and Adolescent Development, pp. 9–24.

Zlatkova, M. (2012). Towns Close to the Border: Spaces of Migration and Inheritance. In: Elchinova, M. et al. Migration. Memory, Heritage: Socio-cultural Approaches to the Bulgarian-Turkish Border. Sofia: IEFSEM – BAS. Available at http://2sidesborder.org/Resettlers%20 and%20Migrants/. [accessed: 31 October 2015.

Zlatkova, M. & Stoyka P. (2012). The children of migrants: cultural heritage strategies and types of crossing the Bulgarian-Turkish border. In: Migration, Memory, Heritage: Socio-cultural Approaches to the Bulgarian-Turkish Border, edited by V. Ganeva-Raycheva and M. Zlatkova, Sofia: IEFSEM – BAS. Available at http://2sidesborder.org/migration%20EN/index.html [accessed: 31 October 2015.], pp.174–198.

Бокова, И. (2003) „Подвижният човек" - в мрежата от топоси. В: Пл. Бочков (съст.). Антропологични изследвания, Т. 4. 78–98, София: НБУ/ИК „Яр". [Bokova, Irena (2003) Mobile man – in the network of topoi. In: Anthropological Research, edited by Pl. Bochkov, vol. 4. 7, Sofia: NBU/Yar Publishing House.], pp. 8–98.

Бочков, П. (2002) „Родината" в дискурса на сравнението. В: Елчинова, М. (съст.). Антропологични изследвания, Т. 3. 57–76, София: НБУ. [Bochkov, Plamen (2002) "Birth country" in the discourse of comparison, In: Anthropological Research, edited by M. Elchinova, vol. 3, Sofia: NBU.], pp. 57–76

Бочков, П. (2004) Българските турци, изселници в Измир – идентичност, адаптация и мрежи на солидарност. В: Лазова, Ц. (съст.). Антропологични изследвания, Т. 5. София: НБУ, 175–190. [Bochkov, Plamen (2004) Bulgarian Turks, out-migrants in Izmir – identity, adaptations and networks of solidarity. In: Anthropological Research, edited by Ts. Lazova, vol. 5, Sofia: NBU.], pp.175–190

Ганева-Р., В. (2004) Разказване и идентичност. София: „Яр". [Ganeva-Raycheva, Valentina (2004) Story-telling and Identity. Sofia: Yar.]

Ганева-Райчева, В. (2012) Миграции и институции: политики и практики при конструиране на памет инаследство. В: Миграции от двете страни на българо-турската граница: наследства, идентичности, интеркултурни взаимодействия. В. Ганева-Райчева, М. Елчинова, М. Златкова, Н. Вуков (съст.), 169–196, София: ИЕФЕМ. [Ganeva-Raycheva, Valentina (2012) Migrations and institutions: politics and practices of constructing memory and identity. In: Migrations on Both Sides of the Turkish-Bulgarian Border: Heritage, Identities, Intercultural Interactions, edited by V. Ganeva-Raycheva et al., Sofia: IEFSE. Available at http://2sidesborder.org/Resettlers%20 and%20Migrants/index.html#/10] [accessed: 29 January 2016], pp. 169–197.

Дичев, И. (2009) Граждани отвъд местата? Нови мобилности, нови граници, нови форми на обитаване. София: Просвета. [Dichev, Ivaylo (2009) Citizens beyond Places? New Mobilities, New Borders, New Forms of Inhabiting. Sofia: Prosveta.]

Елчинова, М. (2012) Преосмисляне на травматичния опит във всекидневните дискурси: наративите за изселването на българските турци в Турция в перспективата на времето. В: Миграции от двете страни на българо-турската граница: наследства, идентичности, интеркултурни взаимодействия. Ганева-Райчева, М. Елчинова, М. Златкова, Н. Вуков (съст.), София, ИЕФЕМ. [Elchinova, Magdalena (2012). Rethinking traumatic experience in everyday discourses: narratives of out-migration of Bulgarian Turks to Turkey from a diachronic perspective. In: Migrations on Both Sides of the Bulgarian- Turkish Border: Heritage, Identities, Intercultural Interactions, edited by V. Ganeva-Raycheva et al. Sofia: IEFSEM, 21–31.] Available at http://2sidesborder.org/Resettlers%20and%20Migrants/index. html#/10 [accessed: 31 October 2015], pp. 21–31.

Желязкова, А. (съст.) (1998) Между адаптацията и носталгията (българските турци в Турция). В: Съдбата на мюсюлманските общности на Балканите. София: IMIR. [Zhelyazkova, Antonina (ed.) (1998) Between adaptation and nostalgia (Bulgarian Turks in Turkey). In: The Fate of Muslim Communities on the Balkans, vol. 3, Sofia: IMIR.]

Златкова, М. (2016) Градски наследства и граници. Пловдив: Контекст [Zlatkova, Meglena (2016) Urban Heritage across Borders. Edirne, Turkey and Tzarevo, Bulgaria. Plovdiv: Context]

Златкова, М. & Стойка, П. (2011) „Противоречията на наследството" – образованието като културен капитал на „второто поколение" мигранти: децата на изселниците в Турция. В: Ловци на умове. Т. 4,. София: НБУ. [Zlatkova, Meglena and Stoyka Penkova (2011) "Contradictions of inheritance" – education as cultural capital of the "second generation" of migrants: the children of out-migrants to Turkey. In: Mind Hunters, vol. 4. 74–100. Sofia: NBU.], pp. 74–100.

Златкова, М. & Стойка, П. (2012) „Завръщания" през границата? Форми на преминаване на българо-турската граница от младите поколения. В: Социологически проблеми, тематичен брой „Мобилност и миграции" 1–2, 152–171. [Zlatkova, Meglena and Stoyka Penkova (2012) Cross-border returns? Forms of crossing the Bulgarian-Turkish border by the young generations. In: Sociological Problems, 1–2.], pp. 152–171

Кръгла, м. (2012) Трансграничното сътрудничество между България и Турция: предпоставки, развитие, проблеми. В: Миграции от двете страни на българо-турската граница: наследства, идентичности, интеркултурни взаимодействия. Ганева-Райчева, В., М. Елчинова, М. Златкова, Н. Вуков (съст.), София: ИЕФЕМ. [Round Table (2012) Trans-border cooperation between Bulgaria and Turkey: premise, development, issues]. In: Migrations on Both Sides of the Turkish-Bulgarian Border: Heritage, Identities, Intercultural Interactions, edited by Ganeva-Raycheva et al. Sofia: IEFSEM.] Available at http://2sidesborder.org/Resettlers%20and%20Migrants/index. html#/10 [accessed: 31 October 2015.] 277–298.

Кръстева, А. (съст.) (2006) Фигурите на бежанеца. София: НБУ. [Krasteva, Anna. (ed.) (2006) Images of Refugees. Sofia: NBU.]

Маева, М. (2006) Българските турци – преселници в Република Турция (Култура и идентичност). София: IMIR. [Maeva, Mila (2006) Bulgarian Turks – out-migrants to the Republic of Turkey (Culture and Identity). Sofia: IMIR]

Маева, М. (2012) Миграция и мобилност на българските турци-преселници в края на 20 и началото на 21 век. В: Миграции от двете страни на българо-турската граница: наследства, идентичности, интеркултурни взаимодействия. В. Ганева-Райчева, М. Елчинова, М. Златкова, Н. Вуков (съст.), София: ИЕФЕМ. [Maeva, Mila

(2012) Migration and mobility of out-migrant Bulgarian Turks at the end of the 20 and the beginning of the 21 centuries. In: Migrations on Both Sides of the Turkish-Bulgarian Border: Heritage, Identities, Intercultural Interactions, edited by Ganeva-Raycheva, V. et al. Sofia, IEFSEM.] Available at http://2sidesborder.org/Resettlers%20and%20Migrants/index. html#/10 [accessed: 31 October 2015.], pp. 45–53.

Пенкова, С. (2009) Бурдийо, Фуко като шанс за една историческа социология на дискурсивните практики. В: Социологически проблеми 3-4. [Penkova, Stoyka (2009) Bourdieu and Foucault – a chance for historical sociology of discursive practices. In: Sociological Problems, 3–4], 50–69.

Пенкова, С. (2013а) Неравенство, дискурс, наследяване. Пловдив: Контекст. [Penkova, Stoyka (2013a) Inequality, Discourse, Inheriting. Plovdiv: Context.]

Пенкова, С. (2013б) Наследяване и дискурсивни практики. Сборник студии. Пловдив: Контекст. [Penkova, Stoyka (2013b) Inheriting and Discursive Practices. Plovdiv: Context.]

Стоянов, В. (1998) Турското население в България между полюсите на етничната политика. София: ИК „ЛИК". [Stoyanov, Valeri (1998) The Turkish Population in Bulgaria between the Poles of Ethnic Politics. Sofia: LIK.]

Socialist family as a biopolitical dispositive

Rositsa Lyubenova

1 Introduction

The following text is an essay on the socialist family. Its purpose is not to look at all of its aspects, but only to outline its contours and characteristics as a biopolitical construct with its existing and newly formed boundaries – those that have been overcome and those that have not been, respectively. In the discourse of socialist policy, family is one of the key subjects. It is a prerequisite for the existence of the socialist society, as well as a result of the construction of the New Man and the New Society[1]. In practice, the socialist family is an artificial construct, which subsequently must be filled with content and brought to life by real living people. The intertwining of ideological goals and biopolitical measures with the family's biography provides the socialist authority with the predictability, clarity, and fate needed in order to achieve flawless social relations.

My main thesis is that the socialist authority exercises a biopolitical control over the processes of birth, mortality, morbidity, and life expectancy. As a consequence, the socialist authority controlled the productivity and usefulness of socialist citizens, primarily through the giving of new roles of women and the mobilization of childhood.

---

1   The notions „New Man" and "New Society are self-nominations of the society of socialism and the "new citizens" comes to differ them from the pre-socialist ideas in terms of way of life, behavior and thinking. The notion "New Society" refers to society which was built from the new socialist citizens. These terms were used in the official documents of the socialist government and also by the ordinary people who lived in the period examined in this text - 1945-1968.

The goal of this text is to trace the main mechanisms through which the biopolitical construction of family and its separate members is achieved, as well as to consider the specific target points of the biopolitical dispositive. In order to accomplish this, I will focus both on explications in archival materials related to the characteristics of the socialist family as a whole, as well as the new roles prescribed to women, children, and childhood. To achieve this, I will refer to archival materials, which are in fact the official documents of socialist institutions. They are a product of the official discourse of socialist power and thus explicate exactly that power, and as a result of this they appear as pre-set, prescriptive, and constructive identities. The following text is part of a larger research project, carried out in 2011, which used documents from the State archives in Plovdiv and Blagoevgrad, as well as editions of the State Gazzette for the period of interest. The funds used for the research are connected to the activities of institutions and organizations corresponding naturally to the family as a whole or its members. The prescriptive explications within the official discourse of the archival documents evidence some basic grounds that make everyday practices of the socialist family possible.

The issues I would like to emphasize and attempt to provide answers to are related to the nature and the intensity of the government measures, that led to the involvement of the socialist family in the implementation of biopolitics in the period of 1945-1968, as well as the reasons they took these measures, the desired outcomes, and the actual consequences that occurred as a result of these measures.

While examining these questions I will refer to Michel Foucault's analysis of the dispositive, his view of biopolitics of the population, as well as other concepts of his theory associated with the creation, distribution, implementation, and management of practices and discourses on sexuality – through which the dispositives of knowledge and power and the dispositive of sexuality are formed. The current study also draws on the theoretical prerequisites of the historical sociology of socialism developed by the Bulgarian sociological school. In order to extract and analyze the archival documents, I use the methodology of discourse analysis and the socioanalysis of documents.

And here, I would like to write a preliminary, and, in my view, essential paragraph for the understanding of the text, a paragraph which will highlight the peculiar historical context in which it is set.

2 The Bulgarian society in the period 1944-1968 in the context of the historical sociology of socialism

Socialism is a specific period in the history of Bulgaria spanning the period from 1944 to 1989. During this phase many new directions for the development of Bulgarian society that differed greatly from the existing ones were established. The beginning of socialism in Bulgaria was initiated with a politico-military coup on September 9th 1944, and the government of the Fatherland Front took the subsequent first steps. In the country, many changes took place: new ministries were legalized and many of the laws adopted by the former government were abolished. The state apparatus was restructured and from 1941 to September 9th, 1944, ministers from all governments, MPs of the Twenty-fifth National Assembly, and senior military officials were detained. The property (movable and immovable) of such persons was barred and participants in the coupe fled the vacated positions. The archives of the royal police were „purged" and the estates of the wealthy associated with the former government were confiscated to be used by the new regime. At the same time, these practices enriched the activists of the Fatherland Front, that is, those who participated in the „fight against fascism and capitalism." The privileges of the „deserving ones" were not limited to small acquisitions. The legal requirements for candidates for certain state and municipal posts were canceled and the senior management positions were occupied without any obstacles, by semi-literate Bulgarians who „fought against fascism and capitalism". The so-called "People's Court" had started the „cleansing" of the state apparatus.

All this was accompanied by the formation of a new social group, which was composed of former peasants who constitute the vast majority of the communist party. The country was in a difficult economic situation: there was a serious capital deficit, a severe inflation, and a lack of goods and savings among the population. The formation of agricultural cooperation began. Settlements, schools, streets and any many other sites in the country were renamed in order to obtain the proper socialist meaning. By this process the past was pushed back, even in the names of streets and squares. This practice was related to Lenin and Marx's views, according to which the old material environment (be it in plates of streets and squares) reproduces the old social relations.

Large-scale construction also took place. In the late 40s, youth brigades were formed and they were sent to sites across the country to support the socialist construction. In the month of May in 1947, the construction of Dimitrovgrad began. In order to build the city from scratch 50,000 young people from 943 cities and villages in the country worked gratuitously. The slogan of the foremen of the „Young Guard" was „We build the city, the city is building us". By using the free labor of Bulgarian youths, residential complexes, chemical plants, factories, roads, railways, and dams were built. The participation in the brigades was voluntary, but it was regarded as one of the proofs of loyalty to the homeland and the Party and this kind of gift to the state could be a ground for a gift in return. As an evidence I will quote the story of Mrs. Abadzhieva-Eliseeva who narrates how to be eligible to apply for a university had to take a special note (named in the quote below FF – note, issued by the district organization of the Fatherland Front), affirming its „reliability" to be a student.

> „I need the FF note. To people like me, however, the FF note is given only after participation in the national brigade or three years of work experience in a factory. And I go. First to Pernik-Voluyak, for work experience on the „Penchov bridge." April-May. Labor. It is cold. Fatigue. My thighs have bleeding wounds. We are dressed in shorts. [...] In June, armed with the FF note they gave me, I was a forewoman – I went to Burgas for an exam. „(ed. Znepolski; Abadzhieva-Eliseeva 2010: 54-55).

During the epoch of socialism in Bulgaria an accelerated program for construction and industrialization was initiated: establishments for food consumption and childcare were built and the pattern of life for Bulgarian families was subjected to significant changes. They were separated from the village and the land and began to make their living by working in factories and industrial plants. A huge migration wave from the villages to the cities emerged, which was a consequence of the policy of nationalization and the lack of means for sustenance in the countryside. This led to a housing crisis that spread throughout the entire country. The men in managerial positions, such as mayors, directors and etc. were arrested and a significant number of them disappeared without a trace, leaving their families with no means of sustenance.

All family members were involved in the process of „building socialism": men worked in factories, plants, and mines, young men and women worked on construction sites around the country and conducted their training sessions on site (the construction process involved minors as well). Women, besides dealing with propaganda in order to attract more members into the women's organizations, were also involved in providing some necessary items to the youth brigades. „Women send letters, packages of vegetables, fruits, pastries, candy, envelopes, sheets of stamps etc./.../ In addition to the above mentioned help that we as women have to give, we will have to periodically arrange to send every week to the brigades and the sites women with the plan for cleaning the premises, and washing and patching the clothes. July 27, 1947" (State Archive Plovdiv, f.30, op.1, a.e.1, l.21[2])

---

2   Abbreviations : f. (fund), op. (docket), a.e. (archival unit)

At the same time, women, more often than not, started working in production plants and were even encouraged to work in the mines. The following quotation is from a letter dated August 8th 1950 from the Bulgarian National Women's Union to the city authorities of the women's association: „It is necessary that the women's associations respond to the appeal of the mining union, by extensive propaganda for women to join the workers community in the mines. The example of those having already joined from Dimitrovo shows that women in this sector of our industry can cope perfectly." (State Archive Plovdiv, f.30, op.1, a.e. 1 l.27)

3   The family in the context of the socialist biopolitics: "an institutional consequence" of this society[3]

Referring to the historical context outlined in the previous paragraph, leads to the formation of sexual discourse as a product of power and knowledge I will explicate its main premises. The authority already has a benefit and desire to maintain the sexual dispositive. The dispositive of sexuality is actually an expression of the interaction between knowledge and power or „knowledge about human sexuality and biological sciences of reproduction" (Foucault 1993: 208). There is enough data from the archives that describe the official socialist discourse on sexuality for the conduction of biopolitics the way Foucault describes. Biopolitics, which has the aim to collectivize, to build a new socialist society: „... power that has a positive impact on life, undertakes to manage it, increase it, to multiply it, to exercise an accurate control over it and to fully regulate it" (Foucault 1993: 184). The socialist biopower and the biopolitics conducted by it, are not limited to „harnessing the bodies" in the manufacturing process. It contacts the masses and is interested in humans as a biological species – the individual bodies are of no interest to biopolitics, unlike the disciplinary authority. Socialism also gives a meaning to basic biological characteristics as politically effective and controllable. It evaluates and calculates the value of the human body by a calculation of its useful effects and by raising the efficiency bounds.

The main targets of biopolitical control are the processes of fertility, mortality, morbidity, and life expectancy, because all of this leads to exercising control over productivity and usefulness. The Socialist authority was interested in the masses and humans as a biological species. The purpose of biopolitics, conducted by the socialist state, was to gain an added value from life. The introduction and control of negative and positive sanctions over fertility and mortality, the application of

---

3   An exact quotation following Mariya Dinkova, 1976: 216

measures for mass hygiene and immunizations – were all measures that aimed to achieve the immortality of the collective body. They were also carried out through processes of mass education, urbanization, and public hygiene.

The enforcement of specially designed laws outline the power mechanisms through which biopolitics was introduced and conducted – incitement to sexuality for reproductive purposes, implemented through economic motivations and sanctions. The dispositive of sexuality is the connecting link between biological reproduction and biopolitical techniques for the exercise of control over birth rates. The official discourse „recommends" controlling and planning for the expansion of a family; it offers „incentives" for families that create the future socialist citizens and dresses the established „relationships of subordination" in this power dispositive. Foucault says that every power dispositive produced by different techniques and different „relationship of subordination" its various subjects. If we follow the logics of Foucault and accept that, in the present case, the establishment of any superior system is a product of a crisis, then it follows that the socialist authority is experiencing a lack of „builders" in order to build the „bright future". The state wants „results" from the sexuality of its socialist citizens and provides „incentives" for this.

In the short term, the citizens of the socialist state would be substantially fed and healthy, and in the long term, they would receive the necessary education to be useful to the state in return. It is expected an increase in the efforts of the scientific work, which focused on reducing the cases of infertility and miscarriage. A specialized center affiliated with the Medical University of Sofia was created in order to deal with these problems limiting the cases of artificial abortion, prohibiting the interruption of the first pregnancy, unless was necessary due to medical reasons, such as rape or in especially severe cases, and conducting recurring events in „protecting the fertility and the health of women" (SG, № 1, 01.09.1968, 2).

On February 23rd,1968 in the State Gazette issued a decree declaring that unmarried men and women, widowed, and married and divorced without children should be taxed (SG, №. 15/ 23.02.1968, 1). The tax was doubled on 30th birthday of unmarried citizens (man and women) and for families without children after 5 years of marriage. Legislative measures were also implemented aimed at supporting large families, pregnant women, and mothers, and improving the work of health establishments and health education in schools.

The Family Code, in essence, interprets biopolitical measures of the authority, derived from the contact with knowledge, and is mostly a product of the sexual dispositive of the legal language. These „legally cloaked" measures „were reported" and respectively legalized through public announcements bringing them to the attention of the subject to whom the measure would be applied. The Family Code was actually a reflection of „social policy" or in Foucaldian terms – of biopolitics. Biopolitical exclusion was implemented by the signature of class and the mechanisms for conducting biopolitics were legalized and ideologized. These practices were directed towards society as a whole, but they were especially used and strictly controlled with regards to children. Children were seen as the future capital of the socialist state and care to limit child mortality, the preservation of health, healthy food, proper nutrition, and good hygiene were in the foreground. The process of educating the population about personal hygiene and hygiene of the house began in the first years of the socialist period. Happiness, health, employability, and their mass demonstration were essential for the country's social policy. Childhood began to take up new spaces; it took place, in its vast majority of the time in the public spaces, different from the private sphere of the family. The residence of the child in the public domain through collective children's activities, children's camps and kindergartens, playgrounds, etc., through active communication with others, and also through distancing from the family (as that is possible at a young age) were all prerequisites for a child's "proper" future development. These measures provided „happiness" to the children, comfort for the parents (associated with more free time, its planning and scheduling which, in turn provided for yet another calculation of the efficiency and usefulness of socialist citizens), as well as the child's trust. And these factors were considered necessary to implement the „tireless work" to reach the communist future. Because the system had already established mechanisms for the socialist education of children and needed resources, it placed emphasis on the dispositive of sexuality, which had a key role in birth control policies.

Much of the turmoil in socialist family life arose from the new role of women in society as a result of the perception of gender equality, the conversion of traditionally female spaces to „uninhabited" ones, the seizure of functions in public spaces intrinsically linked to women (such as kindergartens, canteens, laundries, etc.), and the channeling the potential and energy of women into the service of socialist production. The process of collectivization marked a boundary in the pattern of life, towards which the village family could not return, as it has been deprived of its purely economic function. This forced the members of the village families to join the lines of the so-called proletariat, or in other words – to become workers. From here many changes began in the family's way of life that change the village for the city.

The reasons for the qualitatively new dimensions of inner family relations and practices were numerous, but two were perhaps the most serious. First, urban migration, which is the main reason for the collapse of the traditional „big family" (by Mariya Dinkova[4]), and second – the main instrument of biopolitics – female

---

4   Mariya Dinkova – leading figure of the "Sociology of family" in Bulgaria

emancipation followed by the institutionalization of a new identity of women. The women and the children were perceived as the main tools for the construction of socialist life and for the application of biopolitics in Bulgaria. Adhering to the covenants of Marx and Engels, the socialist regime in Bulgaria made women a part of the industrial life and the children were taken away (to the extent possible) outside the boundaries of the home environment in order to be made useful to society.

4 Instituting of the new identity of the woman: the female emancipation as an instrument of bio-politics

The woman in the city also worked in the factory or factories alongside men. She was employed and financially independent of her husband. This development also determined many changes, the most significant being the removal of the patriarchal model and building new relations "not only a formal, but substantival gender equality." "Winning the September 9th freedom with the help of the glorious invincible Red Army, and the equality which women were granted subsequently, allowed for a broad public political manifestation. For a short time in the city, quite spontaneously, there appeared eighteen female associations with four thousand five hundred members, who provided warm and cordial care for the fighters of the Patriotic War. With such a result the women in Plovdiv for the first time freely celebrated their battle holiday on March 8th " (State Archive Plovdiv, f.30, op.1, a.e. 6, l.11). The new position of women in socialist Bulgaria is described in this way in a letter from the city Trustees of the Bulgarian People's Union Women in Plovdiv 1945 – 1951.

The right and the opportunity for the education of women and the equal access to education are two of the factors that contributed to the new understanding of the family as such. The woman now also had social obligations – she was a member of the socialist party; and took an active role in all kinds of events. She had been supported and protected by the Party, because she had been the main "accomplice" of the educational institutions (from the day care to the university) in the raising of children.

The vision of the socialist authority was for the "liberation" of woman from "heavy capitalistic slavery," from the subordinate position in the patriarchal family model, and from the typical spaces and activities. How successfully this patriarchal model of the Bulgarian family was overcome is a question, the answer to which slightly shines through in some of the documents. The female members of the woman's organizations took part in different educational and informative discourses, and also in biopolitical discourses, which if assimilated by a large aggregation of women, would help the authority with the effective application of the biopolitical measures. The Bulgarian woman from the socialist period bravely stepped beyond the boundaries of her home environment, which until this moment had been clear and emphatic, in order to put her efforts into the "construction" of the new, common for everyone, socialist home.

5 The instrumentalization of childhood

The society must provide for a big part of the children's education – this was a goal of the ruling socialist party. The separation of the children from the family happened with the help of the social educational institutions. The time that children are engaged in the educational institutions was increased by creating study halls, as well as boarding schools and 7-day kindergartens. The role of the parents in the education and formation of the child's personality, as described in the official authority discourse, was mediocre. The substitution of the parents in two of their main functions, upbringing and education, had a triple aim: first, to increase the manufacturing time and the effectiveness of the parents in the "work process;" second, to create free time which they could devote to public and political activities; and last but not least, to prevent the possible education of children in cultural stereotypes that were different from the socialist ones.

In 1945 the Ministry of Social Affairs established the rules for the regulation and management of children's homes.

"Art. 1. Children's homes are designed to take full care of children, mostly of the workers during the time when their parents are involved in the production, administration, public life and for children without parents. Children's homes take care of the social education, health and proper physical and mental development of the children.
Art. 2. There are four types of children's homes: nurseries, children day-care homes, daily children's homes and summer day-care homes. [...]
Art. 8 In children's homes children of workers are mainly accepted and those who are deprived of adequate and proper parenting, due to the absence of parents, poor housing, poor moral environment and so on. The goal, however, is for the children's homes to encompass all children of the people, so that they can develop in themselves social feelings, to give them the necessary education and to form even at a tender age the future citizen. [...] The children's clothing must meet all the requirements of hygiene, to be convenient and to be uniform. " (SG № 77, 04.1945, 6)

The children's and the teenager's physical and moral development was a topic that was recognized and treated as paramount by the socialist state. Children were perceived in a qualitatively different way. What is found and stimulated in them was not the belonging to their families, but the belonging to the state. The entire concept for the education, tutoring, guidance, and treatment of the children was based on the planning of future benefits.

The mobilization of childhood began in kindergarten – the institution with a significant importance according to the socialist authority. This was the place where the direct trilateral relationship kindergarten, children, and parents (family) was strongly harmonized. The children's education was not related to family traditions, the imparting of ancestral knowledge or following family values, rather it was entirely subordinated to the correct ideological and political course of education. The parents were obliged to inform the kindergarten about everything that took place in the family and was directly or indirectly related to the child. The state would yet again peek into the private space of Bulgarian citizens and teach them from an early age to be tolerant and well-disposed to this all-seeing eye. In the intimate child-parent relationship a third element interfered, institutionalizing its presence and breaking the close bond in the child-family relationship.

Due to the necessity that socialist education, regardless of how old the child is, be transferred and continued, ideologies of the socialist family paid great attention to the strength of marriage. "In our country the family is an important link in the education of people. We must not allow children to be wasted; they belong not only to parents but also to society. We need healthy, physically and mentally complete children – future citizens of communism. […] The socialist family subjects the tasks of family upbringing to the most important public purpose – the creation of active and conscious builders of communism" (quoted in Brunnbauer 2010: 401). According to socialist theorists, bad marriage relationships not only affected the raising and education of children in socialist virtues, but also the work performance and the efficiency of the worker. That is why the state and the society interfered with family relations and with the distribution of family obligations; they constantly controlled what happened in the family.

The school institution is "…publicly legitimated, biographically predestined and in this sense is a mandatory fixed period, an event" (Nikolova 2001:71). The socialist authority relied exactly on this legitimated obligatoriness of schooling in order to apply its biopolitics. The student is treated as a "work element", not as a child. Great efforts were taken for tutoring the youth visiting the schools so they would be reliable enough and could take maximum advantage of and efficacy from their bodies. The knowledge for this reality was assimilated and incorporated in the first years of socialist education. The system dictated, controlled, and sanctioned everything that took place in the schools. The entire childhood was bounded with the world of the adults, with state priorities and with economic development.

6 Summary

The official discourse guided the socialist citizens; it prescribed their values and created their identities. This discourse set (and subsequently implemented a control over) the practices of the citizens of socialist Bulgaria, creating the demarcating boundaries between "right" and "wrong" types of behavior regarding sex, family and children. An analysis of the archival materials clearly outlines the ideological discourse that aimed to support and justify the biopolitical measures provided by the Socialist government, and well as attempted to "penetrate" the biography of the family by exercising pressure at several target points simultaneously. These efforts of the government paved the way for social relations that were easily predictable and controllable, and namely this combination provided stability and longevity of every type of power.

References

Брунбауер, У. (2010) „*Социалистическия начин на живот.*" *Идеология, общество, семейство и политика в България (1944 – 1989)*. Русе: ИК „Елиас Канети". [Brunnbauer, Ulf (2010) *"Socialist way of life." Ideology, society, family and policy in Bulgaria (1944-1989)*. Ruse: Elias Canetti.]

Динкова, М. (1976) *Съвременното българско семейство*. София: Отечествен фронт. [Dinkova, Mariya (1976) *Contemporary Bulgarian family*. Sofia: Publishing the Fatherland Front.]

Абаджиева-Елисеева, М. (2010) „Страници от моя дневник". В: Знеполски, Ивайло (съст.) *Това е моето минало. Спомени, дневници, свидетелства. (1944-1989)*. т.2. София: Сиела [Abadzieva – Eliseeva, Mariya (2010) „Pages of my diary", In: Znepolski, Ivaylo (ed.) *This is my past. Memories, diaries, testimonials. (1944-1989)*. v.2. Sofia: Ciela.]

Николова, Н. (2001) *Политанатомия на модерния човек*.София: ИК „Критика и Хуманизъм. [Nikolova, Nina (2001) *Polit-anatomy of the Modern Man*. Sofia: Critique and Humanism.]

Фуко, М. (1993) *История на сексуалността. Волята за знание*. т.1. [Foucault, Michel (1993) *The History of Sexuality: The Will to knowledge*. v.1. Pleven: EA.]

Държавен вестник №2/ 09 януари 1968, 1. [State Gazette №2/ 09 January 1968, 1.]

Държавен вестник №1/ 09 януари 1968, 2. [State Gazette № 1/ 09 January 1968, 2.]

Държавен вестник № 15/ 23 февруари 1968, 1. [State Gazette № 15/ 23 February 1968, 1.]
Държавен вестник № 77/ април 1945, 6. [State Gazette № 77/ April 1945, 6.]
Archival funds:
Държавен архив – Пловдив, ф.30, оп.1, а.е.1, л.21. [State Archive Plovdiv, f.30, op.1, a.e.1, 1.21.]
Държавен архив – Пловдив, ф.30, оп.1, а.е. 1, л.27. [State Archive Plovdiv, f.30, op.1, a.e. 1, 1.27.]
Държавен архив – Пловдив ф.30, оп.1, а.е. 6, л.11. [State Archive Plovdiv, f.30, op.1, a.e. 6, 1.11.]

More than to Raise a Child from a Distance

Mobile Parents and Their Children Left Behind in Bulgaria

Svetlana Antova

1 Introduction

A few days ago my four-year old son asked me where he stayed while we, along with his father and older brother, were in Cyprus in 2012. "You stayed here with grandma and grandpa", I answered. And the deep sense of guilt gripped my throat again. I know that obstacles did not allow us to take him with us for the period of five months while we were there, but still… three years later I continue to ask myself if it was worth traveling to Aphrodite's island because of my academic project. How many children are left behind in Bulgaria by their migrant parents for longer or shorter periods? What is the price for both, the children and the parents? What are the outcomes of repeated periods of separation or permanent separation?

The aim of this paper is to examine one of the main problems that results from labor mobility abroad in the last 25 years or more – the problem of distance-parenting and children left behind in Bulgaria. The main questions are:

- What are the reasons behind the separations of families and why is this preferred over going abroad together or staying at home?
- How do participants in these processes – mobile parents, their children, and their relatives – perceived the situation of separation and how do the families' roles and relations change?
- What are the main consequences resulting from the separation of parents and children?

I use the term "distance-parenting" to describe the distance-parental control of mobile Bulgarians mainly through modern communicative technologies – mobile phones and internet while the children stay with their grandparents or relatives in Bulgaria. In this article I state that the separated families develop and maintain new forms of trans-nationalized ties and relations. Leading transnational, multi-sited lives means that exchanges and interactions across borders are a regular and sustained part of migrants' realities and activities, due to a report of IOM (IOM, 2010: 1). In Western reports the term "left behind children" and "distance-parenting" are used in cases where one or both of the parents are absent from the family because of one reason or another and normally refers to separated couples or families (De la Garsa 2010). All authors notice that these terms are used when one or both parents are abroad.

In this paper I also use the term "remittance-led" migration as a term for seasonal and temporary labor migration, provoked mainly by economic and social reasons and aiming to stabilize incomes. This is not a new phenomenon for Bulgaria. Petko Hristov noticed it in his research of labor forms of migration on the Balkans:

"The tradition of seasonal and/or temporary labour migrations, particularly among the men, has existed for centuries in a number of regions on the Balkans. The model, according to which men earn money somewhere "away" or "abroad" (the neighboring region, the big city, another state/country or "somewhere" in the Balkans), but return every year to their home places and families "here", is known on the Balkans as gurbet/kurbet, or with the South-Slavic term pechalbarstvo" (Hristov 2008:217, cit. in Hristov 2010: 28).

Remittance-led migration increased after 1989 when economic instability became one of the main push factors for thousands of Bulgarians to search for an honest living abroad. Normally people who feel unable to cope with the situation in their own space or who feel in danger of being caught in the poverty trap are oriented to such mobility and migration. Fieldwork data have shown that to some extent these people feel that they have reached the edge of their possibilities for gaining financial and material security in their native country and so stepping into the emigrational flux seems to be the best personal crisis solution: For example, "We went from Belogradchik to Sofia first in 1997. I had worked as a teacher there and my husband was a cook. My son was 3 years old. We lived in lodgings. We became short of money to cover our everyday needs and started living on credits. It was impossible to continue this way. They started to search us from different banks every month and we hardly covered more and more credits we used to take. We even tried to open a small business by opening a small grocery. But we bankrupted soon. So, initially I started to go to Cyprus for the summers. I started first, because I had been there before when we were still in Belogradchik. I started immediately after I gave birth. I did not see when my little son started to walk and I did not hear his first words. Then my husband started to come there too. The child came with us one or two seasons, but it was very hard for us to take care of him and the next few summers he spent with my parents in Belogradchik. This continued until 2007 when we completely moved to Cyprus." (Woman, 45 years old, lives in Paralimni, Cyprus)

My working hypothesis is that it is not the poverty itself, but the fear of falling in the gap of poverty that is the key motivation factor for almost the whole group of studied Bulgarians in Cyprus. Furthermore, the fear of poverty is packaged up as a fear for the future of their children. The same respondent continued: "To stay in Bulgaria without money was unbelievable. What future could I assure to my child?! No money, no opportunities to give him normal living conditions or to think about giving him a good education..." I have to mention that for the group in question, the feeling of poverty itself means not just the absence of existential living conditions but also includes a lack of opportunities to migrate. Mobility needs sources – money, documents, and social networks to support a successful start, as a minimum. The lack of any of these conditions means that the labor mobility cannot start. The fear of poverty is a factor of great importance and a strong factor for mobilization of all resources available.

The field work data have shown that remittance-led migrations crucially affect the family its structure and its members. Most often it leads to separation of spouses, children and parents, which builds transnational families (Castaneda/Buck, 2011: 85). Some scholars conclude that beyond the suffering caused by this separation and the accompanied feeling of insecurity, there are substantial consequences for the future stability of members of the transnational family (Tilly 2007, Cit. in: Castaneda/Buck, 2011: 85). This process increases mainly in gender perspective because women become an extremely active part of it, in contrast to traditionally male-oriented migration processes from the earliest periods of time (Karamihova, 2004).

2 The head burrowed deep in the sand... or about neglecting the problem

The topic concerning left behind children of migrating parents is relatively new for Bulgarian scholars. Not until the last two decades have researchers of migration, ethnologists, and sociologists started working on it (Guencheva, 2010: 51 – 53).

Even more important is that both researchers and institutions intentionally refrain from working on this topic. Castaneda and Buck mentioned that "despite the negative consequences of family separation after migration some researchers may shy away from writing much on these issues out of concern for being perceived as criminalizing or judging migrant parents" (2011: 85). In Bulgarian cases, scholars still keep almost silent on this question. There is only one academic study on this topic, which was published in 2010 (Guencheva 2010). R. Guencheva claimed that children of migrants are not passive victims of their parents' decisions but they are active participants in the decision-making process and in the redistribution of family roles. At the same time, they are independent in their own life choices (Guencheva 2010). This paper is derivative of another one published in 2013, which did a critical analysis of the factors involved in a long separation between parents and children, observing what happens "there" where the migrants are and "here" where the children stay (Antova 2013). In 2015, the results were published from a study done in the first part of 2014 by a Bulgarian NGO – Foundation "Partners – Bulgaria" as part of an international research network devoted to children left behind. The most important conclusion the authors reached is that these children are still not officially represented as an autonomous group at-risk. The official statistics and collected data are poor. Only in the last two or three years have some sort of fragmentary reports in the daily press been published, showing statistics from different ministries, for example, the Bulgarian Ministry of education. From my point of view, it is not the definition of these children as an at-risk group that is important, but the development of mechanism for monitoring children left behind by their mobile parents could be more effective and could give a clearer picture of the situation of such families.

3 Methods

This research was done in few stages. I have been to Cyprus two times – between May and October in 2009 and in 2012. The rest of the time for a period of more than 5 years I have done constant fieldwork in Belogradchik, a place that regularly sends temporary labor migrants to Cyprus. The most active period for labor mobility is determined every year according to the tourist season in Cyprus, which normally starts after mid-March and ends in late October or in the beginning of November. For this, I planned and did my fieldwork exactly at this time. The classical ethnological methods were used for the aims of this study – the qualitative methods of participant observation, semi-structured interviews, daily protocols, and auto-reflections. In this study I use the data from both fields – in Belogradchik and in several places in Cyprus. When I speak about migrants' point of view, I use data gathered in Cyprus and when I comment on the situation of children "here", I use examples mainly from my Bulgarian fieldwork. The strength of my data is that in having it from both countries, I have covered the point of views of all participants in the process I explore. The weakness here comes from the impossibility making in-depth interviews with most of my respondents in Cyprus, because of lack of time. In Cyprus I met my respondents mainly at their work places or in informal spontaneous conversations on the streets. In Bulgaria, in Belogradchik the weakness results from almost the same reasons. Because I could not enter the respondents from Cyprus locked houses, the only way to collect relevant data was to speak with relatives, those taking care of children, or to meet some migrants on the streets for a short conversation. Mostly I made semi-structured interviews, which I reproduced in my field diary immediately after the meetings with the respondents. This method has its weaknesses because I could not remember all the details of the conversations, but I extracted the most important parts of them. The advantage of this way of getting data is that respondents themselves are more open and candid.

I based my research in two regions of two countries – Northwest Bulgaria and the region of Famagusta, Cyprus. Northwest Bulgaria according to Eurostat is the poorest European region. I have chosen Belogradchik as representative place – it is a small border town near Northwest Bulgarian-Serbian border with a decreasing economy, an aging population, and a high level of migration. A subjective factor was that this is my and my husband's birthplace. I started my fieldwork in 2006 when we were living in the capital and in 2009 we moved with my family from Sofia back to Belogradchik where we have settled permanently up to day (Antova 2007, 2009).

Northwest Bulgaria still continues to be at the bottom of statistics according to the Eurostat data from 2013. My fieldwork started there in 2006 by observing the post- totalitarian economy of the small town. During my work I identified that there is a very active process of emigration. Local people move mainly to the capital Sofia or abroad. The main destinations for remittance-led migration are Cyprus, Greece, Italy, Spain, and in the last few years, Austria, Great Britain, and Germany. As for migration outside the state, I noticed a labor mobility in which the local women are more active participants than the men. I determined that the preferred destination for the migration of locals is the Famagusta district in Cyprus. I decided to interview only those economic migrants from the region in question in Bulgaria who had planned this process of short-term migration to Cyprus as a strategy for stabilizing their standard of life. Regardless of time spent there, two months or even more than twenty years, all of the people I observed and/or interviewed were convinced that it is only a question of time until they go back home. What is important to mention is that the fieldwork data showed that there are two main types of mobility – seasonal and temporary. By "seasonal" I mean the cases when one or both parents go to Cyprus for a few months, normally from spring to late autumn, and then come back for the winter time. By "temporary" I mean the cases when migrants stay in Cyprus and come back only for a short time in different seasons, depending on their annual holiday.

4 Profile of the studied group

About 200 people were observed and interviewed. They were men and women from a wide age distribution – from 20 to 60 years old. The economic migrant from Bulgaria to Cyprus is normally between the age of 25 and 55 possesses at least a secondary or high school education, speaks a minimum of one foreign language (Russian, English, German, Greek), and has computer literacy. He or she quit their job in Bulgaria because it was underpaid. and They went to Cyprus looking for any job that did not require specific skills, other than physical strength, and is better paid compared to the previous job in the country of origin. Cases of who migrates and with whom varied too. I met respondents that left their families in Bulgaria, cases where whole families reunited gradually through a chain migration, and also partners that both worked and lived in Cyprus while children were left behind with the closest relatives in Bulgaria. The people I reached in Famagusta worked in services, tourist businesses, restaurants, souvenir shops, chains of supermarkets and fast food, constructions etc (Antova 2010). These economic spheres most often require low-skilled work and are low paid. The relationship with the employers is unstable and there is a real threat of becoming unemployed (Anderson 2007: 5, Ehrenreich 2001). The monthly salary varies from 650–800 Euros for nine or more working hours per day. After 2012, the salaries in the tourist season stayed at the lowest level, between 600–650 Euros per month, while the working hours often increased to between 10–12 hours per day. The additional payments were also cut. All the savings that temporary migrants have are oriented to Bulgaria to cover the needs of the respondent's families and relatives. Most often parts of the money are invested in renovations of houses or apartments, for furnishings, for covering the everyday necessities, or for opening or supporting a small family business. The respondents claimed a large amount of remittances was allocated for the education of children. My observation shows that rarely this covers additional private lessons for studying languages or mathematics, but actually means nothing; more than covering the most important needs – buying new clothes and shoes, textbooks, and consumables. While this is nothing different than the spending of others who live in Bulgaria, the respondents declared that they could cover the needs of their children only if they migrated to Cyprus.

This type of labor mobility is seasonal or temporary. It is gendered, because women are more active participants in searching for a job abroad. The data show that the average mobile Bulgarians in Cyprus are paid a low to middle wage on their jobs, but these jobs themselves are time-consuming and lead to day-to-day orientation. In spite of everything the labor mobility abroad still gives more opportunities for locals than the very limited labor market in the region in question in Bulgaria. Unfortunately, the possibility for earning "fast" money, which secures incomes for subsistence "now and today" regardless of what kind of job became a basic living strategy for many people in Bulgaria. This in itself means a lasting shortening of the horizon of expectations and directly affects the values that parents pass on to their children, especially from being at a distance due to remittance-led migration.

5 Why is it better to go to Cyprus without children?

The respondents confided to me that ,"You come here and start working. You do not have time for yourself, you do not have any spare time – only working" (Female, 43 years old, Agya Napa, Cyprus). And again: "What about children – who will take care of them? When they call you, you have to be ready to go. Nobody will give you rest to stay at home if you or your children are sick. Nobody will understand if you have to be away from your work place." (Female, 30 years old, Proteras, Cyprus). Another interlocutor snapped: "Being here with children is very difficult, actually, it is impossible" (Female, 32 years old, Paralimni, Cyprus). The everyday organization of time was subordinated to the working rhythm, often including time for a second job. Despite the intention to bring their children later after adjusting in Cyprus, reuniting the whole family for many migrants was constantly postponed. Besides many single women who felt urged to leave their children at home, there were also many couples that went one by one but still left their children in Bulgaria. When they were asked why, they answered that at first they feared they would not succeed to organize their time in a way to ensure the adequate care and comfort of the child/children: "How could it happen – I am at work, she is at work, who will bring them to and from school? Who will help them with lessons? Even if one of us will go to a night shift, then you will need a rest. We thought about this – mirrored on all sides – no way!" (Male, 40 years old).

During the tourist season when the working hours are extended, there is an additional problem with the child care – the schools are closed and the limited working hours of kindergartens do not cover the needs of parents working at night time or on breaking shifts. There are possibilities for private care, nannies or private nursery schools, but these are an additional financial expense that only a few people calculate they could afford. When it is possible, Bulgarian grandparents who could come for the tourist season provide an alternative or when possible the children could be sent for vacation to Bulgaria. The children that actually accompany their migrant parents are too low in number in the concrete group I have observed.

There are cases when parents take their child/children with them for around a year stay, but I have noticed that they often lose control of the children's lives, exactly because of a shortage of spare time. This is how children appear in a very stressful environment where they have to learn a new language, build new friendships with strangers, and at the same time cover the minimum requirements to be regular students. They have to build a completely new world, alone and almost without any support from their parents. When the children enter a regular Cyprus school they are just listeners, so long as they learn enough Greek to be capable of continuing as regular students. In many cases, their status as listeners may be prolonged and they may be left to repeat the class or be sent back to Bulgaria. Few of them could become good students and most Bulgarian children finish a form of education close to the Bulgarian vocational schools. This brings them some professional orientation, but does not allow them to apply for higher education. Another problem emerges when an adolescent is successful at school but has a desire to go back to Bulgaria to enroll in Bulgarian University. After years spent in Cyprus, poor knowledge of the Bulgarian language could become a serious problem too. Contrary to the claims of my respondents that they care a lot about their children's education, there is an absence of understanding about child development and future career – both from the side of the parents and from the children themselves. And this, I think, is not because they do not care but because they have to overcome day-to-day crises, and this does not allow them to think in a wider perspective. It happens when someone is finishing school in Bulgaria and decides to go for a job following their parents in Cyprus. Then, after a while, they change their mind and go back home for higher education: "My son came here to try to work and to decide himself what he will do in the future. He started to work at Luna Park in Agya Napa last month. Let's see!" (Female, 45 years old, Paralimni, Cyprus). One year later the same boy came back to Bulgaria and enrolled as a regular student at a university.

Bulgarians in Cyprus have one very strong argument regarding their children. They often repeat that they are there so their children in Bulgaria will not suffer and will not have to work. But in her paper about relations among children left behind and their parents abroad, Guencheva gives examples of children working in Bulgaria and describes cases where children, independently and without parental agreement, decided to start working. The author comments that this is an indicator of early formation of responsibility, calling these children "young adults" (Guencheva 2010). While this orientation to such early earning of their own money indicates an independence from the children's side, it speaks to me about a few more things. First, the job factor takes one of the leading positions in the scale of the values of these children. The widespread postulation in times of socialism "Study and be free of the necessity to work!" is no longer valid, which was the positive side of these processes of transition from a state-controlled economy toward a free labor market. The individual decision making of migrants' children are also valid when it comes to other questions. For example, a woman who used to be a seasonal worker in Spain told me that her daughter entered a university, without asking her and without looking for some help from other relatives. This shows some higher level of independence of left behind children in the decision-making process, compared to children accompanying their parents to Cyprus.

6 "When the state is stepmother, the mother's warmth is in... Skype"

It was proven by Western scholars that the long separation from a parent is almost equal to the loss of a parent (Castaneda/Buck 2011). The traumatic consequences for the children could be very serious. Teachers from the local schools in Belogradchik said that these children are "different from their classmates," some of them are more shy, while others are often absent from classes. Fieldwork data have shown that the children of missing migrants are highly stimulated by their parents and relatives to learn foreign languages, especially English and German, because these languages are considered "perspective" if children decide to go for work abroad in the future. "Let him know languages, so that at least he could run away from here, to study, to find a job outside Bulgaria – there is no justice here, there is no life for these children here! At least they have to do better than their parents and us! My children studied here and so what – nothing. One of them was a teacher, now she cleans houses in Cyprus. Our lives are already finished. I hope these children will live better" (Female, 64 years old, Belogradchik). This is one clear example of how controversially education has been perceived. It is visible that there is a big sense of disappointment and that nowadays a good educational background does not matter a lot. People could not live normal lives in Belogradchik, relaying only on their own education and skill. The effort to study languages is the only stimulation towards education I have observed. Because there is only one secondary school in the town, many people encourage their children to go to study in the neighboring bigger cities like Vidin, Montana, or Vratsa. None of the children left behind went to study somewhere outside the town, because grandparents or relatives that take care of them could not move with them, and also because, if the kids moved alone the parents could not control the situation from such a distance. This is only one example concerning the question of education. However, beyond the claims of migrant parents themselves that they care deeply about the education of their children, they do nothing different than others staying in Bulgaria, except limit the possibilities in some cases concerning the place the child can study. Actually what is packaged as efforts for the well-being of the child has to be well circumstanced – parents take care to regularly send money, not just for sustenance but for purchasing expensive commodities like the newest smart-phones, tablets or computers, cars and motors for mature ones, and expensive clothes and toys for the smaller ones. From conversations with interlocutors I am left with the impression that sending this money for luxury items is, from one side, a compensation for the parents' own shortages. Many respondents still remember how they dreamed about or how they received their first pair of blue jeans or a tape recorder during their youth in the time of socialism. The inferiority complex inherited by times of shortage has been extended after 1989, when the achievement of a normal standard of living became almost mission impossible for many Bulgarian citizens, not only for those from Belogradchik. The efforts to satisfy all the material needs of children left behind is also a kind of compensation for the absence, a kind of excuse. It is an explanation for this way of living and a search for approval from their already old parents after a long-lasting absence; an attempt to excuse of their own feelings of guilt and sense of failure. The migrants often state: "I could never buy these things in Bulgaria." Generally, material satisfaction is the most universal answer given in different variations to the question: "Why you continue to stay here in Cyprus?" Parents express themselves in everyday conversations through Skype and Facebook, sending small gifts and pocket money through those returning to Bulgaria, and "liking" new photos on Facebook or other social media.

Asked how they deal with the pain of separation, migrant parents speak little and they most often reduce the answer to: "It is too hard!" and sometimes continue: "Especially when there is a holiday, Easter and Christmas is the time I hate from the depth of my soul – everybody is with his family and I am alone. This is the time when I really feel pain that I am here alone. And the birthdays... I missed many of the most important moments in my kids' life. Hope one day they will understand why I left them..." (Female, 43 years old, Paralimni, Cyprus).

7 Left in Belogradchik

The practices of elderly people to take care of children in one's family have deep roots in the Bulgarian model of the pre-modern culture. The memory of big families and households is part of communicative culture where everybody lives together and the bigger children take care of the smaller ones. This model is still popular in some minority groups in Bulgaria. But in their households, in contrast to separated migration families, there is the presence of people of all generations and there is no generational gap. When thinking about bringing up of children left behind by their migrant parents, the first and strongest feeling that arises is fear. The fears of elderly people who take care of these children are huge and highly varying. They fear their own growing age: "I wonder if we will be healthy enough and if we will be alive to take care of her as long as her mom and dad work in Cyprus, to give her an education, to put the bread in her own hands" (Male, 68 years old, Belogradchik). The people are not sure if they can ensure a healthy environment and adequate care for the children. Sometimes the fear grows to a kind of panic: "This is my kid, my grandson, but he is not mine, he is another's child. It is not the same as taking care for your own kid. When I used to take care of mine it was completely different and had nothing in common – to be anxious about him day and night is difficult" (Female, 61 years old, Belogradchik). Despite all the incredibly devoted care of grandparents give to the children left to them and despite the parents striving to satisfy all the material needs, the children are situated in a highly stressful family environment. The new generations of transnational parents have to fulfill many hard tasks. They have to meet the expectations of their elderly parents, who often think that their inheritors are somehow obliged to them. Traditionally, elderly generations expect to be pampered by their children in old age. As mentioned before in this paper, migrants often packaged their own decision to migrate with the care of the future of their children too: "I am here because of the kid. What do I need if I was alone? But everything is about the kid" (Female, 33 years old, Agia Napa, Cyprus).

The strong feeling that children have obligations to meet their parents' expectations also comes because their material needs have been satisfied, especially when compared to their coevals in the town. On the other hand, these children have to find their own way to deal with the situation of living long-distance from their parents. After all, they are not the ones who defined the final decisions of their parents, although they may have been participants in the discussion process about possible family strategies. As they stay behind with their aged grandparents, they have to meet their expectations, too. Sometimes, the care taking process needs to change directions. If the health of one of the grandparents' declines, the care of the household becomes a duty of the children left behind. Despite everything mentioned above, one of the main consequences is the change of family roles and dependencies. I heard many times that one or both grandparents had replaced the figure of the parent and had become the most important figure for the child. A grandmother said, "Even now as a student in Sofia we continue to call each other every day, even a few times per day. He could miss-calling his mom in Cyprus, but me – no way." (Female, 67, Belogradchik).

8 Conclusion

These are just a few fragments of a still missing picture of the situation of children left behind by their mobile parents. My observations are from a particular, small place, Belogradchik and the region of Famagusta, Cyprus, where Belogradchik inhabitants often migrate to work for remittances. Seen from this angle, this is a small sturdy at a micro level. But the problem I have just drafted here is substantial for the nation. First of all, I cannot state for sure whether these children form a group at-risk or not. I think it is too narrow and one-sided to be stated definitively, because they are not simply victims of their parents' decisions and the effects of recent migrations. Some of them play an active role in the redefinition of the family and ties inside it, maintaining transnational interrelations with their mobile parents (Guencheva 2010: 63). I know that they are in a specific situation compared to their coevals. Distance-parenting is something that is possible nowadays because of new technologies. It could allow almost constant virtual presence of the parents, but is this enough to replace their physical presence at home? For sure, the children parented by their distance-parents and left to their grandparents and relatives should create their own adaptive mechanisms and strategies to balance between both caregivers. On the other side, they should learn to deal with real everyday life with different and sometimes difficult situations without relying on the help of some adults. Parents could not be "online" at any time and grandparents may not be in an adequate position to react. This in many cases means that these children make more independent decisions than their coevals- and those decisions are not by default the right ones. The reason most often pointed out, that by working abroad migrating parents can provide better educational opportunities for their children, is also subject to critical examination. The fact that none of those children go out of town to seek a better education on the secondary level shows that actually what is secured is the necessary educational minimum. The only compensation here is the higher emphasis on learning foreign languages compared to children whose parents did not migrated. Logically this comes from the mobile parents' personal experience that knowledge of languages gives easier realization on the labor market outside Bulgaria. The very rare continuation to a higher level of education is most often an independent decision of left-behind children. When it happens, this leads to great satisfaction for mobile parents and the elderly relatives who substitute for them here in Bulgaria. After all, this is one of the most sufficient final results for all participants of a transnational family and is perceived as a compensation for the long-lasting separation.

References

Antova, S. (2007). Social Relations, Problems and Trends in Cross-National Families (A Case Study of Belogradchik) In: Ed. Elena Marushiakova: Dynamics of National Identity and Transnational Identities in the Process of European Integration. Cambridge Publ., pp. 123-131.
Antova, S. (2009). Female Migrations from the Border Region of Northwest Bulgaria in Last 20 Years – In: Dialogs about Human and Humane. A Jubilee Collection, Devoted to 70nth Anniversary of Prof. Todor Iv. Zhivkov, Briag, Bourgas, pp. 76 – 99 (In Bulgarian).
Antova, S. (2010). Mobility or Temporary Migration? Cultural-Economic Strategies of Bulgarians in the Region of Famagusta, Cyprus – In: Karamihova M., (Ed.) Readings in the History and Culture of the Balkans. In Support of University Teaching, Paradigma, Sofia, pp. 155-172.
Antova, S. (2013). Bulgarian Migration to Cyprus and Transparenting – In: Bulgarian Ethnology, 3, ISSN 1310-5213, c. 351 – 367 (In Bulgarian).
Anderson, B. (2007). Battles in Time: the Relation between Global and Labour Mobilities, COMPAS Working Paper WP-07-55
Castañeda, E & Buck. (2011). "Remittances, Transnational Parenting, and the Children Left Behind: Economic and Psychological Implications." The Latin Americanist 55:85-110.
De la Garsa, R. (2010). Migration, Development and Children left behind: A Multidimensional Perspective – In: Social and Economic Policy Working Paper, New York, UNICEF.
Ehrenreich, B. (2001). Nichel and Dimed. On (Not) getting By in Amerika, A Metropolitan/ Owl Book, Henry Holt and Company, New York.
Guencheva, R. (2010). Long Distance Relationships: Children and Migration in Contemporary Bulgaria, In: Ethnologia Balkanica, Sofia, pp. 49 – 71.
Hristov, P. (2008). Trans-border Exchange of Seasonal Workers in the Central Part of Balkans (19th – 20th Century). – In: Ethnologia Balkanica, 12, Lit Verlag, Berlin, pp. 215 – 230.
Hristov, P. (2010). Gurbet on the Balkans – Traditional and Contemporary Forms (Introduction) – In: Balkan Migration Culture: Historical and Contemporary Cases from Bulgaria and Macedonia, Paradigma, Sofia, pp. 28 – 44.
IOM, (2010). Migration and Transnationalism: Opportunities and Chalenges, 9-10 March 2010. Background paper, pp. 6 – In: https://www.iom.int/jahia/webdav/shared/shared/mainsite/microsites/IDM/workshops/migration_and_transnationalism_030910/background_paper_en.pdf (Last visited: 15.02.2016).

Karamihova, M. (2004). American Dreams, A Guide among First Generation of Immigrants, Krotal, Sofia (In Bulgarian).
Thilly, C. (2007), "Trust Networks in Transnational Migration." Sociological Forum 22.

ововован
Women and Families: Mobility Strategies

Aneliya Avdzhieva

1 Introduction

Scholars in the fields of social sciences and humanities nowadays widely agree that the world is becoming more and more mobile referring to an increasing mobility of goods, capitals, objects, ideas, technologies, strategies, people, etc. Arjun Appadurai (1996) talks about the *global flows*, Manuell Castells (2011) about the *network society*, and Tim Cresswell (2006) about *on the move* experiences. Cresswell writes: "Mobility is a fact of life. To be human, indeed, to be animal, is to have some kind of capacity for mobility" (2006: 22). We all are on the move in the net of people, connections, and meetings, whether for work or for leisure.

These acts of human mobility are considered an indication of the way life-being is constructed, but they also reflect the social roles an individual plays within the microstructure of the family and the community s/he belongs to.[1] These roles are based on everyday activities as well as the *fields*[2] where interactions and strategy games are played in order to accumulate capital – economic, social, symbolic, and cultural. Women's roles are often linked to the traditional understanding of the social and cultural structure of the group or community, which is fundamentally

---

[1] This contribution is part of the research project "Boundaries and Social Mobility", funded by Scientific Research Fund of University of Plovdiv Paisii Hilendarski, with project manager: Assoc. Prof. Dobrinka Parusheva, PhD.

[2] The term *field* is used in the way Pierre Bourdieu constructed it as a part of the *social topography* and defined by the distinction of status and class (Bourdieu 1985).

defined by patriarchal values. On a symbolic level, their spaces of inhabitation are perceived as linked to nature and home, as men's to culture and the public sphere. This is applicable to the Roma communities too: women's roles refer to household activities and childcare (Pamporov 2004, Ivanova/Krastev 2008), and are not perceived to include building social and economic strategies of gaining symbolic capital and playing on the men's "market field" where this capital is performed.[3] Within the specific discourse of Roma people on gender, this capital is linked to masculine domination, which is slowly transformed and/or detached between other social actors, both men and women. In the *field* of social interactions, mobility is an important element that creates or destroys and reshapes statuses, images, symbols, and roles capital transformation and proliferation appear on the foreground.

This paper presents parts of my research on mobility and the social strategies of the Roma people viewed through the lens of gender in the microstructure of the family. It will focus on the strategies that originate from their mobility choices by addressing the questions:

- For what reasons do Roma people move?
- What are the mechanisms that make them move and the relationships they have established in order to realize the movement?
- What are the social consequences of moving for (predominantly) Roma women especially with respect to their image within the Roma family and community?

However, the paper will not deepen issues related to the everyday strategies migrants (when referring to transnational mobility) apply in the host country of immigration. It will rather tackle the communal perceptions of the performed mobility pattern in the country of origin. It will analyze the process of movement and its consequences for the mobile person, and the specific features one gains with that movement due to her cultural and social virtues and characteristics.

---

3 In Masculine Domination Pierre Bourdieu (1990) widely discusses women's roles and images by the means of diverse dichotomies as male-female, up-down, in-out, culture-nature, market-home spaces, and by symbolic power as measurement for the masculine domination over women.

2 Some preliminary remarks: Roma people and gender

Before describing my research methods and methodology I need to underline that the Roma communities in Bulgaria, where the research has been conducted, are highly marginalized in both positive and negative terms. Their images are constructed on many levels – on a daily life level as verbal narratives between non-Roma; on an historical level; on a project level, for example, programs like the *Decade of Roma inclusion*[4]; on a political level as the "selling votes during election" narratives; on the very important media level where their images are visualized, textualized and communicated to the wide audience. In other words, regardless of the highly romanticized positive images of Roma musicians and singers and of their sense of freedom or ability to live fully, typically images of Roma people, their way of living and traditions, are constructed as a "problem" that needs to be solved for everybody's sake.[5] This attitude marginalizes them (they are often excluded or they self-exclude themselves from the urban or rural life of the place they are settled) but, in addition, it also forces them to build strategies for coping with this marginalization.

In 2010, I started my research about the Roma women's labor mobility in Plovdiv and the region and this research is still ongoing. Since then I have been trying to understand if the Roma women's positions and roles in the family and in Roma communities are changing and if so, how this change takes place. In order to do so I observed their labor activities as traders, seasonal workers, in the grey and/or – some say – black economy (black economy understood as all kinds of illegal criminal activities like prostitution, drug dealing and so on; in my research only prostitution is in the focus of attention). Furthermore, I use biographic and unstructured interviews, case studies and observations methods linked to the labor strategies and mobility of Roma women from the city of Plovdiv and some rural areas in the region of Plovdiv. Very important to the study is the biographic method, which is applicable to my gendered research, because "[...] 'gender' (as 'ethnicity', 'class' or other categories) is not in its 'pure' form but is always the respective concrete interaction with different social orders, in concrete context and modality of the historical-social layers" (Dausien 2004: 15). Crossing of borders and boundaries

---

4   *Decade of Roma inclusion* is an initiative of European Union about Roma peoples' social inclusion and elimination of discrimination. Its period was 2005-2015 and "[...] focuses on the priority areas of education, employment, health, and housing, and commits governments to take into account the other core issues of poverty, discrimination, and gender mainstreaming". For further elaboration, see http://www.romadecade.org/.
5   About media and politically constructed narratives see Lukova (2011).

in order to realize labor practices is also the focus of attention. The activities under research are highly mobile: a trader is constantly moving and exchanging goods in order to satisfy consumers' demands, a seasonal worker moves seasonally to diverse geographical places, and working in the grey economy is often linked to transnational migration. Hence, the term mobility is most appropriate to designate all these choices.

Here only women traders will be in the center of attention due to the specific family cases from my fieldwork – the geographical perspective, religion performed, and language spoken. The other mobility direction of Roma women – the one towards Western-European countries of seasonal workers – will be the object of analysis in another paper. These trader women (also labeled as *suitcase traders* (Craciun 2014: 77-79) and *tourist-traders* (Konstantinov 1996) are traveling mostly to Turkey – some of them weekly, others monthly, but all of them perpetually. They buy and resell commodities, garments, and detergents in Bulgaria. Most of the Roma women under research, who are traders in Plovdiv and the region, are Muslim and speak a variation of the Turkish language. Therefore, the choice of their mobility direction is unsurprisingly a country that is representative of both their religion (in most of the cases) and language.

Images of Roma women in both rural and urban settings are constructed and perceived on a family basis. Already during the eighteenth century some German and Austrian travel writers reported about the basic functions of Roma women: "Women are taking care of the family and household activities and men indulge themselves in various indecent arts, but many in crafts [...]" (Ivanova/Krastev 2008: 146).[6] They continue to be linked to sustaining of family order and preserving and transmitting the family and community's tradition; the latter is nowadays considered a sign of identity and prestige. Marriage is an important event in women's lives as it shows a change in their social status, which is related to the imposition of several restrictions due to the need for defending their "purity". One of these restrictions is the ban to move freely throughout places without permission and an appropriate companion approved by the husband or another (important) family member. This can be associated with Bourdieu's concept of constructing women as the symbolic capital of men, a concept that assures their social prestige within the community (Bourdieu 2001: 42-52). Women in the Roma communities, as in all traditional Balkan cultures, are restricted and have a spatial and social ban of access on the places that symbolically define *masculinity*. Their isolation, as the Austrian social historian Michael Mitterauer states (Miterrauer/Sieder 1982), is divided into two poles. One pole is economic, where women are separated from

---

6   Translation of all quotations from the Bulgarian language in this paper is by the author.

the working places and their function should not be connected to these places. The other pole is related to social performance and authority (of family, of neighborhood, of Roma, of Bulgarians). The man is the main possessor of these poles of social and symbolic capital.

In the book by Evgeniya Ivanova and Velcho Krastev *The Roma Woman – Spaces and Boundaries in her Life*, Roma women's functions and roles within the family and the community are explained as follows: "In the everyday life Roma/Gypsy woman is burdened with important economic functions that consist of the obligation to provide for the everyday survival of the family. She takes care of children and adults, food and clothes, she communicates with people from the community and with the public institutions. We see her around her husband in the workshop, making spindles or daubing walls with mud, we find her to sell in the fair and market place, to wander with begging bag on her shoulder. She is a sorceress or a fortune teller, a prostitute or a dancer. And all this is performed within the society, preserving Roma identity." (2008: 283)

Although the last quote could be considered as trivialized and racist, it disentangles the overall taboos and commonly perceived images of Roma women in history and shows how these aspects continue in the contemporary world. About the value of the family and the role of the individual in it these authors also share that: […] In the traditional value system of Roma people the individual is important to the extent to which s/he is part of the family and the most important thing is to fulfil strictly his/her obligations. Male power is rather political – he represents the family in front of the community. "[…] It is the men's law that rules among us. It can be good or bad, but that is it! It is the man who represents family but he always consults with his wife" (Ivanova/Krastev 2008: 247).

Another important role of the family is linked to the functioning of networks among Roma people. Networking is organized on the basis of family organization, or respectively, on the professionalization of the specific Roma sub-groups in general. This allows the exchange of various (by meaning and power) symbolic, cultural, and economic capital that differentiates ties between the Roma sub-groups. In this sense, social networks, for instance, are extremely enlarged and complicated and exist on a variety of levels, depending on the frequency of circulation and the type of the capitals exchanged. However, the main "arena" in which they are exchanged is the family group.

3 Mobilities, Strategies, Families

Within the social sciences the term *mobility* is widely used and perceived in various aspects. It can describe *spatial mobility*, in the sense of crossing spaces and places and passing from one territory to another, as well as *social mobility*, which refers to a change of status and social positions and not necessarily to spatial movement (Kaufmann/Montulet 2010). Luk Boltanski and Eve Chiapello (2005) were the first to pay attention to the implicit parallelism between spatial and social mobility.[7]

In the following, *mobility* is understood as free movement of people and as becoming the "ironic foundation for anti-essentialism, antifoundationalism and antirepresentationalism." (Cresswell 2006: 46) In other words: mobility is perceived as embodied action that exceeds movement, as the physical enactment of crossing spaces but at the same time as movement into places with their cultural and social specifics. Therefore, mobility passes into the deep gap of social interactions on inter-individual, inter-communal, inter-cultural, and inter-institutional levels.

The other important notion of the study is *strategy*, which Bourdieu describes as a social system of structured and structuring dispositions revealed throughout practice: "[...] as a way of directing practice that is neither conscious and calculated, nor mechanically determined, but is the product of the sense of honour as a feel for that particular game, the game of honour; and the idea that there is a logic of practice, whose specificity lies above all in its temporal structure" (Bourdieu 1990: 22).

According to Bourdieu, it is the *habitus* that pushes the individual to undertake strategy: "[...] it 'produces strategies which, even if they are not produced by consciously aiming at explicitly formulated goals on the basis of an adequate knowledge of objective conditions, nor by the mechanical determination exercised by causes, turn out to be objectively adjusted to the situation" (Bourdieu 1990: 10).

---

7   They emphasize that these two directions in conceptualizing mobility, as it concerns other mobility types too, should not be considered separately and special attention should be paid to the differences. By claiming this, they oppose the opinions of researchers like McKenzie (1927) who argues that mobility thought as movement does not mean mobility in the social space in general (the difference between mobility and fluidity). There are also numerous other scholars who deal with human (and not only) mobilities, such as the British sociologist John Urry (Urry 2000a; 2000b; 2007; Law / Urry 2004), the American human geographer Tim Cresswell (Cresswell 2006; 2010a, 2010b), and the Bulgarian political scientist Anna Krasteva (2014). See also Canzler et al. (2008), etc.

In this sense, Roma women develop their *habitus* for building *strategies*, which negotiates different statuses and helps in "accumulating" different sorts of economic, symbolic, and social capital. When thinking of the Roma people and researching them, it is important to stress what *family* means for its members. "It stands right next to freedom, which goes hand in hand" explains Yosif Nunev (1998: 30), and is the main functioning unit in the Roma communities' social and cultural organization. He divides Roma families into three subgroups: *traditional* (and most common), *abnormal*,8 and *untraditional* (family members who do not identify themselves as Roma) (1998: 31-34). Usually the Roma family is extended – so that at least three generations live together and this extended family-group functions as one household. Although there are nuclear families too, where only two generations live together. Roma families are organized according to the patriarchal norms. Scholars who did research on Romani (Marushiakova/Popov 1997; Pamporov 2004, 2006) refer to the existence of a social stratification within the families that members occupy and describe the functions that members perform. These stratifications are based on the age factor (power distribution and hierarchy between its members), as well as a gender division of spaces. Traditionally associated with nature, home, and household (Bochkov 2009: 151-183), women (in general perspective) are "imprisoned" in the frame of family.

Roma communities are perceived to be highly mobile (according to the spatial aspect of the notion) and their marginality is partly caused by this perception. Mobility is considered to be performed mainly by the whole sub-group (such as kalderash, kalaidjii, etc.), or by family groups, kin group, or the individual. How often are women mobile and to what extent? What are the strategies they build in order to be on the move and to whom are they connected? What is the role of the family?

---

8   *Abnormal families (anormirani semeystva)*: "This subgroup is slowly abandoning its own culture without accepting another one on its place. This problem is followed by: lack of family member; generation misunderstandings; lack of income; divorcing parents or misunderstanding between them, and a like. Here it could be easily found problems, driven from the transition toward democracy regime: unemployment; alcoholism; prostitution practicing; breathing glue as a form of drug abuse amongst youngsters; small thefts; vagrancy; begging; searching for food in the garbage; lack of interest toward education as spiritual value. Abnormal families live in small cribs, in garbage in the so called Roma ghettos. Their families are the most crowded" (Nunev 1998: 32).

4 Cases and families

In one of the Plovdiv neighborhoods, Stolipinovo, trade is a common labor practice. Stolipinovo has a high population density where one can usually notice there are many people in the public places, where street and pedestrian spaces are filled with stalls and shops and everything is cheaper in comparison to the central urban spaces. However, placed at the periphery of the city, this part of Plovdiv is audibly isolated and the inhabitants are separated from the other (Bulgarian) urban inhabitants. Entering the inside, there are new borders and boundaries of difference visible by layers that shape the neighborhood as "town within the city", whereat other mechanisms and structures of social organization and functioning are set. Although the neighborhood is urbanized, it has many problems linked not only to the infrastructure but also to the diverse ethnic communities and groups living in it. Thus, it is presented as the primary problematic zone in the city.

Considering trade, more often women are traders and they travel to Turkey on a weekly or monthly basis by using organized transport or their own vehicles. In the organized transport pattern, they travel in groups, sometimes accompanied by their husbands, as the minibus is set specifically for this purpose. The border crossing happens in a day only, they do the shopping and come back without staying in Turkey. The same applies to the other mobile labor pattern. Mostly the women are traders, because of their *habitus*, their *practical reason* (after Bourdieu 1998). As one of my male respondents puts it: "Uhhmm, they have the flair to trade, generally and a very big part of them, after the recession time and the economic crisis [in the late 1980s – A. A.] is practicing trade. Uhhmm for many years after the changes many of women, uhhmmm, and not only women, this is, they are some kind of family business… women are most commonly the ones who sell, mostly the woman is the one that is staying on the stall and is selling" (Anton K., Stolipinovo, 2010, quoted from Avdzhieva 2011: 157).

In addition, mostly women are selling on the stalls and shops relying on the data from the focused observation of the research. They are active social actors and "players" on the symbolic capital scene where masculinity is usually performed. Their image is strongly marginalized due to the new functions they have incorporated. However, by being mobile, they have the freedom to act outside of the social ban and to contact the Other, the other man.

Due to high levels of unemployment and high levels of poverty among the Roma people in Bulgaria[9] it could be claimed that the main push factor for mobility is

---

9   More about socioeconomic situation of Roma people in Bulgaria see Dimova et al. (2004).

an economic one. For my respondents in Sheker mahalla, another neighborhood in Plovdiv, being a trader is a first place work that secures the physical survival of their family. In one of the cases under research (Jane[10] and her family), only the mother was working. The main reason for mobility and traveling to Turkey as a trader is because this is the only way to provide income for the extended family. On the question "Why did she go?" the daughter answered: "Because my father was always drunk, always gambling. He was stealing the money, he was gambling. [...] There was nobody else who could take us, my mother had to work. And my mother was always traveling. [...] It was always my mother. My father not so much [traveling – A.A.]. It was my mother who was usually wandering to Turkey" (A woman, 27 years, Sheker mahalla, 2010, quoted from Avdzhieva 2011: 138).

Jane's household consisted of three generations and only the oldest woman provided subsistence for her three children, their wives/husbands and six grandchildren. They lived on selling cigarettes and detergent bought in Turkey. Jane had been practicing this labor mobility for more than 20 years, passing through different phases of trade – trading various garments and traveling on diverse ways. All the family members had a certain role in this "family business"– grandchildren and daughters were selling the purchased commodities in Plovdiv, men sometimes accompanied Jane or were protecting the sellers from a distance.

Currently, Jane is constantly traveling to Turkey, where she had already established a labor partners network with Turkish traders. Trade becomes life-being. The participation of all family members is a basis for conditionally determining this practice as a "family business," even though it is not legalized. In this specific case, the woman trader inevitably becomes extremely mobile and transforms movement into embodied experience that exceeds crossing borders by its spatial transition with temporal determination. This movement can be discussed as social mobility, firstly within the family hierarchy, and secondly within the local community. This family labor mobility is highly genderized and re-constructs the life-being of the entire household.

Defining female status on the basis of housewife qualities is not the only resource for determining Jane's position. The change of symbolic capital possession, sign of power, and high position in the hierarchy is influenced by the economic changes in Bulgaria and also by reshaping breadwinning roles within the family. In addition, "Bargaining models of labour supply and time allocation suggest that family members' power increases as income increases. Therefore, as a woman's income increases, the more power she should have within the household" (Addabbo et al. 2010:6). The network nature of the relationships assumes power and helps

---

10 The name is a pseudonym.

in building strategies for ruling and applying a set of characteristics that create an image of masculinity. Acknowledging the transfer of a part of the symbolic and economic capital from men to women can be analyzed as a step towards a change of women's status, framed within the family structure. In his book *On the Move* Cresswell (2006) explains: "In contemporary social thought, words associated with mobility are unremittingly positive. If something can be said to be fluid, dynamic, in flux, or simply mobile, then it is seen to be progressive, exciting, and contemporary. If, on the other hand, something is said to be rooted, based on foundations, static, or bounded, then it is seen to be reactionary, dull, and of the past" (Cresswell 2006: 25).

Despite the fact that this female mobility is not well accepted on the symbolic level, it is recognized as common practice. This may result from the perception that this is a "family business" and may also be explained by the understanding (among Roma) that women traders work with the upper half of their body, with their head – they think and bargain rather with the lower part of the body (the example of practicing prostitution and the other labor mobility pattern of my research), which automatically transfers them into the "shameful" symbolic level.[11]

As a conclusion, the cases I have observed during the fieldwork since 2010 lead to a few working conclusions. First, the image of the mobile working woman, in the Roma people's case, is different from the one of a Roma woman who lives and works in Bulgaria. Second, by becoming mobile, women inevitably cross the symbolic "purity-shame" boundary that might lower their and their family's status within the social hierarchy of the Roma community. This influences their inclusion in the community via marriage, which is a fundament of Roma social organization. This differs according to the labor mobility pattern and direction.

Having a peculiar perspective in (re)thinking mobility, anthropology pays attention to the changes that follow the mobile experiences while considering various social and cultural factors such as gender, ethnicity, religion, norms, values, as well as the social and cultural structure of the community and society. In this sense, borders and boundaries are important when analyzing the role of main functioning units of an individual way of living and their influence on individual's strategies and operational *fields* on a daily and symbolic level. Therefore, the labor mobility of Roma women and its inevitable link to family can help to disclose how border crossing influences the gendered body and what the social consequences for the actor are. As Dichev states, the border is a powerful *attractor* (in terms of Urry),

---

11   For "purity-shame" division and the division of the Roma female body into two halves see Stewart (1997) as well as Avdzhieva (2011).

and "[T]he firmer borders become, the more powerful also the vectors of desire to cross them are" (2009: 40).

In the field of human geography, Cresswell states that, "Mobility, as a social product, does not exist in an abstract world of absolute time and space, but is a meaningful world of social space and social time. Mobility is also part of the process of the social production of time and space" (2006: 5). And I am inclined to add to this, mobility is not only a social product, and as such a part of the production of time and space, it is also a social interaction with various cultural dimensions and consequences, both positive and negative. It deeply influences individuals' images and identities and helps establish communal relations. It can solve and/or create problems, and it can be an instrument for building economic or social strategies, with different endpoints.

5 Final remarks

When discussing the labor mobility of Roma women, the family is very important since family determines to a large extent the women's position in the local community. Considered to be organized on the basis of the patriarchal model, Roma people are perceived as extremely traditional – the woman has to be a virgin until the day of her wedding, the man has to be the breadwinner and secure the economic independence of the family by providing income. The woman has to inhabit and stay at home and take care of the offspring and other inhabitants. All these perceptions are thought to be an "anachronism," due to the globalization and feminization. Women's mobility strategies are determined by the men's power, depending on the extent to which men operate with the capital, defining it within the family.

Considering the aforementioned, it is important to share what Cresswell argues about the notion of mobility in spatial science: "[...] mobility is suspicious because it threatens the quite explicit moral character of place – threatening to undo it" (2006: 32). I will add that this statement is applicable not only for the place as a spatial characteristic of the idea of *sedentarism*, but also for the connection between the symbolic normalization of the social reality of different communities and the everyday practices and strategies of physical survival. So, taking into account the case of Roma people, it is important how women cross state borders. If they cross them alone (without companion), men's trust toward them decreases and malign communal gossips are exposed – due to the lack of masculine control needed to defend the symbolic power of men that is revealed by the means of men's honor (in the way Bourdieu 2001 refers to it). Therefore, a woman's image acquires "shameful" virtues that might change her position in the family and community.

This image is a basis for creating and establishing prejudices. Different mobility strategies have various positive or negative perceptions in rethinking Roma women's mobility, gender roles, and identity. In the Roma communities, the image of women is linked to household activities and roles: "the woman of good quality is the housewife-woman".[12] In the time of the *second modernity* (after Beck 1992) women started to share obligations with men, one of which was providing food and money for the family members. By being traders, women fulfil this new breadwinners' obligation. Nevertheless, Roma women's "best" image in the family and in the community remains the one of housewives and mothers. Still, trade is quite a well-accepted economic mobile strategy, and even though they are marginalized *per se* by the idea of movement, these women possess a specific purity that justifies the family's honor and status, not only the men's but in general. In terms of flexibility and fixity, this is an example of a cross-point feature that connects positivism and criticism in the perception of global change and flows. Since the Roma people are considered to share "modest" patriarchal values, they are expected to subordinate to the virtues that are subject to masculine dominance. Crossing symbolic boundaries that enhance masculinity might be achieved by mobility conceived in positivist terms[13] of the *metaphysic of nomadism*, and not in terms of threatening *sedentarism* (compare to Cresswell 2006). This leads to a change of the social order within the Roma family and community. On the contrary, immobility of the community and a state of fixity in a certain place like home reveals the existing social order and is deeply territorialized by the people. On the one hand, cultural specifics of the group are being changed through a mixture of fixity and forming boundaries. On the other hand, mobility and crossing borders and boundaries lead to a transformation in social relations and the distribution of roles within the family and the local community's everyday life. This stance, highly positivist at first glance, attempts to disentangle the complex processes of movement and their connection to labor practices and images of Roma women within the family framework. Nevertheless, it does not exclude the apparent distinctiveness between positivism, rational choice, realism and a critical analysis of social reality's rendition.

---

12   A statement by my respondent Anton K., Stolipinovo 2010.
13   To induce a change in a positive direction – social change, economic development, gender and citizenship equality, and so forth.

References

Addabbo, T. et al. (eds.) (2010) Gender Inequalities, Households and the Production of Well-being in Modern Europe. England: Ashgate Publishing Limited.
Appadurai, A. (1996) Modernity al large: cultural dimensions of globalization (Vol. 1). USA: University of Minnesota Press.
Beck, U. (1992) Risk society: Towards a new modernity (Vol. 17). Sage.
Bourdieu, P. (1990) In Other Words: Essays towards a Reflexive Sociology. Stanford: Stanford University Press.
Bourdieu, P. (1998) Practical reason: On the theory of action. Stanford University Press.
Bourdieu, P. (2001) Masculine domination. Stanford: Stanford University Press.
Canzler, W. et al. (eds.) (2008) Tracing Mobilities. Toward a Cosmopolitan perspective. Aldershot: Ashgate Publishing Limited.
Craciun, M. (2014) Material Culture and Authenticity. Fake Branded Fashion in Europe. London: Bloomsbury Publishing Plc.
Castells, M. (2011) The rise of the network society: The information age: Economy, society, and culture (Vol. 1). UK: John Wiley & Sons.
Cresswell, T. (2010a) "Mobilities I: catching up". Progress in Human Geography. 35(4), pp. 550-558.
Cresswell, T. (2010b) "Towards a politics of mobility". Environment and planning. D, Society and space. 28(1), pp. 17-31.
Cresswell, T. (2006) On the move: mobility in the modern western world. NY: Taylor & Francis.
Decade of Roma inclusion 2005-2015, Available at: http://www.romadecade.org/ (accessed 16 January 2016).
Kaufmann, V. & Bertrand, A. (2008) 'Between Social and Spatial Mobilities: The Issue of Social Fluidity', in Canzler, Weert et al. (eds.). Tracing Mobilities. Toward a Cosmopolitan perspective. Aldershot: Ashgate Publishing Limited, pp. 37-55.
Konstantinov, Y. (1996) "Patterns of reinterpretation: trader-tourism in the Balkans (Bulgaria) as a picaresque metaphorical enactment of post-totalitarianism." American Ethnologist. 23(4), pp. 762-782.
Law, J. & John U. (2004) "Enacting the social". Economy and society. 33(3), pp. 390-410.
Marushiakova, E. & Popov, V. (1997) Gypsies (Roma) in Bulgaria. Frankfurt am Main: Peter Lang.
Mitterauer, M. & Sieder, R. (1982) The European family: Patriarchy to partnership from the Middle Ages to the present. Chicago: University of Chicago Press.
Stewart, M. (1997) The time of the Gypsies. USA: West View Press.
Urry, J. (2000a) "Mobile sociology1". The British journal of sociology. 51(1), pp. 185-203.
Urry, J. (2000b) Sociology beyond societies: Mobilities for the twenty-first century. London: Routledge.
Urry, J. (2007) Mobilities. Cambridge: Polity Press.
Авджиева, А. (2011) Трудовата миграция на ромските жени (Столипиново, Шекер махала, Хаджи Хасан малаха в гр. Пловдив). Пловдив: Катедра Етнология към ФИФ на ПУ „Паисий Хилендарски" [Avdzhieva, Aneliya (2011) Labour Migration of

Roma Women (Stolipinovo, Sheker Mahalla, Hadzhi Hassan Mahalla in Plovdiv city). Plovdiv: Department of Ethnology of FFH in PU "Paisii Hilendarski"].

Бочков, П. (2009) Ние и другите. Студии по етнология. София: НБУ. [Bochkov, Plamen (2009) We and the Others. Ethnology Etudes. Sofia: NBU].

Даузин, Б. (2004) "Биографичното изследване. Теоретични перпективи и методологически концепции за едно конструктивно изследване на половете". Българска етнология, бр. 4,. [Dausien, Bettina (2004) "Biographical research. Theoretical perspectives and methodological conceptions for a constructive research about gender". Bulgarian Ethnology, 4], pp. 8-25.

Димова, Л. et al.. (съст.) (2004) Ромите: другото измерение на промените. София: Фондация „Партньори-България". [Dimova, Lila et al. (eds.) (2004) The Roma people: the other dimension of changes. Sofia: Foundation "Partners-Bulgaria"].

Дичев, И. (2009) Граждани отвъд местата? Нови мобилности, нови граници, нови форми на обитаване. София: Просвета. [Dichev, Ivaylo (2009) Citizens beyond places? New mobilities, new borders, new forms of inhabitating. Sofia: Prosveta].

Лукова, К. (2011) Темата етнос в медийния език на пресата преди и след присъединяването на България към Европейския съюз–психолингвистични и социолингвистични аспекти. [Lukova, Kalina (2011) The ethnicity theme in the media language before and after the accession of Bulgaria to the European Union – psycho- and socio-linguistic affects].

Иванова, Е. & Кръстев, В. (2008) Ромската жена – пространства и граници в живота й. Стара Загора: „Летера Принт" АД. [Ivanova, Evgeniya, Velcho Krastev (2008) The Roma woman – spaces and boundaries in her life. Stara Zagora: "Letera Print" AD].

Кръстева, А. (2014) От миграция към мобилност: политики и пътища. София: НБУ. [Krasteva, Anna (2014) From migration toward mobility: politics and roads. Sofia: NBU].

Нунев, Й. (1998) Ромското дете и неговата семейна среда. София: IMIR [Nunev, Yosif (1998) The Roma child and its family environment. Sofia: IMIR].

Пампоров, А. (2004) Ромското семейство: аспекти на всекидневието. София [Pamporov, Aleksey (2004) The Roma family: aspects of everyday life. Sofia].

Пампоров, А. (2006) Ромското всекидневие в България. София: МЦПМКВ [Pamporov, Aleksey (2006) The everyday life of Roma people in Bulgaria. Sofia: MCPMKV].

Children and Socialization: Crossing Social and Cultural Boundaries

Svetoslava Mancheva

1 Introduction

The various definitions of the word *child*[1] are determined by the cultural and social reality. One assumes therefore that childhood is constructed[2] and as such it should be approached in the context of reality today, as well as with regard to different social and cultural processes occurring in the groups under research. In the contemporary world, we witness the creation and consolidation of various *boundaries* in human relations, which could be physical and/or mental and they could be crossed in a real and/or symbolic way. According to Fredrik Barth the "boundaries define the group," and the social ones may have "territorial counterparts" (Barth 1969: 15). For the purpose of this paper, I use a symbolic *boundary*, meaning the diversification between actors in a variety of youngster groups by social and cultural indications, as well as between Roma and non-Roma – a division constructed by the majority and seen in the public discourses.[3] Relying on Barth's theory (1969), these differentiations appear when symbolic *boundaries* are observed in social and cultural contexts. The social boundaries are already determined and thus show the lack of equality and social differentiations. The cultural boundaries, on other hand, show differences between groups and their cultural dimensions (religion,

---
1   I use the term *child* to designate a minor according to the law.
2   See Aries (1962), James and Prout (2005).
3   In my master thesis (2013) I observed the images of and about children in the context of media discourses in Bulgaria and the usage of the notion *child* in the institutional context about Roma.

beliefs, practices, ethics, etc.)[4]. Barth uses this otherness as an "ethnic boundary" that, in his words, "canalizes social life" and entails "a frequently quite complex organization of behaviour and social relations" (Barth 1969: 15). Methodologically, the social and cultural boundaries are research instruments that are interconnected and cannot be observed separately or distinguished at all. Furthermore, they can be visible or invisible and are understood as symbolic boundaries requiring that not only physical, but also mental aspects be taken into consideration. In the *child*'s world, the divisions and *boundaries* have a specific character and expressions. Examining the moments of crossing social and cultural *boundaries* in order to take part in a group or testify prestige allows an understanding of the processes of exchange and communication among children and youngsters. Such processes can be discussed as cultural learning (in its wider meaning). In this context, changes can be observed in the social statuses and roles, as well as in individual pursuit and inclusion in a particular cultural environment. These transitions constitute a large part of everyday life for youngsters and become very important for them in many cases. Fredrik Barth points out that "the cultural features that signal the boundary may change, and the cultural characteristics of the member may likewise be transformed, indeed, even the organizational form of the group may change..." (1969: 14).

Research on childhood as a social and cultural phenomenon and on children has a relatively short history. A basis for a change in thinking about childhood and directing the attention of researchers to the *child* and his world was provided by the French historian Philippe Aries (1962), who approached the *child* and childhood as constructs of modern times. Among the scholars who have contributed to the development of the subfield of the anthropology of childhood were Montgomery (2009), James and Prout (2005), and last but not least, David Lancy (2008; 2010; 2013; Lancy/Grove 2011).

In Bulgaria, studies of childhood are dominated by approaches used in the fields of pedagogics, psychology, and sociology. They often cover topics related to ethnic issues and the Roma community in particular (Koleva, et al. (ed.) 2012; Pashova 2003, 2005; Nunev 1993, 1998), although in most cases they deal with Roma children's "integration" in school (Nunev 2006, 2008, 2009, Nuneva 2003, Kyutchukov (ed.) 2004, 2006, Topalova/Pamporov 2007). This results in categorizing and unifying of ethnical and cultural characteristics for the purposes of the educational system by putting all Roma communities within a common group.

---

4   This paper is part of the research project "Boundaries and Social Mobility," funded by the Scientific Research Fund of University of Plovdiv Paisii Hilendarski with project manager: Assoc. Prof. Dobrinka Parusheva, PhD

Problems arise in trying to link theory with practice, i.e. when it is impossible that the theory be applied in every context. In this sense, the anthropological approach allows the use of methods that give meaningful results to implement field research related to childhood. Exploring the boundaries of childhood via crossing and observing the socialization of the body, (a symbolic boundary by itself), the socialization between children, between the child and the other children of the group, between them and the adults, etc., helps to better understand the notion of childhood among Roma and how the interpersonal and group relations during childhood changes.

This article aims to discuss how children socialize (in its wider meaning) in and out of their community. To answer this question, I will present a few examples of crossing social and cultural *boundaries* between Roma and non-Roma children through a demonstration of the body practices and techniques of sport and dance activities. These result are from fieldwork carried out in different cities and villages in Bulgaria. The object of observation and analysis are young people from different Roma communities involved in some type of a team sport, through which they learn new skills, acquire prestige, and gain more friends in and outside the community. The moments of child *socialization* (after Berger/Luckmann 1996) outside the Roma community can be traced through an understanding of human body perception. From a cultural and social point of view, different body practices and techniques create *boundaries* that could be crossed over at some times in the lives of children.

The text is part of a larger study of the world of childhood in which a holistic anthropological approach is applied.[5] In an article commenting on the widely used term "agency" (Oswell 2013: 9-33), the cultural anthropologist David Lancy gives several recommendations for research methods of childhood as "participant observation, interviews with key informants (adult and children), studying the cultural context in which children live, comparative analysis of childhood in other societies (Ethnology), photography, oral audio recording video" (Lancy 2012a: 9). According to him, one of the main problems of the research is that it is based only or mainly on interviews with children as a source of information. In an attempt to avoid such pitfalls, I have observed directly and indirectly, children in several communities by carefully looking at specific details of the lives of both children

---

5 "In anthropology 'holism' refer to a theoretical and methodological approach that tries to avoid a particular view on what is being studied and remains open for new and unexpected connections (see Otto and Bubandt 2010 for a thorough discussion)" (Hesse 2014: 371). For a deeper discussion of the methods in anthropological research see e.g. Bernard 1998 and Bernard 2006.

and adults. Furthermore, I conducted interviews (unstructured, semistructured and free conversations) with – again – both children and adults.[6] The presented examples and the analysis that results from them have no intention to generalize; rather they aim to raise new questions related to the anthropology of childhood among Roma.

2 Crossing Boundaries

As already mentioned, the processes of crossing social and cultural *boundaries* among children as a means of socialization could be observed through the human body as a symbolic and physical way of expression and communication, and as a marker of identification. By learning new skills, practices, and body techniques a *child* gains new friends, prestige, and social and cultural capital (after Bourdieu) in and outside the community. These become a way of his/her socialization. The connection between learning and socialization is interrelated from a socio-cultural perspective and offers a large field for observation. "In classical anthropological monographs learning is generally used synonymously with concepts like 'socialization' or 'enculturation' or as an explanation of cultural transmission" (Hasse 2014: 372). Perhaps a bit more discussion of *cultural learning* is necessary.

I use the term *cultural learning* here to designate any informal inter- and/or intra-group practices and processes of exchange of information and experiences that accompany the lives of children. The school, which is often a place where many practices of this kind are performed, is not the focus of attention here; attention will be paid rather to people who determine the life of the *child* in the family, community, and in informal groups of friends. For example, participating in a sport team or in a group of with common interests becomes a way of cultural transmission and learning for children.

The anthropologist David Lancy (1975, 1980, 2010, 2012) insists on focusing on cultural features in the learning process, not on the practice itself as a physiological condition of the person. The physical act of learning and the cultural characteristics of the training cannot be divided as they are interrelated. Understanding the body as symbolically laden is a way to track the different ways of cultural learning among children. This may be done through observing the processes of crossing the symbolic *boundaries* among youngsters and tracing them in the everyday practices and ways that children live among adults. "Learning takes place all the time and

---

6   Sometimes I enriched my instruments by also using visual methods and mental maps, but because of ethical considerations I will not present them here.

everywhere and affects not only knowledge, language and individual identities but whole communities of learners" (Hasse 2014: 379). Not only are the parents and relatives important, but also other people in and outside the community – friends or other adults that take part in their lives such as teachers from school, neighbors, etc. According to Hesse, "the main contribution to the development of notions of practice-based learning are, however, found in the detailed descriptions of children learning outside of formal schooling systems" (Hesse 2014: 371). Family and the larger circles that Roma children live within are most influencial to their lives and building their perspectives.

According to Allison James, "the family' has long been regarded as a key site of socialization" (James 2013). The Bulgarian ethnologist Petya Bankova also claims that the family is a key institution through which the instinctive impulses of the individual modify themselves to satisfy the conditions for the survival of the community (1998: 31). Furthermore, she insists "the interaction of the individual with the community and the culture determines the formation of major part of his/her patterns of behavior" (Bankova 1998: 30). Most scholars share the opinion that the main role for "developing" the child and his/her "secondary socialization" (after Berger and Luckmann) is played by the community he/she lives in and by valuable "others" (Pashova 2003, Nunev 1998, Pamporov 2004).

A great part of the *child*'s life in Roma communities depends not only on the closer family but also on the larger community he/she lives in. There are different interactions to be observed in children's everyday lives between kids of the same age and/or older youngsters that show an understanding of the social and cultural perspectives of childhood among Roma. "When children learn from other children instead of from adults, many factors may influence the course of interactions. These range from age, gender, or status hierarchies, to the basic cognitive or emotional levels of the parties, to the cultural setting" (Maynard/Tovote 2010: 183). The refraction of the body boundary is a way to track changes in interpersonal and group relations during childhood. Body as "socially constructed" (Bourdieu 2001: 13) and actually perceived is related directly to the understanding of belonging to a group or community.

Sports as a global phenomenon and other types of physical practices are often used as a means of communication and exchange in various social spheres and allow in some situations for team interactions. David Andrews and Michael Giardina review Gruneau's approach to sports "as created by society but is correspondingly one way in which social beings are able to maintain and develop a sense of themselves" (2008: 397). According to them, "sport is at the same time constitutive of the *boundaries* framing social experience and a forum for the manufacturing of individual identities" (Andrews/Giardina 2008: 397).

Football, freerunning[7], dancing, and other types of examples came up during my fieldwork. These are widespread practices that have their own specific features of activity and skills needed. The observation shows that young people are interested in practicing current popular trends and their universal application in the current environment.[8] The communal character of the three activities specifically mentioned above is important for the topic. Learning a new commercial skill is difficult because, according to Suzanne Gaskins and Ruth Paradise, "it is often an unmarked, fully integrated, almost invisible, part of everyday interactions" (2010: 87). "... [l]earning through observation, however, involves more than just picking up a discrete skill; it is complex and culturally situated" (Idem: 85). In some circumstances it is part of crossing already existing symbolic *boundaries* between children.

As they are permeable and dynamic, social and cultural *boundaries* are frequently crossed and one of the reasons is the widespread mobility among children. Because of that, in most of the cases these *boundaries* may be visible or not, and they intersect and become interrelated as part of the youngsters' lives. Therefore, social and cultural boundaries could be understood in a symbolic sense when the boundaries become visible through crossing and/or overcoming them. My observations indicate that crossing the already determined symbolic boundaries between Roma and non-Roma is a means of socialization and presence for young Roma people outside their community. Another important step in this process is the adoption of new social roles and acquiring prestige. Now I will discuss the three activities separately and try to outline their social and cultural aspects through the way youngsters participate in a group and/or a sport team and their interactions with others.

3 Freerunning

The first example shows crossing of already determined social *boundaries* between Roma and non-Roma children through practicing a collective sport with common interests. These results come from my fieldwork in 2009 in the town of Tsarevo, which is a small town situated in the southeast part of Bulgaria on the South Black Sea, where communities of Bulgarians and Roma live. This exam-

---

7   Freerunning is an acrobatic activity that is developed from the earlier style Parkour – developed from military obstacle course training. For freerunning see Pargova (2010).
8   About research on youth subcultures in Bulgaria see Georgieva and Koleva (2010); Neikova (2010).

ple presents an interaction with a group of freerunners – only boys, all from the town and from both Roma and non-Roma communities. At that time, it was a self-formed teenage group, whose main objective was practicing freerunning. The skills of each member were a main condition to participate in the group: everyone "able" to do "tricks" was a worthy member of the group.[9] The organization of these youngsters showed hierarchy in relation to the "most capable" member in the group. The leader was one of the boys who was the most experienced in freerunning and was a "teacher" for the rest. For these boys the learning process was realized through their experience in the culture of freerunning and the characteristics of behavior attached to it. By body practices, techniques, and the introduced knowledge, the members of the group acquired a new social status as freerunners. Among them were boys from the local Roma community. One of them defined the leader of the group as "the best" and also as his "brother," although they had different cultural and social backgrounds – Roma and non-Roma. This observation indicates a strong connection between some of the members and the way they identify themselves within the group. The interpersonal interactions of the boys depended on their social status, experience, and on their progress and realization outside the group, for example taking part in competitions, performances, acquiring new and complex skills, etc. By participating in the freerunning group, the members expressed affection and dedication to the sport, which defined them as a community.

In this observed youth group social and cultural *boundaries* existed. These *boundaries* were crossed over in some circumstances. Firstly, we should consider the public dimension: the very formation of this group and the presence of boys from different ethnic backgrounds in it. They were visible for the rest of the society and enjoyed a certain social status. This allowed for the initial social and cultural differences to lapse. Secondly, another moment of crossing symbolic *boundaries* was at the level of personal relationships. In a conversation with one of the boys from the Roma community, it came out that despite the unifying freerunning activities, outside the group the boys were not as "united" as they were in the group; a kind of "disunion" existed. Nevertheless, the common interest of these young people unified them and decreased the differences that obviously existed, offering a new field of personal expression.

This kind of formal crossing and seemingly overcoming social *boundaries* could be observed at different levels of interpersonal relations. The very *boundaries* are designed according to the stages of relationships between individuals – at an individual or group level. The mobility of youth groups helps to observe

---

9   This is the discourse used by the participants in my conversations.

frequent changes in the perspectives and the field of performance of youth in the public domain.

4   Dance 1

Another case of crossing social and cultural *boundaries* I observed among youngsters from a dance group from the village of Dink. It is a small village located in Maritsa Municipality, in the Plovdiv Province of Southern Bulgaria on the northern bank of the Maritsa River. The village is very near the city of Plovdiv and Bulgarians, Roma and Turks live there. The attitude towards the type of activity of young people in the example of the freerunning depends on performance in front of the audience. Such an attitude existed also within the dance group and their attendance at the festival called "We sing, dance and live together" on the occasion of the International Roma Day (May 6th) in 2013 in the village of Manole, Maritsa Municipality.

This group was organized institutionally by the so-called *chitalishte* in Bulgaria (a local cultural community center), but the self-regulation within the group depended on its members and the prestige each of them had. The repertoire of the group was different and combined modern and oriental dances, choreographed by their tutor. This mixture widened the dimensions of the dance and made it more international. Their performances were on a local level and in front of a small audience mainly from the nearby villages. At the time I carried out the fieldwork, the members of the group were boys and girls with different ethnic backgrounds – Roma, Bulgarians, and Turks, with relatively minor age difference – most were between 14 and 17 years old. A unifying factor for the members was the dancing and performing in front of the public in terms of competition with other groups during the time of the dance festival. Despite being institutionally organized, this group does not exist today because of personal misunderstandings between the members and mainly between those with more and less prestige. This unsustainability confirms the dynamic in youngster's participation and group activities.

During the youngsters' performance, I recognized one of the girls as the daughter of the woman who was their organizer (and did not mention it at first). Later in our conversation my observation was confirmed. The daughter, despite her Bulgarian origin, had participated in the group for a long time, because, according to her mother, "she likes it." This girl distinguished herself from the others in the group by her clothes. Visually her outfit was slightly different from the other girls, but there was no other obvious distinction between the members and their performance on the stage. The process of crossing symbolic *boundaries* happened through demonstration of body practices and techniques in front of the audience and with continuing legitimization and communication among the dancers from the village of Dink. The organizer[10] of the youngsters was a direct witness to the socialization among the children. According to my observation, the presence of her two daughters in this group, surrounded by young Roma and Turks, was part of their family's everyday social interactions. On the one hand, they lived in the village of Dink and, on the other hand, the youngsters had a common desire to perform dance in front of an audience.

The presence of young Roma boys and girls in a different situation and location among non-Roma, and vice versa, is an example of crossing *boundaries* at different levels – on a group level and towards the outsiders of the group (adults, audience, community, etc.). In the case in Tsarevo, Roma boys were numbered fewer compared to others in the group. The case with the dancers from the village of Dink represents the opposite pattern of presence – non-Roma girls were numbered fewer as part of a dance group consisting of Roma and Turk kids.

The group interactions are defined by the performance on the stage and the body skills of each member. The public performance is a kind of testifying point in which the private experience of the person enters into a public form. Both the freerunners and the dancers from the village of Dink have this main private-public crossing of *boundaries* where personal interactions and diversifications between the members occur. The *boundaries* of the groups have their own terms for participation, whether formal or not, but with obvious inside-outside group dimension and rules. The freerunners' audience was organized (school celebrations), or could also be spontaneous and random (witnesses in the street). The extent of crossing the visible and invisible *boundaries* of the group members was expressed by contact with the others. During the performances the members of both the freerunning and dance groups proved the existence of the required skills that aimed to legitimize their participation in the group and also each member's prestige. The performance of the dancers from the village of Dink was organized and happened on the stage. Their spontaneous performances happened among "insiders" – the circle of dancers and friends during rehearsals at the community center. The learning process helped them not only to acquire new skills, but also to build new friendships and get involved in the group's life with an aim to create an atmosphere of more confidence and comfort. Crossing the *boundaries* in front of an audience happened in an organized manner and this increased the extent of overcoming the symbolic *boundaries* between the dancers in everyday communication, i.e. when the group is together, the members feel secure. At another level, the symbolic

---

10 Later I learned that her other daughter also was part of the same dance group.

boundaries within the group were overcome, which confirmed the role of dance and expression as a socializing factor among young people belonging to different communities.

The mobility among youth and the rapid change of their status and position in the community and the family can affect the participation or presence in a group with common interests. Performing in front of an audience brings a certain prestige and symbolic capital to the participants – fame, recognition among the community, new friends, girlfriends, etc. Overcoming certain symbolic *boundaries* through physicality is a type of a *game* (after Huizinga) that depends on a set rules and models of implementation. If the presence and participation in youth formation will bring certain capital to the members, the *game* can start with the stages of initiation, demonstrating skills and presence among the group, and overcoming certain physical and mental limits.

5 Dance 2

Another case of a group, related to breakdancing,[11] was observed in 2011 in the Stolipinovo neighborhood in the city of Plovdiv located on the outskirts of the city in its northeastern part on the right bank of the river Maritsa. Compared to the previous two places, the town of Tsarevo and the village of Dink, Stolipinovo is a larger neighborhood and part of the city of Plovdiv, which is the second biggest in Bulgaria. It is considered as "Roma neighborhood" by the media, but according to my observations, it is not a homogeneous district with clearly identified inhabitants and communities live there who are self-declared Roma and Turks. In 2011, the breakdancers were an informal group of youngsters with no specific number of participants. They were boys gathering to practice breakdancing and learn new skills. Nowadays some of them, particularly their leader, are trying to engage more young people to practice dance. As Catherine Hasse claims, "children learn by doing, observing, imitating or by being praised and reacted to by grown-ups" (2014: 373). The breakdancers have specific potentialities and skills during their performance ("game") in front of their community and beyond. Their group performed during public events and concerts. In response to the question of how the youngsters from the neighborhood were organized to do breakdancing, their leader answered: "I go out in the neighborhoods, gather four guys who are very famous

---

11 Breakdancing is known also as B-boying and is part of the hip hop culture and its basic elements: Graffiti, DJing, B-boying, and Emceeing. The person who is practicing it is called b-boy or b-girl. For Breakdancing/B-boying See Simard (2014).

names with their dance, and tell them 'guys, need to get your groups to come to see you, to talk, we'll go somewhere to dance', that's it" (Chakara[12]). Close observation indicates that two kinds of public performance of the youngsters exist: formal – in front of the community, as on the occasion of International Roma Day in 2011, and informal – among friends from the community and small audiences from outside where there was no competition but self-expression on the stage and beyond it. To outline the difference, the idea of breakdancing as a style and part of the hip hop culture is to perform in so-called battles with other competitors, to prove skills, to earn respect, and to overcome interpersonal boundaries without physical assaults. Moreover, the b-boying battles are used as a means of communication and aim to compete to legitimize personal skills and style, and to contribute to the crew. Some stories of getting involved in the hip-hop culture and how it could change the youngsters' lives were shared in my conversations with some members of the breakdance crew in the Stolipinovo neighborhood: "Breakdancing educates them a lot… Because the neighborhood […] It is tricky to live in this neighborhood and young people mostly avoid hanging out in such places and with such people. (Chakara) […] And through this dance they avoid stress and encourage themselves. Just fall in love with the game and want to play." (Yashi*).*[13]

The process of proving and presence in the group depended on the abilities of the members and the acquaintances they had. By practicing this type of activity Roma children gain prestige that influences their position within the community and their social status outside their group. The public performances of the group represent a way of legitimization and demonstration outside their community. They mark the moment of testifying prestige in or beyond it, by presenting the individual body practices and techniques. When personal skills and qualities are manifested and proven within the group, socialization happens. The process of learning new skills is an important part of youngsters' lives and becomes their way of self-expression, through which they overcome certain symbolic *boundaries* in their social and cultural interaction with others. Breakdancing and teaching is culturally determined, firstly by the "imported" hip hop characters, and secondly, by the *glocal* way of interpretation in new surroundings. In addition, breakdancing, like free running, leads to physical assimilation of public and common areas of the city and neighborhood, thus it constantly questions the borders of the neighborhood and the *boundaries* of the community.

---

12 Now and later in the text I will use only the nicknames of my respondents.
13 Chakara and Yashi participated in one conversation.

6 Football

The last case outlines sports as a mediator and as a means of socialization explicitly in the lives of Roma children. It was observed in Stolipinovo neighborhood in Plovdiv in 2010 and 2011. I met some members of the local football club "Jutvari" (this was the way they write the name in English; it means "Harvesters"), and several times I met their coach Segun Phillips.[14] The coach provided me with basic information about the lives of young people in the neighborhood in his words "through sport" and discussed the role sports played in it. He was a mediator in the process of the socialization of boys from "the ghetto" (in his words) into the society.[15] Being a coach and a pastor simultaneously he had a different social status on the "border" between the football club as a community and the rest of the society. Through his institutional role, the coach was able to influence the children – mostly boys[16]. In a conversation with him, it became clear that his aim was to "educate" (in his words) the children from the neighborhood through football and to help them develop in "the right way. "You do not just play football, I get you involved in ... life ..." (S. Ph.). Football as a worldwide sport was legitimized in front of the majority of the Roma community and provided the players with prestige and a higher social status. "Through football, and I love football, everybody loves football, you know true football is a general game, I mean it is a discipline game and ... so I used that form, that area, to get them, to trust them in football, at the same point get them involved and disciplined in life" (S. Ph.).

The adolescents in Stolipinovo, according to the coach, lived in an environment of bad practices and habits – theft, drugs, termination of school, etc. Football and his educational purpose shaped children as personalities to become "significant" and "legitimate" in the adults' world and the macro-society. "You know before they were so quick to get angry and they want to be violent [like] in their nature, you know. But, Praise God, that's not who they are again, they've changed. And the good news is that they all want to finish their school" (S. Ph.).

---

14 He was a professional football player in FC "Spartak" – Plovdiv for some time, terminated his career and became coach of FC "Harvesters" until 2014. His relationship with the Roma community in the Stolipinovo neighborhood happened through commitment to the Evangelist Church and his role as pastor.
15 For research about life in the ghetto see Bauman (2003).
16 Observations showed extra sport activities organized by the coach in which girls from the neighborhood participated too; this however was the case only when the pastor was pastor and sport leader at one and the same time, which happened usually on Saturdays.

Children and Socialization: Crossing Social and Cultural Boundaries 175

The socialization of children from the Stolipinovo neighborhood among non-Roma happened in an organized way, through sports and by the mediation role of the coach who aimed at offering presence and interactions with others outside the neighborhood, which was seen as a "closed" district. Due to his support, the young boys experienced cultural learning of new skills and new social roles simultaneously. Despite the efforts of the young people for acceptance and presence outside the Roma community, they often faced negative attitudes from the other players. The communication of youngsters from the local community with others, i.e. non-Roma outside the neighborhood, according to the coach, was difficult: "We win four to one and they [...] get angry, they're [...] calling us names, they're insulting the players, they're insulting everybody, and one [...] gave my player a slap" (S. Ph.). The presence of his football team in another city was an event of great importance to the players and their parents.[17] This communication through sports was part of their legitimacy as a community to the other football groups and a way to prove their skills.

On the one hand, there was a differentiation between Roma and non-Roma players that was visible as a space division, for example, during football matches. The observation, on the other hand, indicated differentiation between the youngsters in the Stolipinovo neighborhood that depended on social status, religion, spoken language, residence in the area, etc.[18] Social and cultural *boundaries* are crossed in some circumstances – when the boys take part in the activities of the football club like training, meetings, vacation trips, competitions, etc., and that brings them a sense of belonging to a team. The common objectives and characteristics of the football team make young people come together in a community. The activity of the group appears liminal, both in spatial and social terms for the Roma community in Stolipinovo. First, the team is situated geographically by their living area and common activities, and second, there is a social and cultural differentiation of the players as Roma who are living in the neighborhood that is a symbolic *boundary* between Roma and non-Roma.

Empirical data confirm the hypothesis about the existence of social and cultural *boundaries* among youngsters in the Stolipinovo neighborhood. These *boundaries* are symbolically crossed at times for a purpose. Through sports and other collective activities socialization of children within and outside the community happens. This is an important part of their social status–because through the adoption of

---

17 For the work with FC "Jutvari" see the award winning documentary movie 'The road to Rudozem' at https://vimeo.com/11162253
18 They referred to themselves as respectively Roma, Turks, Bulgarians, etc. depending on the area of the neighborhood where they lived.

various roles they acquire the necessary prestige and can enjoy a "better" image and status among others.

Both contemporary cultural exchanges and changes in the way and style of life in the Roma groups in Bulgaria create new fields and practices of socialization among young people in and outside their community. There are people with intermediary roles – leaders, mediators, etc., who use the prestige they gained in the community and beyond, who exercise influence on children, and transmit skills and knowledge to adolescents in order to make their socialization possible and easier. However, as Maynard and Tovote claim, "in many cultures, children's interactions with other children are more prevalent in their day-to-day experiences than their interactions with adults" (2010: 183). Indeed, there are moments of intercultural exchange and cultural learning among youngsters belonging to different ethnic groups. As in the cases from my fieldwork briefly presented here, when the social and cultural *boundaries* are crossed by various Roma and non-Roma communities, whether on a group or interpersonal level, knowledge of body practices and techniques are transferred, with an aim to achieve prestige and accumulate more social capital. These frequent boundary crossings allow youth to actively participate in new cultural environments within and outside of their community. Liminal markers of identity and self-identification are: the spoken language, religion, and personal skills. Undoubtedly, practicing a team sport and ways of expressing physical skills may be discussed as one of the successful ways of socialization.

To sum up, crossing social and cultural *boundaries* creates new connections and relationships between individuals and thus develops paths for cultural transmission of knowledge and skills. In the case of children, it suggests their presence in one or another group, or in both simultaneously. Similar phenomena construct a new identity, which helps the *child* to socialize in the living conditions of the group and/or outside it and to acquire a new status and position. Young people manage to create their network of relationships with others through bodily practices and by overcoming mental and physical limitations.

Crossing social and cultural *boundaries* through sports as a means of socialization and communication allows the Roma children to express themselves at different levels outside their community and to prove themselves in the eyes of the others. In this way they acquire prestige and a sense of belonging to the sport team that is respected by most members of the Roma community.

References

Банкова, П. (1998). Културна среда – семейна среда – медийна среда. [Cultural environment – family environment – media environment], В: Българска етнология, бр. 3-4, 21-37.
Бауман, З. (2003). Най-ниското равнище: гетото. [The lowest level: the ghetto], В: Бауман, Зигмунд. Общността. Търсене на безопасност в несигурния свят. София, 132-148.
Георгиева, В. & Колева, Д. (2010). Младежки субкултури – що е то? [Youth subcultures – what is it?] В: Семинар_BG, бр. 3. Available at: http://www.seminar-bg.eu/spisanie-seminar-bg/broy3/item/274-%D0%BC%D0%BB%D0%B0%D0%B4%D0%B5%D0%B6%D0%BA%D0%B8-%D1%81%D1%83%D0%B1%D0%BA%D1%83%D0%BB%D1%82%D1%83%D1%80%D0%B8-%D1%89%D0%BE-%D0%B5-%D1%82-%D0%BE?.html (accessed 13 July 2015)
Колева, И. & Живка Иванова, Г.Х. (2012). Етнопсихопедагогика на детето. [Ethnopsychopedagogy of the child], Романи Бахт, Самоков.
Кючуков, Х. (2006). Между традицията и образованието. [Between the tradition and the education], София: Балканска фондация "Дайвърсити".
Кючуков, Х. (съст.) (2004). Аспекти на интеркултурното образование на ромските деца. [Aspects of intercultural education of the Roma children], София: Делфи.
Нейкова, Н. (2010). Субкултурите – поглед „отвън". [The subculture – "outside" view], В: Семинар_BG, бр. 3. Available at: http://www.seminar-bg.eu/spisanie-seminar-bg/broy3/item/275-%D1%81%D1%83%D0%B1%D0%BA%D1%83%D0%BB%D1%82%D1%83%D1%80%D0%B8%D1%82%D0%B5-%D0%BF%D0%BE%D0%B3%D0%BB%D0%B5%D0%B4-%D0%BE%D1%82%D0%B2%D1%8A%D0%BD.html (accessed 13 July 2015)
Нунев, Й. (2009). Ромският етнокултурен дискурс в организацията и управлението на интеркултурното образование. [The Roma ethnocultural discourse in the organization and the management of the intercultural education], В: Технологични аспекти на етнокултурното образование. Сборник с научни доклади. Изд. на ЮЗУ „Н. Рилски", Благоевград.
Нунев, Й. (2008). Формиране на образователна политика по интеграция на децата и учениците от ромското етническо малцинство. [Formation of the educational politics for integration of children and students from Roma ethnic minority], В: Социологически проблеми. Специален брой, 210-229.
Нунев, Й. (2006). Ромите и процесът на десегрегация в образованието. [The Roma people and the process of desegregation in education], София.
Нунев, Й. (1998). Ромското дете и неговата семейна среда. [The Roma child and its family environment], София.
Нунев, Й. (1993). Ромското дете и неговата възпитателна среда. [The Roma child and its educational environment], София.
Нунева, Д. (съст.) (2003). Образованието на ромската общност в измеренията на мултикултурализма. [The education of the Roma community in the dimensions of multiculturalism], София: Агато.
Пампоров, А. (2004). Ромското семейство: аспекти на всекидневието. [The Roma family: aspects of everyday life], София.

Пашова, А. (2003) Ромското дете и проблемите на неговата социализация. [The Roma child and the problems of its socialization], В: Пашова, Анастасия. Попкочев, Траян (съст.). Социализация на ромското дете. Благоевград, 5 – 11.
Пъргова, Я. (2010). Фрийрън – уличен спорт или начин на живот. [Freerun – a street sport or a way of life], В: Семинар_BG, бр. 3. Available at: http://www.seminar-bg.eu/spisanie-seminar-bg/broy3/item/273-%D1%84%D1%80%D0%B8%D0%B9%D1%80%-D1%8A%D0%BD-%D1%83%D0%BB%D0%B8%D1%87%D0%B5%D0%BD-%D1%81%D0%BF%D0%BE%D1%80%D1%82-%D0%B8%D0%BB%D0%B8-%D1%84%D0%B8%D0%BB%D0%BE%D1%81%D0%BE%D1%84%D0%B8%D1%8F-%D0%BD%D0%B0-%D0%B6%D0%B8%D0%B2%D0%BE%D1%82%D0%B0.html (accessed 13 July 2015)
Топалова, В. & Пампоров, А. (съст.) (2007). Интеграцията на ромите в българското общество. [The integration of the Roma people in the Bulgarian society], София: Институт по социология при БАН.
Andrews, D. & Giardina, M.D. (2008). Sport Without Guarantees: Toward a Cultural Studies That Matters. Cultural Studies. Critical Methodologies, 8(4), Sage Publications, pp. 395-422. Available at: http://csc.sagepub.com/content/8/4/395 (accessed 13 July 2015)
Aries, P. (1962). Centuries of Childhood. New York.
Barth, F. (1969). Ethnic Groups and Boundaries. The Social Organization of Culture Difference. Boston.
Berger, P. L. & Luckmann, T. (1996). The Social Construction of Reality. Penguin Group.
Bernard, R. (2006). Research methods in anthropology: qualitative and quantitative approaches. London, AltaMiraPress.
Bernard, R. (1998). Handbook of Methods in Cultural Anthropology. London, AltaMira-Press.
Bourdieu, P. (2001). Masculine Domination. Stanford University Press.
Gaskins, S. & Paradise, R. (2010). Learning through observation in daily life. In: Lancy, David. Bock, John and Suzanne Gaskins. The Anthropology of Learning in Childhood. New York, pp. 85-117.
Hasse, C. (2014). The Anthropological Paradigm of Practice- Based Learning. In: Billett, S. et al. (eds.). International Handbook of Research in Professional and Practice-based Learning, Springer International Handbooks of Education, pp. 369-391.
James, A. (2013). Socialising Children. University of Sheffield, UK.
James, A. & Prout, A. (2005 [1997]). Constructing and Reconstructing Childhood. Contemporary Issues in the Sociological Study of Childhood. London, Taylor & Francis e-Library.
Lancy, D. (2013). 'Babies aren't Persons': A Survey of Delayed Personhood. In: Keller, Heidi and Otto, Hiltrus (eds). Different Faces of Attachment: Cultural Variations of a Universal Human Need. Cambridge: Cambridge University Press.
Lancy, D. (2012). The Chore Curriculum. In: Spittler, Gerd and M. F. C. Bourdillon. African Children at Work: Working and Learning in Growing Up. Berlin, LIT Verlag.
Lancy, D. (2012a). Unmasking Children's Agency. In: SSWA Faculty Publications, Paper 277. Available at: http://digitalcommons.usu.edu/sswa_facpubs/277 (accessed 3 February 2015)
Lancy, D. & Grove, M.A. (2011). Getting Noticed. Middle Childhood in Cross-Cultural Perspective. Hum Nat, 22, pp. 281–302.

Lancy, D., Bock, J. & Gaskins, S. (2010). The Anthropology of Learning in Childhood. New York
Lancy, D. (2008). The Anthropology of Childhood: Cherubs, Chattel, Changelings. Cambridge: Camridge.
Lancy, D. (1980). Becoming a Blacksmith in Gbarngasuakwelle. Anthropology & Education Quarterly, 11(4), pp. 266-274.
Lancy, D. (1975). The Social Organization of Learning, Initiation, Rituals and Public Schools. Human Organization, 34(4), pp. 371-380.
Mancheva, S. (2013). The World of Chilhood among Roma – Images and Models of Representation. Master Thesis of Ethnology, Plovdiv University 'Paisii Hilendarski'.
Maynard, A. & Tovote, K.E. (2010). Learning from Other Children. In: Lancy, David. Bock, John and Suzanne Gaskins. The Anthropology of Learning in Childhood. New York, pp. 181-205.
Montgomery, H. (2009). An Introduction of Childhood: Anthropological Perspectives on Children's Lives. Oxford. Blackwell.
Oswell, D. (2013). The Agency of Children: From Family to Global Human Rights. New York, Cambridge University Press.
Simard, H. (2014). Breaking Down the Differences Between Breakdancing and B-boying: A Grounded Theory Approach. Montreal.

Parents' neighborhood integration in two ethnically diverse low-income neighborhoods

Banu Çıtlak

1 Introduction

Although, compared to other urban areas in Europe today, ethnic segregation in German cities is rather low (Schönwälder/Söhn 2009: 1454), the close link between poverty and education, and also social resources, still forms neighborhoods which have a disadvantaging effect on children and youth (Oberwittler 2007; s. Çıtlak in this Book). While unequal opportunities for children and youth lead to a wider interest in neighborhood and school segregation, the consequences of local segregation on perceived parental trust as a mediating variable for parental behavior is widely overseen thus far. However, international research predicts a high sensitivity of parents of adolescents towards neighborhood characteristics and effects, suggesting that parents adjust their parental strategies with respect to the deemed risks and perceived mutual trust in other inhabitants and families within the neighborhood. The wider spectrum of contextual effects on families, children, and youth has been reviewed by researchers (Jencks and Meyer, 1990; Leventhal and Brooks-Gunn, 2000) indicating that a high level of generalized trust strengthens families and leads to less protective parenting and less parental stress during adolescence (Jencks/Meyer 1990; Nieuwenhuis 2014: 38). In fact, studies show that higher levels of perceived trust and confidence in other inhabitants go together with assumed similar normative ideas and values among neighbors. In that case, parents can rely on the positive social control of other adults in the neighborhood (collective efficacy for children). Very broadly, Coleman (1988) has investigated this positive effect of local family communities on parenting and children's educational achievement and defined it as social capital. Coleman concluded that higher levels of local social capital (social cohesion) are positively related to parental engagement in the community and are leading to positive youth development as well as to school success. Moreover, the perceived positive social control of other adults in the neighborhood, as well as higher intergenerational closure, reduces family stress. Thus, if parents feel secure and are more confident with their own parental supervision, they show a higher parental sensitivity which on the other hand leads further to positive effects on school achievement of children and adolescents (Coleman 1988; Sampson/Moronoff 1997; Darling/Steinberg 1997, for ethnic minorities: Portes 1998). In addition, the level of community cohesion is being investigated, not only by parents' and children's local engagement and social networks, but also through intergenerational closure, measuring the quantity and quality of relationships between parents of peers. New research, on the relationship between local engagement of parents and children's social capital in urban neighborhoods underlines that children are not restricted to the social capital of their families alone but actively create their own local networks, and in doing so they build their own social capital (Weller/Buegel 2009). However, Coleman's conclusions have been criticized for describing nothing but the well-known suburban communities and that his results are therefore not applicable to today's urban family life outside of wealthy homogenous suburban environments. In a well-recognized study of Furstenberg and colleagues, it is shown that the variance of parental strategies within the same neighborhood is even higher than between different districts of the whole city (Furstenberg et al. 1999; Ardelt/Eccles 2001). Applied parental strategies were particularly dependant a lot more on parents' resources, their perception of the neighborhood and on families' local engagement (local social capital) than on the specific neighborhood itself. Drawing on these findings so far, the important research question for the following study is which family resources and characteristics on the individual level play a significant role in parents' neighborhood perception. More specifically, do family characteristics such as family structure (single parent families), minority status, and parents´ educational status predict the perceived trust in neighbors and the intensity of involvement in the school environment? For minorities in the US, Portes (1995) showed that Hispanic families benefit from the positive child centred social control within the ethnic community by stabilising parental authority and giving local mutual support which further contributed to children's school success. However, Putnam (2007) brought quantitative evidence for decreasing trust in ethnically diverse neighborhoods supporting the conflict theory. In particular, his analysis showed that inhabitants of ethnically diverse neighborhoods tend to withdraw from collective life, have less social contacts, distrust their neighbors more and have rather shrinking collective efficacy beliefs. Portes and Vickstrom (2011) questioned this hypothesized lack of social cohesion in ethnically diverse neighborhoods recently by giving evidence of a long history of contradictory empirical findings about the interrelationship between trust, local engagement, and ethnic diversity. As a major argument, they show that most past research studies measured influences of social inequalities and ethnic segregation whereby poverty and discrimination were the main mediating variables explaining the withdrawal from social life (Portes/Vickstrom 2011: 472).

Although neighborhood poverty is of significance for educational pathways of children and for positive youth development, there is a considerable variance between poor neighborhoods with respect to these disadvantaging ecological effects (Bronfenbrenner 1979). Thus, not all poor neighborhoods have been characterized by high mobility, anonymity, high rates of single parenting families or even by high rates of ethnic diversity. Moreover, past research indicated that neighborhood organization and culture makes an important difference by explaining the ecological effects on negative versus positive youth development in poor neighborhoods (Elliott et al. 1996: 393). The methodological challenge that rises from the spatial inter correlation between poverty, segregation, and ethnic diversity will be met in the following research by using two equally disadvantaged neighborhoods with differing grades of residential mobility and ethnic heterogeneity. With respect to length of residence as an indicator for residential stability and neighborhood social embeddedness a representative family survey taken from the city Mülheim in the Ruhr area in 2007 calculated significant differences between the two neighborhoods which are selected in the following study. According to this representative family survey, families in the former working class neighborhood lived there for a significantly longer time than families in the city centre (Familienbericht Mülheim an der Ruhr 2007).

2 Research questions and sample area

In line with the theoretical framework above, some questions are of major interest in this study: A first explorative research question on the individual level is whether family characteristics (parents' years of education, family construction such as single parenting, and migration background predict families' social integration and trust in child centred social control in low income neighborhoods. In line with research about parenting and neighborhood trust there is a strong expectation that high levels of local social capital will go along with higher levels of trust in other inhabitants in terms of believing in shared values and positive social control. In addition, research reveals residential stability to be of significance in explaining higher levels of local integration, intergenerational closure, trust, and neighborly exchange (Sampson at al. 1999: 644-656). In order to test this hypothesis, the data for the following research has been collected in two neighborhoods, one with a high rate of residential stability, and one with a high rate of fluctuation compared to the city average. Thus, it is probable that higher residential instability in the city centre will hinder the development of local social ties and foster anonymity, while residential stability within the former working class neighborhood will foster a feeling of locale familiarity. Therefore, on the aggregate level, I shall test the hypothesis that families in the inner city neighborhood are locally less integrated and trust families around them less, than those families from the stable traditional working class neighborhood. Finally, a last research question is concerned with the role that educational settings and institutions play on the locale integration of families. On the one hand, school engagement may function as a door opener for parents to build networks in the neighborhood. On the other hand, to be a part of the school parents' community can also function as an alternative to neighborhood social capital for families. In this case, parents who have less locale social capital might engage more in school context in order to compensate or gain more networks in the neighborhood.

Research area: Like in other urban areas of Europe, the neighborhoods in the cities of the Ruhr area are segregated with respect to the demographic, ethnic, and socioeconomic status of their residents (Strohmeier 2002, 2010, s. Çıtlak in this Book). The city, from which both neighborhoods of the following study have been collected, is on state average with respect to the socioeconomic position of the population, demographic characteristics, and rate of immigrants. The investigation took place in two secondary schools in the city of Mülheim an der Ruhr. Geographically, the structural indicators within city segregation (Shevky/Bell 1955) show a southeast division, whereby most families live in the east part of the city, which is also rather poor and ethnically diverse. Compared to the city average, both sample neighborhoods have a younger population with higher rates of population below 18 years. Both have also higher shares of unemployed (26% and 24.3 %) and of immigrant population (26.2 and 23.9) than the city average of 5.9% and 11% respectively. One of the selected neighborhoods is located in the city centre, where the rents are low and the unemployment rate is above average. The second neighborhood is geographically located outside the town centre in a former working class district. With regard to the family structure, 16.9 percent of the family households in the former working class neighborhood are single parents. This share is somewhat below city average (17.9%) which is partly explainable by the ethnic composition of the residents with a high percentage of Muslim families, mostly of Turkish origin. In contrast to the former working class district, the share of single parents within the surveyed neighborhood in the city centre, reaches 23.4

percent. In addition, the share of immigrant population in both neighborhoods is about equal while the composition of ethnic groups is more diverse in the city centre. The residential stability with regard to length of residence differs remarkably between the two neighborhoods. Thus, the population turnover is higher and the length of residence for family households is shorter in the city centre than in the former working class neighbourhood. In order to make the article more readable, I will refer to the former working class neighborhood as *alpha (α)* and the neighborhood in the city center as *beta (β)*.

2.1 Research Design and Measures

Questionnaire: The "parents' neighborhood trust questioner" (PNTQ) is a standardized instrument which consists of 34 items. It was developed during the research process in order to assess a wide spectrum of parental beliefs and assumptions regarding the surrounding neighborhood and pre-tested several times to achieve comprehensibility even for low educated participants. The content items were chosen using the *"Collective efficacy for Children"* questionnaire presented by Sampson and colleagues (1997, 1999) with its subscales: 1) child centred social control (CCSC), 2) social integration and closure in neighborhood, and 3) neighborly exchange. However, since parents' *school related social contacts* were also of interest in this study, a fourth scale with further questions about engagement in the school context was added. For example, the original item "People in this neighborhood can be trusted" has been divided into two items each of which corresponds to the neighborhood and to school context: 1) "Parents in this neighborhood can be trusted." 2) "Parents of this school can be trusted". Similarly, the general statement "Parents in this neighborhood know their children's friends" has been changed to: 1) "I know the children in this neighborhood." 2) "I know the friends of my children." and 3) "I can tell the names of most of the classmates of my children." Parents' answers were conducted using a four point Likert Scala ranking from "fully agree" to "strongly disagree". The frequencies of certain events (like school meetings or neighborly interactions) were also measured on a four-point scale from "never" to "often". In addition, family characteristics were noted using a short *demographic screening* at the end of the questionnaire, including parents' years of education, home language, and family composition. In order to reach immigrant families of Turkish origin, the questions were translated.

Data Collection: In line with the above mentioned considerations two secondary schools were contacted – one was a secondary school (Realschule) located in the city centre and the other (Gesamtschule) in a former working class neighborhood. In both schools, 480 questionnaires were handed out and collected by teachers in 16 classes of grades seven and eight. In order to ensure anonymity, parents got the questionnaires in a cover, and they could fill it out at home and send it back with their children in a closed envelope. To children with a Turkish origin, the teachers were instructed to hand out questionnaires in both languages, Turkish and German respectively. The survey period was in spring of 2012[1]. The closed envelopes were collected in a box in the classroom and were picked up by the research team after two weeks. In the survey, 257 parents of adolescents between 13 and 14 years of age participated. The response rate was only 53.5 percent.

2.2 Results

Sample: Mothers (75.5 %) rather than fathers (15.2%) or both parents (8.1%) filled out most of the questionnaires. Table 2 provides an overview of the relevant sample characteristics. A quarter of the sample consisted of single parents, whereby all were mothers. Parents of girls and boys were represented almost equally (119/120). A test for mean variance, however, did not show any significant differences between the responses of parents and the gender of the target child on any item at all. With respect to parents' education, only 26 % of the sample had a school degree above 12 or 13 years of schooling, which signals the threshold for access to higher education in the German educational system. However, immigrant families made up 30 percent of all respondents, with parents of Turkish background making up the largest share within this subgroup. Overall, the sample characteristics (Table 1) are quite similar to the described family characteristics in the district in general, suggesting representation at least for adolescent parents in comparable neighborhoods.

---

[1] The School of Education at the Ruhr University Bochum/Germany funded this research. The grand was given to Prof. Dr. Klaus Peter Strohmeier at the Faculty of Social Science in 2012.

Table 1 Neighborhood and sample characteristics (N=257)

	working-class neighborhood (α)	city-centre neighborhood (β)	Total (city)
Neighborhood characteristics			
foreign citizen (%)	23.9	26.2	9.9
single parents (%)	16.9	23.4	17.9
unemployed (%)	8.5	7.4	6
Sample			Total (sample)
N	152	105	257
childs gender: female (%)	77	45	122
Parents' characteristics			
immigrant (%)	27.3	38.2	31.7
single parents (%)	23.7	28.4	25.6
average years of schooling	10.79	10.73	10.76

Effects of residential stability and ethnic diversity: On the group level, it was expected that families in the residentially more stable working class neighborhood would have more social capital within the local neighborhood than families in the city center. For this purpose, ANOVAs were performed to evaluate mean differences between the perceptions of parents from both neighborhoods on the relevant subscales of the questionnaire (see table 2). Most of the items did not reveal any significant differences with four exceptions. First, as expected, parents in the former working class neighborhood were socially more integrated within the neighborhood context. Two items particularly captured the families' social capital within the neighborhood revealing significant differences. Parents who reside in the former working class neighborhood agreed more often with the statements *"I have many friends / many relatives in the neighborhood"* than parents in the city center ($p < .01$ (0,001); $p < .05$ (0,013) respectively). The difference between parents´ local social capital in the two neighborhoods at hand is in line with former research, which concludes that families' local integration is positively related to residential stability and negatively related to ethnic diversity. To avoid any misunderstanding, the share of immigrants is about equal in both neighborhoods in this study. However, ethnic composition and length of residence of the ethnic groups differ remarkably.

Table 2 Mean responses to the items of PNTQ by neighborhood

	α	β	total
Neighborly support (9 Items)			
I have many friends in this neighborhood.	2.60**	2.13**	2.41
I have many relatives in this neighborhood.	2.28*	1.90*	2.13
How often do you and your neighbors…	2.94	2.80	2.89
…do a favour for each other?			
…barrow things?	2.16	2.25	2.19
…sit each other's children?	1.83	1.92	1.86
When a neighbor is not at home, how often do you and other neighbors …	2.15	2.10	2.13
…watch over their property?			
…visit each other?	2.46	2.44	2.45
…get together for events?	2.29	2.17	2.24
…ask your neighbors for advice?	2.38	2.26	2.34
Trust in child centred social control (CCSC) (6 Items)	α	β	total
Parents in this neighborhood are trustworthy.	2.88	2.85	2.87
Here in the neighborhood adults have a watchful eye on all children.	2.64	2.73	2.67
Our neighbors will do something if children …	2.33	2.54	2.42
… skip school and hang around outside.			
… damage someone else's property.	2.97	3.18	3.06
… behave disrespectfully towards older people.	2.83	2.89	2.85
… show unfair behaviour or physically threaten peers.	2.79	2.71	2.76

	α	β	total
Integration in the school context (8 Items)			
Do you know the names of the classmates of your child?	3.03	2.79	2.93
Parents in this school are trustworthy.	2.80	2.70	2.76
Parents in this school know each other.	2.59**	2.32**	2.48
I talk with other parents from the school about the school activities.	2.53**	2.21**	2.40
I talk with other parents in the school about the school success of my child.	2.18	2.19	2.18
How often do you meet with other parents from the school?	1.94	1.88	1.92
How often do you talk with other parents about the school and the activities there?	2.25	2.13	2.20
How often are you engaged in school activities?	2.36	2.34	2.35
Intergenerational closure	*α*	*β*	*total*
I know the friends of my child.	3.57	3.51	3.55
How often do you have friends of your child/children over for visit in your house?	3.33	3.23	3.29

Second, two items from the subscale prepared to measure parents' integration within the school context also revealed significant differences. Particularly parents from the school placed in the former working class neighborhood agreed more often with the statement *"parents in this school know each other."* and *"I talk with other parents from the school about the school activities"* than parents from the school placed in the city-center (p < .01 (0,003)).

2.3 Individual characteristics:

Single Parenting: ANOVAs were calculated in order to analyse the interrelation between parents' characteristics and their mean agreement on the items of the subscales. Mean differences were calculated for single and two parent families, immigrant and native parents, and between parents with years of schooling below and above sample average. The results indicate that the responses to the subscales "neighborhood integration" as well as "neighborly support" differ significantly only with respect to family composition. In particular, single parenting correlated negatively with neighborly support F (.870), p < .01 and integration F (.681), p=.01 in both neighborhoods. In order to get a stronger result, a multivariate model using the parents' individual characteristics were calculated with the program STATA. The results revealed that single parenting is the only individual parent characteristic that predicts "neighborhood embeddedness". Since this subscale included items which measured the frequencies of real supportive neighborly exchange, these results indicate a higher risk of social isolation for single parents in both neighborhoods.

Ethnic Diversity: Differences between immigrant and native families have only been found in the entire sample on one subscale, where immigrant parents were significantly more integrated in the neighborhood (p < .01), than were native families. In addition, comparing the subsamples of immigrants and native parents in each neighborhood separately, immigrant parents from the traditional working class neighborhood have been found to have more neighborly support (mean: 2.3/ 2.6) and were more socially integrated (mean: 2.7/ 3.1) than native parents (both p <.01) respectively. Since the majority of this subsample was of Turkish origin, the results suggest high social cohesion and mutual support within the ethnic community in the former working class neighborhood. Whereas in the inner city neighborhood, which has a more heterogeneous ethnic structure and higher rates of fluctuation, immigrant parents' mean responses to these subcategories did not differ at all from the responses of native parents.

3 Conclusions

While it is true that the process of increasing social disparity and unequal local opportunities for children become more visible in urban areas, very little is still known about parenting in these inner city neighborhoods in Germany, especially with respect to the social integration of families or the generalized trust that families set in local people and families.

In the study summarized here, the sample included parents of children attending the seventh and eighth grade of two secondary schools. Both schools were located in neighborhoods with a disproportionally high rate of unemployment, high rates of youth and children dependent on the social welfare system, and high rates of immigrant population, compared to the state and city average. One of the schools was located in the town centre and the other in a traditional working class neighborhood out of the town. Both schools were the only secondary schools in the neighborhood. The results of the study confirm that residential stability is of significant importance for parents' neighborhood integration in ethnic diverse and low SES neighborhoods. As had been expected, parents who resided in the former working class neighborhood knew more people in the neighborhood than parents in the city centre, which has been characterized as residentially instable. For immigrant families these differences were even more visible, suggesting that residential stability and local integration is an important resource for immigrant families. Research with Turkish immigrants in different European countries reveals that integration and identification with the local neighborhood is particularly of importance for this group of immigrants (Crul et al. 2013). Particularly for parents of adolescents, the local ethnic community can help in preventing negative youth behaviour and supporting parental supervision. However, at the same time, those ethnically social coherent local communities can foster conformity in its members and influence parental attitudes and practices (Portes 1995, 1998; Harwood et al. 2006, Çıtlak/Schwegmann 2015).

With respect to school engagement and social integration within the school context, the correlation between the subscales of the PNTQ suggests different patterns of parents' integration in both neighborhoods. Parents' integration to the school context did not correlate with their level of neighborhood integration in the β neighborhood, which might indicate that the school community functions as an alternative to local social contacts for parents in the city centre. In contrast, parents resided in the former working class neighborhood might benefit from the intersection between the neighborhood and the school context. The positive correlation between the school involvement subscale and the other three neighborhood subscales in this neighborhood suggests that those parents, who know and trust others in the neighborhood and have children over to their house frequently, are more engaged in school related activities. However, it is evident that educational settings have a high potential to reach families and engage in the everyday life of adolescents, thus leading to higher educational success and emotional stability. In addition, as research from middle class neighborhoods proves, parents' school engagement influences parental civil engagement positively. Thus, schools work as mediators to bring parents with similar interests together in order to provide a wider selection of programs and so a more stimulating environment for children and youth in the neighborhood (Colemann 1988, Nieuwenhuis 2014: 43). The comparison here underlines the importance of parents' integration in school context especially in low SES neighborhoods with higher population mobility and high ethnic diversity. However, since parents' school engagement is related to the extent to which schools implement services for parents and reach their interests, it is important that particularly secondary schools in unstable inner city neighborhoods make efforts to include parents in school related activities.

Another subgroup of parents which needs particular attention is single parents. In both neighborhoods, single mothers had the least social contacts within the neighborhood, had fewer friends around, and knew less families living nearby than two parent families. In addition, they also received less neighborly support. Since both subscales (social capital and neighborly support) correlated positively on a high level with each other, this significant difference might be an indicator of shared traditional values which the majority of neighbors in the former working class neighborhood hold and which socially excludes single mothers. Nevertheless, it is also possible that these mothers practice the strategy of prevention, by avoiding social interaction with families in the neighborhood (Eccles et al. 1992; Ardelt/Eccles 2001). However, both possible interpretations indicate a lack of integration and signal a need for policy interventions. Programs which bring single mothers with older children living nearby together would help to reduce this stage of disintegration.

Finally, this research study has many limitations mostly concerning the representativeness of the sample. First, the respondents were parents of two secondary schools that are geographically placed within the selected neighborhoods but a part of the parents in the former working class neighborhood were living in the neighboring city of Oberhausen. Thus, they were not within the close neighborhood of the school. Second, the sample included only parents of 13 and 14-year-olds pupils in these two schools but excluded those parents in the neighborhood, with same age children attending other forms of secondary schools (Hauptschule, Gymnasium). Third, due to a restricted response rate it is possible that parents with far less engagement in the school context, as well as those who lack the required language abilities to fill out the questionnaire were excluding from the sample. Therefore, the study might underestimate the perceptions of immigrant parents as well as overestimate the perceptions of those parents (immigrants and natives) who are well integrated in the school and neighborhood environment.

References

Ardelt, M. & Eccles, J. (2001) `Effects of Mothers' Parental Efficacy Beliefs and Promotive Parenting Strategies on Inner-City Youth´, Journal of Family Issues, 22(8), pp. 944-972.
Bogumil, J., Heinze, R., Lehner, F. & Strohmeier, K.P. (2012) `Viel erreicht – wenig gewonnen. Ein realistischer Blick auf das Ruhrgebiet´ [Achived a lot but won less. A realistic view on the Ruhr Area], Essen: Klartext Verlag.
Bronfenbrenner, U. (1979) `The ecology of human development: Experiment by nature and design´, Cambridge: Harvard University Press.
Brooks-Gunn, J., Duncan, G. J. & Aber, J.L. (1997) `Neighborhood Poverty – Policy implications in studying neighborhoods´. Vol II, New York: Russell Sage Foundation.
Çıtlak, B. & Schwegmann, A. (2015) `Soziale Einbettung von zugewanderten Familien im Nachbarschafts- und Schulkontext´ [Social embeddedness of immigrant families in neighborhood and school context], in El-Mafaalani, A., Kurtenbach, S., Strohmeier, K.P. (eds.): „Auf die Adresse kommt es an" Segregierte Stadtteile als Problem und Möglichkeitsräume, Weinheim: Beltz Juventa.
Coleman, J.S. (1988) `Social Capital in the Creation of Human Capital´, American Journal of Sociology, 94, Supplements, pp. 95-120.
Crul, M., Schneider, J. & Lelie, F. (2013) `Super Diversity – A new perspective on Integration´, Amsterdam: University Press.
Darling, N. & L. Steinberg (1997) `Community Influences on Adolescent Achievement and Deviance´, in: Brooks-Gunn, J., Duncan, G.J. and J.L. Aber (ed.) Neighborhood Poverty: Policy Implications in Studying Neighborhoods. Vol. II, NewYork: Russell Sage Foundation, pp. 120-131.
Eccles, J. S. et al. (1992) `How Parents Respond to Risk and Opportunity in Moderate and High Risk Neighborhoods´. Paper presented at the Biennial Meeting of the Society for Research on Adolescence. Washington D.C.: March 1992.
Elliott, D.S. et al. (1996) `The Effects of Neighborhood Disadvantage on Adolescent Development´, Journal of Research in Crime and Delinquency, 33 (4), pp. 389-426.
Familienbericht der Stadt Mülheim an der Ruhr (2007) Faktor Familie (ed.), Bochum.
Furstenberg, F. F. Jr et al. (1999) `Managing to make it: Urban families and adolescent success´. Chicago: University of Chicago press.
Harwood, R.L., Yalcinkaya, A., Çıtlak, B. & Leyendecker, B. (2006) `Exploring the Concept of Respect among Turkish and Puerto Rican Migrant Mothers´, in: Schwalb, D. W. and Schwalb, B. J. (ed.) New Directions in Child and Adolescent Development, 114, San Francisco: Jossey-Bass, pp. 9-24.

Jencks, C., & Mayer, S. (1990) `The social consequences of growing up in a poor neighborhood´, in: L. E. Lynn & M. F. H. McGeary (ed.), Inner-city poverty in the United States, Washington DC: National Academy Press, pp. 111-186.

Leventhal, T. & Brooks-Gunn, J. (2000) `The Neighborhoods They Live in: The Effects of Neighborhood Residence on Child and Adolescent Outcomes´, Psychological Bulletin, 126 (2), pp. 309–337.

Nieuwenhuis, J.G. (2014) `Neighborhood effects on youth´s achievements: the moderating role of personality´. Utrecht: University of Utrecht.

Oberwittler, D. (2007) `The effects of ethnic and social segregation on children and adolescents: Recent Research and Results from a German Multilevel Study´, in: Arbeitsstelle Interkulturelle Konflikte und gesellschaftliche Integration (AKI), Wissenschaftszentrum Berlin für Sozialforschung (ed.), Discussion Paper Nr. SPIV 2007-603, Berlin.

Portes, A. (1995) `Children of immigrants: Segmented assimilation and its determinants´, in: Portes, A. (ed.) The economic sociology of immigration: Essays on networks, ethnicity, and entrepreneurship, New York: Russell Sage Foundation, pp. 248-80.

Portes, A. (1998) `Social Capital: Its Origins and Applications in Modern Sociology´, Annual Review of Sociology, 24, pp. 1-24.

Portes, A. & Vickstrom, E. (2011) `Diversity, Social Capital, and Cohesion´, Annual Review of Sociology, 37, pp. 461-479.

Putnam, R. D. (2007) `E Pluribus Unum: Diversity and Community in the Twenty-First-Century´, In: Scandinavian Political Studies, 30(2), pp. 137-174.

Sampson, R. J. & Morenoff, J. D. (1997) `Ecological Perspectives on the Neighborhood Context of Urban Poverty: Past and Present´, in: Brooks-Gunn, J., Duncan, G. J., Aber, J.L. (eds.) Neighborhood Poverty – Policy implications in studying neighborhoods, Vol II, New York: Russell Sage Foundation.

Sampson, R. J., Morenoff, J. D. & Earls, F. (1999) `Beyond Social Capital: Spatial Dynamics of Collective Efficacy for Children´. American Sociological Review, 64, pp. 633-660.

Shevky, E. & Bell, W. (1955) `Social area analysis; theory, illustrative application and computational procedures´. Stanford University Press.

Schönwälder, K. & Söhn, J. (2009) `Immigration Settlement Structures in Germany: General Patterns and Urban Levels of Concentration of Major Groups´, Urban Studies No. 46 (7), pp. 1439-1460.

Strohmeier, K.P. (2002) `Bevölkerungsentwicklung und Sozialstruktur im Ruhrgebiet´ [The development and social structure of the population in the Ruhr Area], Projekt Ruhr (ed.), Essen.

Strohmeier, K.P. (2010) `Soziale Segregation – Herausforderung der Städte im 21. Jahrhundert´ [social segregation – a challenge for cities in the 21. Century], in: Publikation der Abteilung Wirtschafts- und Sozialpolitik der Friedrich-Ebert-Stiftung (ed.), WISO-Diskurs: Das Programm Soziale Stadt, Bonn.

Weller, S. & Bruegel, I. (2009) `Children´s ´Place´ in the Development of Neighborhood Social Capital´, Urban Studies No. 46(3), pp. 629-643.

Comparing seemingly different living environments

Focusing on children's perspectives

Maren Hilke

1 Introduction

The living environments of children differ in many respects and there is not only *one* childhood. Numerous studies reveal that childhoods vary in material resources, barriers to education, leisure behavior, activities, and health (for example, KiGGS-Study, PISA, IGLU, World-Vision-Studies). The living conditions of children turn out to be different in relation to social class, gender, ethnicity, and family form (Betz 2008). Childhood is influenced particularly by the affiliation belonging to social class and milieu.

The World Vision child study (Andresen/Hurrelmann 2010b) proves that children receive inequalities according to the socioeconomic status of their parents. Depending on their social class, children have a different leeway. Poverty and missing material resources of the family lead to low participation possibilities. In contrast children of a higher social class are able to embrace better possibilities from the beginning (ibid.).

Child poverty appears in the form of educational and material poverty, poorer health, and more limited social participation (Strohmeier 2008: 495). This has a strong influence on the living conditions and development of children and can be seen as an expression of inequality in childhood. The German long-term study of the Arbeiterwohlfahrt and the Institute for Social Work (AWO-ISS-Study) investigated the situation, life course and opportunities of children from 1997 until 2004. It revealed that poor children are rated significantly worse in various dimensions than other children. This is particularly evident in the material aspects of life but also the differences in cultural and social activities are considerable between the groups (Hock et al. 2014). Child poverty appears in form of educational and material poverty, poorer health and more limited social participation (Strohmeier 2008: 495). This has a strong influence on the living conditions and development of children and can be seen as an expression of inequality in childhood.

In this article, the disparity of childhood is extended by the dimension of the residential area. In addition, the relationship of urban space to the disparity of childhood is explored. It is assumed that the social environment influences the development of children whereby socialization in relation to social class is extended through a social ecological viewpoint. This article is based on a qualitative study that compared childhoods in poorer parts of cities in different social contexts. It sought to determine whether similarities exist in the experiences of children in poorer parts of the city, even though their physical space is different and conditions of their societal framework generally differ.

Numerous studies show that childhoods are different. While many of these studies focus on issues such as how children grow up, how they form their living environment, and which resources are at their disposal, they do not contain any information about how children experience and perceive their childhood itself. So far, there is no research available that concentrates on the views of the children (Bock 2010). Therefore, the purpose of this article is to reveal how children – as experts of their own living environment – may be actively involved in the process of research to capture and evaluate the environment from their point of view. Therefore, the focus of this study is not to include the children merely as objects but rather as subjects. By including the subjective views of children, the comparability of different childhoods is possible.

In the first part of the article spatial reference is revealed to derive the imprinting of social environment in dissimilar childhoods. By using spatial theories and knowledge of urban sociology, it is pointed out that poor districts, in relation to the entire town respectively, are designed comparably = by social environments. To highlight the significance of the district for children, social-ecological approaches that regard the child's environment as a context-condition are described. The main aim of the research was to explore childhood from the perspective of children. This article shows selected results.

The change of perspective from research *about* children to research *with* children within childhood research is explained. To meet the requirements of children, the methodology this survey used was a combination of photo interviews and group discussions. Photographs of the children taken prior to the interviews extended the group discussions. The pictures were used as a basis for conversation. A summary of the results and conclusions for a comparison of different childhoods complete the article.

2 Unequal childhood against the background of social and physical spaces

Manifestations of child poverty are always found in the same parts of a city due to polarization of living forms and situations. Child poverty can mostly be found in the segregated poor parts of cities (Strohmeier 2010). Particularly, segregated poverty milieus have extensive consequences for the residents (e.g. Strohmeier 2008; Farwick 2001) and childhoods differ according to the part of the city the children grow up in.

Growing up in different social areas of the city opens up different chances for children and teenagers whose everyday lives take place in specific spaces, which in turn influences their childhood. The neighborhood with social infrastructure, institutions of education, and cultural offerings influences life prospects for children and youths (Mack/ Bruhns 2001: 9). It must be assumed that social spaces influence the development of children whereby socialization specific to social class is extended by a social ecological viewpoint. Society, and correspondingly childhood, takes place in spaces and are characterized by these.

Childhoods differ according to the part of the city children grow up in, precisely because the structures of a society's social inequality are reproduced by social segregation within the social spatial structures. Social inequalities reproduce themselves spatially. The place agents occupy in the physical space is, according to Bourdieu (1991), an indicator for the position in the social space. "Agent and groups of agents are thus defined by their relative position within that space" (Bourdieu 1985: 732). Bourdieu contrasts physical and social spaces which are linked, and notes the physical space contains the geographical space and the social space consists of sub-spaces, which he also calls fields. "Social space is an invisible set of relationship which tends to retranslate itself, in a more or less direct manner, into physical space in the form of a definite distributional arrangement of agents and properties" (Bourdieu 1996: 12).

The physical space as an acquired physical space is always a constructed space (Bourdieu 1991: 28), which is characterized and created by the agents. "The position of a given agent within the social space can thus be defined by the position he occupies in different fields, that is, in the distribution of powers that are active within each of them. These are principally economic capital, cultural capital and social capital" (Bourdieu 1985: 724). The space fulfills the function to make a differentiation and distribution (Schroer 2006: 109). The occupied position in physical space is thus an indicator for the position in social space, whereby the structures of social space are inscribed into physical space (Bourdieu 1997: 160).

Bourdieu assumed that, depending on the volume of the capital, agents have different preferences that influence their choice of living quarters. The individual volume of capital determines the possibility to acquire a space. Social structures are shown in physical space, whereby it is possible to draw conclusions about, for example, the position of an agent in social space due to his location (Schroer 2006: 111). Referring to Hamm (1974) and Schroer (2006), this unilateral connection is extended to the effect that space also influences the individual. The relation between social and physical space is considered mutual. On the one hand, the space shape has an effect on the social behavior. On the other hand, the social behavior has an effect on the spatial creation (Hamm 1974: 14). Schroer explains that Bourdieu assumed a unilateral relationship in which social space becomes apparent in physical space.

Instead, it is also possible that the physical space has an effect on the social space and vice versa. This reveals, for example, the fact that the environment that individuals grow up in is internalized and condensed to a habitus. Thus, the interaction of space structure and the actions of individuals are mutually influencing. The space is constructed by the actions of humans and the construction of the world happens by persons themselves. Therefore, built structures are structured not only socially, but also have an effect on the individual structure of persons. The relation of behavior-forming spatial circumstances, on the one hand, and space-forming social processes, on the other hand, must be understood as an interdependent relation between humans and the environment (Tippelt et al. 1986: 18).

The social inequality of cities is reflected in a dissimilar distribution of the population within districts with different living conditions, which simultaneously determines unequal childhoods. An increasing concentration of poverty in a few parts of the big cities is observable because different social classes and groups of urban populations dispense unequally into the neighborhoods of a city (Häußermann 2010: 1). Explicit forms of social-spatial differentiation (meaning community oriented) as well as separation can be recognized in cities, in particular when members of the upper and lower social classes are separated strongly from each other (Farwick 2001: 27).

Where disadvantaged demographic groups are concentrated, it is possible to make a comparison of areas that are disadvantaged materially, as well as by infrastructure. The origin of forms of segregation in these areas can differ on the basis of historical developments. Therefore, this comparison concerns constructed social spaces, which illustrate social inequality spatially in relation to the whole of the respective city. Particularly disadvantaged neighborhoods have extensive effects on the inhabitants and accordingly on the children who grow up there.

3 Socialization in the context of space

The relevance of the area and neighborhood can be indicated by referencing social-ecological socialization theories, in particular on the basis of the social-ecological socialization theory from Bronfenbrenner (1976, 1981). It can be derived theoretically that not only does the family have an influence, but also the family surrounding the "Mesosystem", the immediate environment, plays a role for the children's development. This system consists of different microsystems, such as the neighborhood or the peer group, that affect the adolescents' socialization. In this process the environment and therefore the neighborhood are important aspects. Children want to explore their environment, developing a personal relation to the spatial-concrete and social environment (Muri/ Friedrich 2009: 78).

The spatial environment is both an objective structure stamped by adults and a subjective category, which can be conquered and acquired (ibid.). The quarter has a meaning for individuals because there are specific spatial and socio-cultural facts that influence the social status and behaviors. While these facts are not, in principle, individual characteristics, they concern many individuals in terms of the characteristics of the social-ecological environment in the same way (Strohmeier/ Herlth 1981: 111).

Particularly, if social contacts are limited to the neighborhood, it has a high influence on development. Locality is especially relevant in lower social classes (Häußermann/ Siebel 2004: 167; Friedrichs/Blasius 2000: 194). With regard to childhoods in disadvantaged neighborhoods, this influence has the possible effect of segregation. Segregation can to additionally disadvantaging effects on the inhabitants with social, material, and symbolic dimensions (Häußermann/Siebel 2004). This paper focuses on the results of a study concentrating on children's perceptions of the effects of their environment.

4 Research with children – methodological approaches to compare different childhoods

The early studies of Martha Muchow (1935) focused on the living environments of children, primarily focusing on the subjective cognitions that children develop in their environment. The study came to the realization that the way individuals perceive their world influences their behavior (Tippelt et al. 1986: 22). Referring to this, the interest of this research was the children's assessment of their own environment, centering on the perspectives of children who grow up in the poor parts of the city. How do children experience grow up in a poor part of the city? How do they assess and appreciate their living quarter? What does it mean from his/her point of view to grow up in the poor part of the? Do they experience the inequality and do they perceive the effects of segregation and poverty?

Until the middle of the 1990s, there were only a few studies that examined childhood from the perspective of children; childhood was researched from adults' point of view (Bock 2010: 24). The scientific opinion was that children were not competent enough to give information about their life world (Andresen/ Hurrelmann 2010a: 70). This perspective has changed in new childhood research, characterized by the fact that it researches not only *about* children but *with* children. Children are seen as experts on their own life world in the context of the research process because they can give the best information about themselves and the areas of their life.

The basic assumption is that research questions referring to childhoods can only be answered if you listen, talk to, and interact with children (Heinzel 2000a: 17). Children are involved in the research process actively and questioned about their perspective. Research about children and childhood is therefore research with children. This came along with the knowledge that the world of adults is completely different from the world of children (Fuhs 2000). Childhood is a form of reality, which may be hardly understandable for adults, and in which they project a variety of their own wishes, fears, and images (Fuhs 2000: 88).

The intention of ecologically oriented socialization research is to try to comprehend the environment as perceived by the people who are involved. The main interest is the subjective perspectives of the individuals and not the objective conditions of the environment (Tippelt et al. 1986: 23). Therefore, children were centered in this study as respondents and were interviewed as subjects and not only as objects. A comparison of childhoods in different contexts is possible by comparing the subjective perspective, although the physical space and the objective reality are different.

The prospects of children and adults are different and children's thought and behavior are not accessible for adults from the beginning. If the aim of childhood research is the comparison of subjective living environments from a child's point of view, the central basic ideas of qualitative research (e.g. openness and strangeness) are well suited and the decision for qualitative research methods seems reasonable (Heinzel 2010). This makes it possible to grasp children's attitudes and perspectives while also discovering new facts. Furthermore, complete information about the activities of the children can be expected.

5 Focusing on children's perspectives: participatory photo interview and group discussion

A methodological challenge of researching with children is recording children's perceptions. In childhood research, classic social research methods are partly modified to integrate children better in the research situation and to correspond to their development status (Heinzel 2000a: 21). A general methodical problem of childhood research is the "power of the education situation in child life" (ibid.: 25).

The everyday lives of children are laced with hierarchical relational conditions and situations, which are formed by educational intentions. It is not possible to prevent this power structure in the research process completely and it must be taken into account. It must be clear for the children that they are addressed as experts so they do not feel forced to answer correctly always (Andresen/ Hurrelmann 2010a: 71). Moreover, typical forms of child expressions and restricted ability to verbalize have to be paid attention to in younger children.

Allowing for the special demands of children as a target group of the research, it one cannot revert to a classic social research method for data collection. The chosen methodological approach depends on the communication skills of the children, focused questions, and the main aim of the research. In a study where the central question is orientated towards the subjective perspectives of children on their environment, the answer may only be associated by involving the children themselves. The method choice and modification must take into account and do justice to the demands of children. To satisfy the special demands of children, a combination of photo interviews and group discussion procedures are offered.

The interviewed children take photographs that are used as a conversation basis in the group discussions. Referring to Wuggenig, the technique of the "Fotobefragung" can be combined with that of the "photo interview" of Collier. In the method of photo interview developed by Collier "a professional photographer took pictures of local living situations, and interviewees used photos to introduce and explain their lives" (Kolb 2008). The aim is to stimulate respondent communication and memory in the interview situation because on the basis of the photos they can give additional detailed information about the objects or the scene of the photographs (Collier 1957 after Wuggenig 1991: 112). For Collier, because the photos are taken in their own social environment, they active memory, place children in the role of expert, and can be taken advantage of to promote motivation (ibid.)

Wuggenig (1991) used the method of Collier with his "Fotobefragung" and modified it to incorporate the photographs. He used them in a participatory way. Compared to Collier, in this method the interviewees take the photos themselves, so that the respondents are both photographer and interviewee. The respondents get a camera and are asked to take photos. They, not the researcher, chose what to photograph and from this choice, it is possible to deduce the respondent's perspectives of their everyday life. An interview with the respondents in which the photographs are the basis of conversation follows. During the interview open questions concerning the choice of photographed objects were asked (Wuggenig 1991: 116).

To analyze collective, group-specific positions and experiences of children and dependence on their environment, children were interviewed in small groups and not on their own. Therefore, the method was changed referring to the interview situation. Group discussions are especially well-suited to reconstruct collective positions and orientations of peer groups (Bohnsack 1989). Milieu specific experiences cannot be surveyed in the same way on the basis of single interviews (Bohnsack 2001). Furthermore, the group discussion method is well-suited for research with children to counteract the hierarchical intergenerational relationship of the majority relationship between children and adults (Heinzel 2000b: 117). In a second meeting, a group discussion is conducted subsequent to the photo interview. The researcher presents the self-taken photographs to the children and uses them as a foundation for discussion. On the one hand, the interviewees were asked to comment on every photo and, on the other hand, they were asked to answer further questions in the group discussion. Hereto the method of an open guideline-based interview is quite suitable.

The photos, taken by the children themselves, made it possible to move them into the role of expert. They were addressed as experts of their own life world, through which the asymmetrical relationship between interviewer and respondent could be relativized. Furthermore, the photos as a conversation basis offered the advantage that children were stimulated to describe their environment in greater detail. They encouraged children during the interview and met the requirements for an interview with children. The difficulties of international culturally comparative childhood research could be avoided because it was a language-independent method.

6 Analyzing of Photo Interview Material

Qualitative content analysis is suited for analysis of data. The data bases of research are interview notes taken from memory and photos taken by the children. The photos are only analyzed only in combination with the group discussions and not only independently with image recognition methods.

Experiences from different research projects have shown that photographs are hardly valid without the comments of the children (e.g. Deinet/Krisch 2009; Hilke

2013). This corresponds to the described theoretical assumption that perspectives of children are not accessible from the beginning and views of children and adults may differ. In the analysis of photos, without the statements of the children, the problem could be transferring images from the adult's world and perspective. Focusing on children's perspectives and perceptions in this research, the photos are analyzed only in combination with the comments of the interviewed person. Therefore, the pictures are more important for the data collection than for the analysis.

7 Similarities of living environments: An example

The study was realized in a disadvantaged and segregated district of Oberhausen, Germany, and in a structurally similar residential quarter of Windhoek, Namibia. For the interview, groups of children who stayed together in the outer area of the district were approached. It was considered that there were at least two people between 9 and 13 years old, but the age structure and sex did not need to be homogeneous within the group.

The central commonality of the groups was that they are a real group, meaning they know each other and spend free time together. This should contribute to the fact that the children feel comfortable in a familiar atmosphere. Altogether, 21 children in five groups have taken part in the study. As described above, a combination of participatory photo interviews and a group discussion based on the self-taken photographs were chosen as a method. After explaining the research and gaining the agreement of the children to take part in the research, each group got a single-use camera. Then they were given a paper with questions and about an hour for taking pictures of the appropriate places.

The children should take photographs of places in their neighborhood which they especially like places they do not like, those they are afraid of, and those where they meet with their friends. The main aim was to get a subjective view for reconstructing collective views of children. After finishing this exercise, they brought back the single-use cameras and thus the first part of the photo interview was completed. In a second meeting, the group discussion was held. The self-made photographs were shown to the children and they were used as a basis for the discussion. In the group discussion, the children were asked to explain the photographs to the researcher. Here, an open guideline-based interview was used. To obtain a natural conversational setting, tape recorders were relinquished and interview notes were taken from memory subsequently. As described above, a qualitative content analysis was applied.

The results of the study show that socially constructed environments have similar effects on the living environment of children. Irrespective of different framework conditions by society, poor parts of the cities are valued in a way that is subjectively similar. Since the individuals have the same position in society as in the areas of research, it is apparent that small-scale contextual effects characterize the children and influence their lifeworld. The ambivalent reference to the socially segregated poor part of the cities was proven to be a central similarity of the children's assessment. The children evaluate their district based on the same categories that clarify both a positive and negative spatial reference, although the structural environment and infrastructure are not comparable. A central aspect of the negative assessment of their neighborhood is its material external condition in the form of dirt and dilapidation.

Figure 1 Trash in the public area Havana & Public toilets Havana

Figure 2 Graffiti on the walls Bebelstraße II

Furthermore, the children experience their quarter as a place lacking safety and calm. The identification shows that children feel noticeable fear in certain areas of their quarter. All children can identify these different areas of fear because it is through them they have learned restrictions in their behavior. The connection of areas of fear with other residential groups has to be named as a further similarity.

Figure 3 Staircases to the underground garage Bebelstraße & Shebeen Havana I

The children experience inequality in the form of small scope and lacking opportunities for participation depending on their living environment. All children describe a neighborhood-related leisure as having a low range of activities and neighborhood-bounded friendship relations. As children, they do not have modernized, individualized, and educated lives (e.g. Zeiher/ Zeiher 1994; Du Bois-Reymond et al. 1994) and are disadvantaged also by the combination of a lack of offers and possibilities for mobility in the quarter. A further similarity is the future described by the children. The central element within their idea of the future is leaving the current place of residence. However, the children have no concrete ideas regarding their future place of residence or a strategy for how to leave their quarter. Therefore, these ideas about the future are primarily an expression of escape from the present because they experience a lack of opportunities. Furthermore, the analysis reveals that children experience the effect of segregation in terms of symbolic discrimination. They are conscious of the bad image of their quarter since they are aware of the neglect of the neighborhood and dissociate themselves from other residents in the district.

Altogether, the dimensions of negative assessment clarify the *dissociation* of the children to their own district. Besides the dissociation, the district is their home, as characterized by social relations, attachment, and familiarity that reveal also *identification* with their quarter. A common dimension of positive assessment within the survey groups is connected to their peer group. The children assess places in their quarter positively when they are linked to the peer group in which they spend time together.

Figure 4   Table tennis table Bebelstraße & sports field Havana I

Moreover, identification is expressed by social relations, which bind together the children in their quarter. This cohesion in the peer group seems to have only a temporary character since the peer group disappears in the future ideas of the children. The common experience of children who grow up in a poor part of the city is an *ambivalent relation* to the district. Furthermore, social inequalities pervade the scope of design, for example in the form of recreational activities, and influence opportunities to participate.

Besides the described similarities, there are only two assessment dimensions that cannot be explained by conditions of socially constructed environments. For children in Namibia, for example, plants as food were very important. The assumption is obvious that these-find their grounds in conditions of physical space and cultural context.

Figure 5   Garden Havana I

8 Discussion of approach – Perspective of comparative research with children

The prospects of children and adults are considerably different and the way children think is not always accessible to adults. Hence, it made sense to integrate children as experts of their own life world into the research process and emphasize their point of view. The approach of focusing on the subjective assessment, rather than comparing the objective conditions of the childhood made it possible to analyze similarities and differences in the life worlds of children in apparently different worlds.

The method of the photo interview in combination with group discussion was very suitable to integrate children into the research process. The photos taken by the children put them into the role of experts and motivated them to participate in an interview. Since they were addressed as experts of their living environment, the asymmetrical relationship between interviewer and respondent could be relativized. Furthermore, the pictures, used as the basis of discussion, support that children are motivated to describe their environment in greater detail and give additional information about the portrayed objects.

Photos helped the children to describe something in detail and were suitable for interviewing children. The choice of a group discussion also proved useful since the numerical dominance of the children was contrary to the hierarchical relationship. Furthermore, a familiar setting was created by the joint interview of the peer group. Thus, collective group-specific patterns within the thinking and experiences of children were worked out in reference to their environment. With regard to comparative childhood research, advantages arise by treating children as subjects and not only objects of research. The central focus is on children's perspectives of their own living environment, making the comparison of initially incomparable childhoods possible. Not only the external living environments are contrasted, but the positions and perceptions of children are at the center in the comparative analysis. Life worlds are described from the perspective of children and not from the perspective of researchers for whom the living environments are considerably different. This makes it possible to contrast living environments, since the same effects on the individuals living there exist.

The analysis resulted from the respective living environment of the children and not from the researcher's perceptions. Because the method does not include a questionnaire, including apparently objective considerations of conditions can be avoided and the problem of transferring the researcher's perceptions and expectations into the research process ban also be avoided.

The research method presented in this article opens further perspectives concerning international, culturally comparative childhood research. On the one hand, it is a language independent method, meaning it is possible to avoid the difficulties of translating a questionnaire, especially when there are specifics in a culture. On the other hand, the method prevents ignoring culture-specific characteristics because of openness in the research process and the inclusion of children's perspectives.

References

Andresen, S., Hurrelmann, K. (2010a). Kindheit [Childhood]. Weinheim und Basel: Beltz Verlag

Andresen, S. Hurrelmann, K. (2010b). Kinder in Deutschland 2010. 2.World Vision Kinderstudie [Children in Germany 2010. 2. World Vision children research]

Betz, T. (2008). Ungleiche Kindheiten. Theoretische und empirische Analysen zur Sozialberichterstattung über Kinder [Unequal childhoods].Weinheim und München: Juventa Verlag.

Bock, K. (2010). Kinderalltag – Kinderwelten. Rekonstruktive Analysen von Gruppendiskussionen mit Kindern [Every day life from children. Analyzing of group discussions with children]. Opladen & Fermington Hills: Verlag Barbara Budrich

Bohnsack, R. (1989). Generation, Milieu, Geschlecht. Ergebnisse aus Gruppendiskussionen mit Jugendlichen [Generation, milieu, gender. Results from group discussions with teenager]. Opladen: Leske + Budrich

Bohnsack, R. (2001). Die dokumentarische Methode und ihre Forschungspraxis. Grundlagen qualitativer Sozialforschung. [The documentary method and their research practice. Basics of qualitative social research] Opladen: Leske + Budrich

Bourdieu, P. (1985). „The social space and the genesis of groups" in: Theory and Society, November 1985, 14, (6), pp. 723-744.

Bourdieu, P. (1991). Physischer, sozialer und angeeigneter physischer Raum. [Physical, social and possessed physical space] In: Wentz, Martin (Hrsg.): Stadt-Räume. Frankfurt a.M.: Campus-Verlag. pp 25-34

Bourdieu, P. (1996). Physical Space, Social Space and Habitus. Institutt for sosiologi og samfunnsgeografi, Universitetet i Oslo.

Bourdieu, P. (1997). Ortseffekte [Effects of places]. In: ders. Et al.: Das Elend der Welt. Zeugnisse aus dem beständigen Leben. Kostanz, pp. 159-167.

Bronfenbrenner, U. (1976). Ökologische Sozialisationsforschung [Ecological socialization research]. Stuttgart: Ernst Klett Verlag

Bronfenbrenner, U. (1981) Die Ökologie der menschlichen Entwicklung [Ecology of human development]. Stuttgart: Ernst Klett Verlag

Deinet, U., Krisch, R. (2009) Stadtteil-/ Sozialraumbegehungen mit Kindern und Jugendlichen [Inspection of districts with children and youth]. In: sozialraum.de (1) Ausgabe

1/2009. URL: http://www.sozialraum.de/stadtteil-sozialraumbegehungen-mit-kindern-und-jugendlichen.php, Datum des Zugriffs: 04.09.2015

du Bois-Reymond, M., et al. (Hrsg.) (1994). Kinderleben. Modernisierung von Kindheit im interkulturellen Vergleich [Childhood. Intercultural comparison of modernisation of childhood]. Opladen: Leske + Budrich.

Farwick, A. (2001). Segregierte Armut in der Stadt. Ursachen und soziale Folgen der räumlichen Konzentration von Sozialhilfeempfängern [Segregated poverty in the city. Reasons and social consequences of urban concentration of paupers]. Opladen: Leske + Burich.

Friedrichs, J. & Blasius, J. (2000) Leben in benachteiligten Wohngebieten [Living in disadvantaged neighborhod]. Opladen: Leske + Budrich.

Fuhs, B. (2000). Qualitative Interviews mit Kindern. Überlegungen zu einer schwierigen Methode [Qualitative interviews with children. Consideration of a difficult method]. In: Heinzel, Frederike (eds.): Methoden der Kindheitsforschung. Ein Überblick über Forschungszugänge zur kindlichen Perspektiven. Weinheim und München: Juventa, pp 87-103.

Hamm, B. (1974). Grundzüge einer Siedlungssoziologie. In: Hamm, Bernd/ Atteslander, Peter (eds.): Materialien zur Siedlungssoziologie. Gütersloh: Verlag Kiepenheuer & Witsch Köln. Pp. 11-32

Häußermann, H. & Siebel, W. (2004). Stadtsoziologie. Eine Einführung. [Urban sociology. An Indroduction] Frankfurt: Campus Verlag

Häußermann, H. (2010). Armutsbekämpfung durch Stadtplanung [Control of poverty by urban planning]. In: Aus Politik und Zeitgeschichte. (52-52/2010)

Heinzel, F. (2000a). Methoden und Zugänge der Kindheitsforschung im Überblick [Overview of methods of reasearch with children]. In: Heinzel, Frederike (Hrsg.): Methoden der Kindheitsforschung. Ein Überblick über Forschungszugänge zur kindlichen Perspektiven. Weinheim und München: Juventa Verlag, pp. 21-35.

Heinzel, F. (2000b). Kinder in Gruppendiskussionen und Kreisgesprächen [Children in group discussions]. In: Heinzel, Frederike (Hrsg.): Methoden der Kindheitsforschung. Ein Überblick über Forschungszugänge zur kindlichen Perspektiven. Weinheim und München: Juventa Verlag, pp. 117-130.

Heinzel, F. (2010). Zugänge zur kindlichen Perspektive – Methoden der Kindheitsforschung [Approach to infantile perseptions – Methods of childhood research]. In: Friebertshäuser, Barbara/ Langer, Antje/ Prengel, Annedore (Hrsg.): Handbuch Qualitativer Forschungsmethoden in der Erziehungswissenschaft. Weinheim und München: Juventa Verlag, pp. 707-721.

Hilke, M. (2013). Wie arme Kinder die Unterstadt erleben. Ungleiche Kindheiten und städtischer Raum in Oberhausen und Windhoek. [How children experience the ‚Unterstadt'? Unequal childhoods and urban areas in Oberhausen and Windhoek] ZEFIR-Forschungsbericht Band 4, Bochum, online unter: http://www.zefir.rub.de/zefirpub.html

Hock, B., Holz, G. & Kopplow, M. (2014). Kinder in Armutslagen, Grundlagen für armutssensibles Handeln in der Kindertagesbetreuung. Weiterbildungsinitiative frühpädagogische Fachkräfte. [Children in circumstances of poverty] WiFF Expertisen Band 38. München 2014

Kolb, B. (2008). Involving, Sharing, Analysing – Potential of the Participatory Photo Interview. In: Forum Qualitative social Research. 9 (3), Art. 12

Mack, W. & Bruhns, K. (2001). Einleitung. In: Mack, W./ Bruhns, K. (eds.): Aufwachsen und Lernen in der Sozialen Stadt. Kinder und Jugendliche in schwierigen Lebensräumen [Growing up and learning in the social city. Children and youth in difficult living environments]. Opladen: Leske + Budrich, pp. 9-17.

Muchow, M. & Muchow, H.M. (1935/ 1980). Der Lebensraum des Großstadtkindes. [Living environments of children living in large cities] Bensheim: Päd.-Extra Buchverlag

Muri, G. & Friedrich, S. (2009). Stadt(t)räume – Alltagsräume? Jugendkulturen zwischen geplanter und gelebter Urbanität. Wiesbaden: VS Verlag für Sozialwissenschaften.

Schroer, M. (2006). Raum, Macht und soziale Ungleichheit. Pierre Bourdieus Beitrag zu einer Soziologie des Raumes [Space, power and social inequality. Pierre Bourdieus contribution to a sociology of space]. In: Leviathan : Berliner Zeitschrift für Sozialwissenschaft, 1(34), pp. 105-123.

Strohmeier, K.P. & Herlth, A. (1981). Sozialräumliche Bedingungen familialer Sozialisation. Eine Vergleichende Untersuchung von Wohnquartieren in Bielefeld, Gelsenkirchen und Münster. [Social spacial conditions of familiar socialisation] In: Walter, Heinz (eds.): Region und Sozialisation. Beiträge zur sozialökologischen Präzisierung menschlicher Entwicklungsvoraussetzungen. Bd. II. Stuttgart- Bad Cannstatt: Frommann Verlag, pp. 95-136.

Strohmeier, K.P. (2008). Unterstadt – für wen ist Segregation gefährlich? [,Unterstadt'- For whom is segregation dangerous?] In: Groenemeyer, Axel/ Wieseler, Silvia (Hrsg.): Soziologie sozialer Probleme und sozialer Kontrolle. Realitäten, Repräsentationen und Politik. Festschrift für Günter Albrecht. Wiesbaden: VS Verlag für Sozialwissenschaft, pp. 488-501.

Strohmeier, K.P. (2010). Oberstadt und Unterstadt- Zwei Kindheiten in Zeiten des demographischen Wandels. [,Uptown' and ,Downtown' – Two childhoods in times of demographic change] In: Leshwange, Martina/ Liebig, Reinhard (eds.): Aufwachsen offensiv mitgestalten: Impulse für die Kinder und Jugendarbeit. Essen: Klartext Verlag, pp. 51-67.

Tippelt, R., Krauß, J. & Baron, S. (1986) Jugend und Umwelt. Soziale Orientierungen und soziale Basisprozesse im regionalen Vergleich. [Youth and environment. Regional comparison of social orientations] Weinheim und Basel: Beltz Verlag.

Wuggenig, U. (1991): Die Photobefragung als projektives Verfahren. [] In: Angewandte Sozialforschung: Zeitschrift für Mitteleuropa, 16 (1991). pp 109-129

Zeiher, H. & Zeiher, H. (1994) Orte und Zeiten der Kindheit. Soziales Leben im Alltag von Großstadtkindern. [Places and times of childhood. Social living in every day live of urban children] Weinheim und München: Juventa Verlag.

Growing up in a disadvantaged neighborhood

Preventing neighborhood effects and promoting positive youth development through sports using the example Plovdiv-Stolipinovo

Ina Schäfer

1 Introduction

The immigration of the Romani people is at the center of attention in the European media since Bulgaria and Romania joined the EU in 2007, strengthened since the freedom of movement for workers in 2014. Media reporting on the so-called "poverty migration" is mostly negative and includes stereotypes that impair the people's needs. The fact that Roma migrate mostly to specific neighborhoods (Castañeda 2014: 6ff.), for example, from Stolipinovo in Bulgaria to the city district of Dortmund in Germany, shows that they also live segregated in their countries of origin. Life affected by poverty and discrimination is seen as a push-factor for migration and as one of the main factors behind creating transnational networks.

Social work must pay attention to this and provide opportunities to help fulfill hopes for better living circumstances. Therefore, it needs to include the transnational background of the target group. The increasing transnationalization also has to be taken into account. This is defined as a "bordercrossing phenomena, which – local anchored in different national societies – constitutes relatively permanent and close social relationships, social networks and social rooms" (translated from: Pries 2010: 13). Social-spatial-orientation must overcome a uni-local view, which only focuses on social proximity, and instead estimate a pluri-local view that focuses on the living-environments of individuals (Pries/Kurtenbach 2016). The observation of these factors helps social work to perceive the experiences and specific needs of the target groups. Beyond the necessity to include this for a holistic view, it also helps to orientate on the options for action and create coping structures and thus is important for an improvement of opportunities and future prospects. The restrictions and opportunity structures of everyday life in the country of origin must be involved to notice and reduce disadvantage through social work. Therefore, the orientation of the living circumstances of the neighborhood must be considered because these have a high influence on the chances and behavior of the inhabitants. "Cities are 'opportunity structures' because the opportunities and restrictions that a city offers determine the behaviour of individuals – The opportunity structure has a high impact on the opportunities of the individuals" (translated from: Friedrichs 2011: 37).

Discrimination against the Roma leads to their exclusion by the majority of citizens, as well as to a spatial dislocation. Due to this exclusion there are poorer opportunities to participate in different subareas. Moreover, districts of the Romani people are embossed of lower infrastructure for the inhabitants. This is fatal because when integration fails, the social space and the work of the community play an increasingly important role (Reutlinger 2008: 215). That is why an opportunity structure that provides enough offers inside and outside of disadvantaged neighborhoods is especially important. If disadvantage exists, it is necessary for social work to provide this in order to avoid solidification of disadvantage.

In this paper, I will examine how the neighborhood and institutions influence individual outcomes, by investigating the living conditions and opportunities in disadvantaged areas using the concrete example of Stolipinovo. With this example, I will underline the necessity of opportunities and offers from social work to reduce disadvantage.

Youth are especially the focus of this research because the development of this age group is important for their further life. Also, this age is particularly marked by a higher importance of the social-spatial area. By replacing the parents, the peers play a more important role, and with this-staying in public places also becomes more important. While youth research focuses primarily on increasing pluralization of living environments, which is linked to isolation and a reduced influence of the social proximity, research with disadvantaged youth must focus on the influence of the neighborhood. In this study, the youth's subjective point of view on their environment and leisure activities is included. The framework that the neighborhood provides is considered. The situation of the young people in terms of movement and socialization is also in focus in order to examine how this is organized under certain conditions of poverty. The influence of the effects of living in a disadvantaged neighborhood is also considered. Therefore, the emphasis is on the arrangement of youth's spare time, the places where they pass this time, and what happens at these places. The main focus of the study is on locations and situations they associate with movement and sports in their everyday lives, to consider the influence they have on preventing negative neighborhood effects. Especially in movement situations, the adolescents are able to make important experiences, which have an effect on their socialization and everyday lives. Additionally, the way social work can prevent and reduce negative neighborhood effects and create new opportunities for youth through the medium of sports will be regarded. Therefore, specific offers and the methods the trainer uses are in focus.

The concrete leading research question at the foundation of the research is: What effects does youth work, through the medium of sports as an opportunity structure, have for adolescents under different conditions of socialization? And how is this arranged within the context of their everyday lives?

To answer this question, the results of a two-week long fieldwork in Stolipinovo, Plovdiv, Bulgaria will be presented. Through an empirical and theoretical examination, I will produce a more accomplished understanding of growing up in disadvantaged areas. To include the point of view of the youth, a participatory method called reflexive photography is used. Additionally, expert interviews with the trainers of two sports clubs were conducted. In the focus is the influence of the environment and how it impacts the youth. Also examined is the prevention of negative neighborhood effects through creating new opportunities and control through social institutions.

This paper is divided into a theoretical and an empirical part. Firstly, the discrimination and segregation of the Roma in Europe will be regarded, with the focus on Bulgaria. After that, neighborhood effects and their mechanisms will be represented. Then, the importance of opportunity structures for adolescents will be constituted. After that, in the empirical part, at first the research question and the methodical design are in focus. Moreover, a description of the research area, the research itself, its limitations will be given. Finally, the results will be presented and a conclusion developed.

2 Discrimination and segregation of Roma in Europe

Of 10-12 million Roma worldwide, 7,5 million live in Europe, most in Southeast Europe (Benz 2014: 58). They are a heterogeneous group with different subgroups. Besides living in different countries under different conditions and with different cultures, they do not even have the same religion. Even if they have the same language, Romanes, many different dialects exist.

One commonality in every European country is that they live mostly under poorer living conditions because of discrimination. Especially in Eastern Europe the situation of the Roma can be characterized as full of hate, exclusion, and discrimination (Matter 2015: 23). The German Association of cities describes the

Roma people as "excluded of the social participation" (2013: 23). Discrimination and less opportunities and are also a push-factor for migration.

Roma people officially make up 4.7% of the whole population in Bulgaria, although unofficially they are approximated to be 10% (Leiserowitz 2010: 260). Discrimination and disadvantages go along with bad living conditions and restricted chances to overcome poverty. Being Roma is one of the factors that leads to the highest risk of poverty in Bulgaria (Ringold et al. 2005: 14). Even though Bulgaria is the poorest country in the EU, there is a huge difference between Roma and ethnic Bulgarians. They are ten times more likely to be poor than ethnic Bulgarians (ibid.: 29). Additionally, they are not only poor but also excluded from all social areas of society based on ongoing discrimination. Antiziganism is very common and goes along with an ascription of negative characteristics. Roma are stigmatized by the discriminating label "Gypsie," which involves stereotypical thinking (End 2011: 16). These stereotypes lead to exclusion. While the concept of poverty was orientated for a long time on the income of a person, an expanded concept of poverty and exclusion pays attention to the holistic life situation. The livelihood approach describes the life situation as scope for action (Groh-Samberg 2009: 80.). The circumstances of under supply restrict different trading options, which block the individual in his free development. (ibid.: 83).

The situation of disadvantage for Roma in Bulgaria has a long historical background. During the liberation from the Ottoman rule (1878-1944) their needs were mostly neglected, their presence mostly ignored, or they were seen as unequal (Marushiakova/Popov 2013: 135). They lived mostly in separate neighborhoods called "mahallas" (ibid. 1997: 5). This was also reflected in the educational situation; even if education was free for everybody during this time, Roma were underrepresented in school and up to 90% were illiterate (ebd. 2013: 136). After that, in the time of communism (1945-1989), policies for Roma as full-fledged citizens started. In this time, most had jobs, but even if they were not excluded from all social sections, they were discriminated against, too. New schools were constructed, but they were separate Roma schools in separate Roma *mahallas* (ebd.: 136), which underlined that they were still seen as different and not included in society. Later, in the 1960s, they even transferred to special educational schools with reduced general subjects and more vocational training (ebd.: 137). Simultaneously they had to change their name to Bulgarian names under the regime of Todor Zhivkov. Instead of voluntary integration, there was a repressive assimilation through these politics (ibid.: 1997: 7).

After the revolution in 1989 and the end of communism, many Roma lost their jobs, because they were less qualified. Since then, racism has been practiced more publicly (Breadley 2001: 551). Now, most Roma are still excluded from the labor market and affected by long-term joblessness. Some of them live in rural areas and do not go to segregated schools, but many live segregated in urban areas. They are characterized as having poor infrastructure, bad health conditions, and poverty. Even though negotiations with the European Union led to the acceptance of the *Framework Program for Equal Integration of Roma into Bulgarian Society* which among other things wanted to promote school desegregation, the implementation ultimately failed (ebd.: 139). Similarly, unsuccessful was the *Decade of Roma Inclusion* (2005-2015). However, through the accession to the European Union, the topic is more in focus and since 2011 there is a more detailed plan called *National Roma Integration Strategy of the Republic of Bulgaria (2012-2020)* (ibid.: 140).

All in all, the educational situation has not become better with time and it is nearly impossible for Roma children to reach higher education. Only 35% finish primary school, 10% secondary school and only 0.5% high school (Goodwin 2009: 9). This low qualification hinders their integration in the labor market. According to these graduation percentages, the unemployment rate varies between 70-100 percent in some settlements and long-term unemployment is common (Ringold et al 2005: 39). There are also some informal forms of employments that are not measured. Also long-term unemployment is common (ibid.: 2005: 40).

Even out-of-school activities are fewer for Roma and opportunities for adolescents to create their own development spaces are limited. But mainly in adolescence it is important that youth can acquire their own spaces and have the chance to use youth-specific offerings. Segregation, which means the unequal distribution of inhabitants through the neighborhoods (Häußermann/Siebel 2004: 140), stands against these needs. Roma in Bulgaria mostly live spatially segregated in two ways, socially and racially.

Segregation is not inevitably connected to disadvantage, as you can see for example at the rich. But even if one group is not excluded through segregation, it can lead to the exclusion of other groups. So segregation is the result of social inequality and also reflects this. It is through the consequences of economic processes of marginalization that discrimination takes effect (Wilson 1989: 70). On the one hand, poverty reduces the alternatives on the housing market. On the other hand, not only financial aspects but also prejudices and exclusion are important. How segregated a group lives can be an indicator for how well an ethnic group is integrated (Friedrichs/Triemer 2008: 17). Exclusion is reproduced spatially, but is more than this. It is not only spatial, but social (Kronauer 2008). They are excluded from all social areas. Symbolic boundaries strengthen this.

Segregation reproduces inequality and solidifies the existing unequal power structure. It "undermines equality of opportunity, and it emphasizes inferiority" (O'Nions 2010: 2).

Simultaneously it intensifies disadvantage. "Differences in where people live must simply reflect differences in what they can afford" (Briggs 2007: 10). Through social and ethnical segregation opportunities are restricted. Particularly, through restriction of contacts to the neighborhood, the effects of segregation are strengthened.

3 Neighborhood effects

Segregation leads to specific neighborhood effects. A neighborhood-effect is the assumption, that the neighborhood has an influence on the behavior and actions, besides individual factors (Friedrichs/Blasius 2000: 17). The presumption of neighborhood effects is distinguished from the presumption of compositions effects, which assumes, that individual characteristics are enough to explain the behavior of the inhabitants (Oberwittler 2004: 137). This enables a holistic view.

Negative contextual effects can influence the individual actions and norms and hinder them to overcome poverty and solidify social marginalization. Segregation strengthens disadvantage and poverty, if fewer opportunities for overcoming it are available.

If social contacts are limited to the neighborhood, this has a particularly high influence. Oberwittler (2004) shows that neighborhood effects on adolescents are important and get transmitted through the peer-group, if their friends are from the same neighborhood. If schools are also segregated, it affects the spatial orientation on peers. When contacts are limited to the disadvantaged residential area, this lead to more disadvantage because not enough opportunities are available. Then the living area could become a negative learning space for children and youth.

Research on the effects of disadvantaged neighborhoods is in focus since the early 1920s. Shaw and McKay explained with their theory of desintegration about higher rates in delinquency when effective social control in the neighborhood was missing and the transfer of these norms from one generation to the next (Oberwittler 2004: 136). Firstly, Wilson (1987) showed the connection of ethnical (social and spatial) exclusion and poverty and the far-reaching consequences of segregation. He points out that in disadvantaged areas role models are missing. He underlines this with the example that if fewer people are working, they could not be role models of a regulated working life to youth. Not only role models are missing, but also contacts that might help youth to find a job are missing, too. So restricted access to resources influences and limits the opportunities of inhabitants. However, the social environment is especially important there, because under poverty mobility is restricted and obtained on the closer environment. Also it creates norms that differ from the mainstream.

Neighborhood effects are complex and affect the inhabitants through different mechanisms. Several explanations have been offered by examining different mechanisms. Some focus only on the macro-level, the influence of the neighborhood, and some only on the micro-level, the influence of individual factors.

Friedrichs and Nonnenmacher (2011: 469) differ between direct and indirect effects. This is based on the rational-choice-theory, which includes the macro-micro-macro-model of social acting by Coleman and additionally a meso-level, where institutions are located. Direct effects are characteristics of the residential area influencing the structure of the individuals' behavior.

Indirect effects develop when the residential area influences the structure of the inhabitants on the meso-level. The neighborhood influences the availability and quality of institutions and this has an impact on the individual. The values and norms of the social networks influence the behavioral outcomes. The availability of institutions and social offers is of fundamental importance, since these factors influence the inhabitants and create social networks. Morrisey and Wilson (2004) showed that being integrated in leisure activities has a positive influence on social behavior which makes the positive development of youth and social learning possible (66). These social contacts and interactions produce norms. But activities for youth can only be practiced if they are available (Friedrichs 1988: 67), therefore opportunity structures in the neighborhood are essential.

Direct effects include primarily the equipment and opportunities of the neighborhood, secondarily the collective socialization, and tertiary the role models and contagion effects. The area provides opportunity structures, for example youth specific places and offers that are central to the socialization and development of youth. Opportunity structures like offers for qualitative good education and non-formal education are not available or only limitedly available in disadvantaged neighborhoods. These restrictions and limitations negatively affect the adolescents by leading to more solidified disadvantage. Also it shows that direct and indirect effects of the neighborhood overlap and influence each other.

Furthermore, collective socialization and the need for role models on the socialization of the inhabitants is important. That neighborhood effects get spread through a collective socialization of the inhabitants is a main assumption (Friedrichs/Nonnenmacher 2010: 472). Therefore, Collective Efficacy in the neighborhood, defined as "social cohesion among neighbors combined with their willingness to intervene on behalf of the common good" is needed (Sampson et al. 1997: 918). If this is not existent, delinquent behavior is more probable.

Moreover, the theory of contagion effects by Crane assumes that delinquent behavior appears through social contacts. He emphasizes the meaning of the peer group. Furthermore, the peer group has a greater influence on poor, male youth than on female youth (Crane 1991: 1227). Additionally, comparisons of neighborhoods with different levels of poverty show that especially youth in disadvantaged neighborhoods spend a lot of their time with older peers, which is called "cross-cohort-socialization" (Harding 2009: 7). This can have a positive function, but also negative effects if the older friends are unemployed or/and delinquent.

This is based on the theory of social learning. Behavior and norms are transmitted through observation and interaction (Bandura 1979: 3). The consequence of a behavior and thereby the legitimization of it influences the acting. Because of this, positive role models must be present. A basic assumption in all approaches is that neighborhood effects influence socialization through different mechanisms, and in most cases through interaction.

Based on the preceding elaboration, the meaning of the peer group, role models, and youth work as opportunity structures in adolescence will be briefly outlined now. Especially, in adolescence social networks and opportunity structures (such as instances of education and socialization) play an important role in the development of young people. This serves as a basis for their future life, like getting a job through education. In the period of adolescence, social networks outside of the family become more important. An increasing replacement of the family goes along with an increasing importance placed on the peer group and other role models. Adolescents spend most of their spare time with their friends which influences their norms and behavior. Besides the norms of the others, the strength of relationships is also important. Weak amicable ties produce an increasing likeliness of delinquent behavior (Thornberry 1987: 883). Not only the interactional aspect but also the aspect of creating a self-image is important. Through observation of others, this is established (Reutlinger 2008: 34). A self-image also includes norms. The high influence of the peers is illustrated by Du Boys-Raymond (2000) with the term peer capital: "informal learning under and with peers produces specific competences, which institutional learning relationships can't produce, [...] but influences the live chances of children and youth" (241).

Spending time with peers outside of institutions takes place mostly in public spaces. Generally, youth spend more time in public spaces; their acting is more spatially orientated. Moreover, in adolescence, role models, particularly adult role models outside the family, become more important. "Mainstream role models are needed who help keeping alive the perception that education is meaningful, that steady employment is an alternative to welfare. And family stability should be a norm, not the exception" (Wilson 1989: 56). So the availability of role models influences the norms of the individuals. Not only at school, but also next to school there are activities influencing education through non-formal learning. In this, social competences through social learning are generated. Furthermore, social problems are closely connected to having few possibilities. Social work is needed to create new action alternatives and to try to balance disadvantage. Therefore, a resource-orientated point of view, focused on the everyday lives of individuals is indispensable.

The following research is based on the importance of the neighborhood, but also the social networks. It concentrates on the subjective point of view of the everyday life of the youth. Furthermore, it wants to consider the local social youth work taking place through the medium sports.

4 Research question and design

The research was conducted during a two-week fieldwork in August 2014 in Stolipinovo, Plovdiv, Bulgaria. A flat was rented within the neighborhood to get accommodated in the field. The research question was: What effects does youth work through the medium of sports have as an opportunity structure for adolescents under different conditions of socialization? And how is this arranged within the context of their everyday lives? Therefore, the actions within the peer groups, as well as in the sports club were in focus. For a holistic view of the individual, as well as institutional and neighborhood factors, the research questions were analyzed by the use of two methods.

The theoretical foundation of neighborhood effects in disadvantaged districts and the need for specific opportunity structures in adolescence require a holistic consideration. The cohesion of the neighborhood and the effects on the inhabitants under research were described according to the macro-micro-macro-model of social acting from Coleman and combined with the social ecological model from Bronfenbrenner. Coleman's model builds on the rational-choice-theory, which is based on the fundamental assumption that "social phenomena, are explained through the acting of individual actors in the social context" (Lüdemann 2000: 89). Friedrichs transferred this model in 1988 to urban sociology to describe mechanisms that influence segregation. He explained collective results on the macro-level with individual behavior on the micro-level and explained that processes can be traced back to the social situation on the macro-level. The social situation is here the social-spatial environment, thus the influence of the neighborhood as "contexts, which have effects on the norms and behavior of the inhabitants through opportunities and restrictions" (Friedrichs/Nonnenmacher 2010: 470). However, the meso-level, where institutions, social networks, and social work are located, is also important. Therefore, parts of Bronfenbrenner's (1981) socio-ecological theory of socialization are added, which consider the connection of spheres of life and events. In addition to a macro-system and a micro-system in which individuals are included, it contains a meso-system, which connects different spheres of life (ibid: 41).

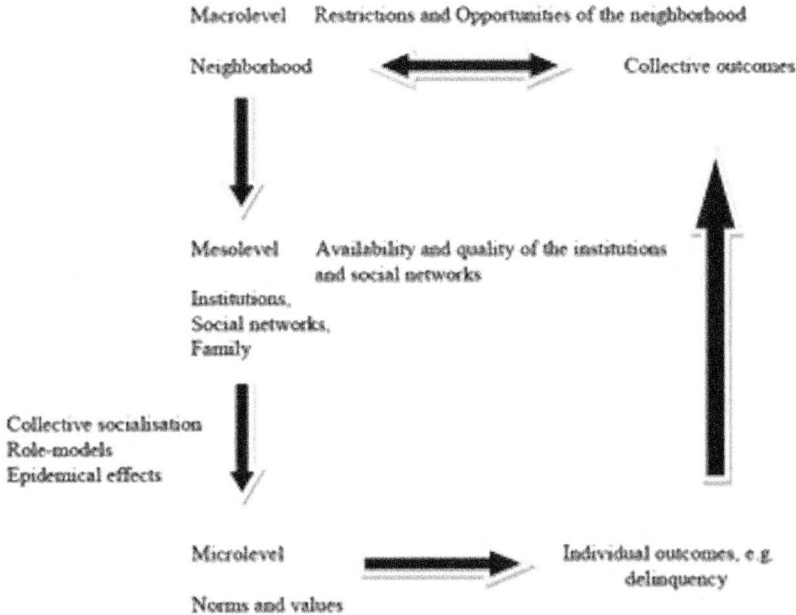

Figure 1 Macro-micro-macro-model
Source: Own representation

In order to apply the model to the research in the conclusion, the different factors that affect adolescents, including the neighborhood as well as the influence of social work are regarded in the following. Therefore, the cohesion of the neighborhood and the effects for the inhabitants are represented holistically.

The methodical work was divided into two parts. The first method of data collection was conducting guideline-based interviews with experts. Therefore, two trainers of different sports clubs were asked as experts who work with youth in the field of sports. In the following, I will only present the football club in Stolipinovo. The second method of conducting data was the method of reflexive photography. Therefore, a target group of 4-6 youth per group from the ages of 12-16 was determined, although the research and these chances refer to an age up to 21. Altogether, three groups were asked. Because of the many limitations of group 3, it will not be considered in the following.

The research method, called "reflexive photography" was used to gain and deepen insights of their lives. The adolescent took a series of photographs with two single-use-cameras per group. The method of reflexive photography itself was divided into four different parts. The conduction is divided into three parts, provided by Kolb (2008). The first meeting was the opening period and I explained my research to the group and we arranged a time for getting back the cameras, based on the preferences of the youth. Up to this meeting they were in the "active photo-shooting phase" and took pictures along the research question. They were asked to take photographs first of places they liked, second, places they do not like and, third, places they associated with sports or movement in general. These photographs visualized their impressions-and showed their arrangement of how and where they spend their spare time.

After that the photographs were discussed in a focused interview called a "decoding phase". Here, the youth explained the photographs to the researcher, which enabled good access for the interview and improved the communication (Kolb 2008: 8). The methodology of "reflexive photography" represented the young person's point of view and attitude and thereby showed that movement was an important part of their spare time activity. They also took pictures of places associated with movement by themselves, which enabled the young people to have a high level of participation in the research process. Finally, the "analytical scientific interpretation phase" included the evaluation of the interviews in connection with the photographs.

The field access was enabled through Sebastian Kurtenbach, a social scientist, who is connected to the NGO in Stolipinovo. Locally the research was supported by the Roma Organization, who helped to find interview partners, addressed the youth and arranged the first meeting. The interviews were held in English and translated into Bulgarian through a Bulgarian translator. The interviews were recorded with a dictaphone and their length varied between 25-34 minutes.

5 Research conditions, description and limitations

Plovdiv is famous for its old city and culture and is, in fact, the European Capital of Culture for 2019. The treatment of minorities is not regarded. Many Roma live segregated in four districts. Stolipinovo is a segregated district and with ca. 50.000 inhabitants, which is the biggest Romani District in Plovdiv – and even in Europe. These inhabitants form a heterogeneous group composed of different religions, for example, Muslims and Christians. The spoken languages are Romanes, Turkish and Bulgarian.

The living conditions in this area are worse than in the rest of the city. Exclusion leads to isolation in different social subsections. School segregation leads to lower education and less qualification. The unemployment rate is approximately. 90%, but there are some other informal employments. Disadvantage goes hand in hand with a bad infrastructure. The health situation is problematic; diseases like HIV and tuberculosis appear more frequently.

There is less mobility than the rest of the city, due to discrimination that goes along with social distance and restrictions (Kanev 1996: 41). Also there is a "spatial sorting", for example the children learn in segregated schools in the district (Sampson et al. 1999: 637). Purchases can be bought at a street market and many other supermarkets, which are operated by inhabitants.

The research has some restrictions. Because of limited time, I could only consider one part of the neighborhood and its effects and therefore, a holistic understanding of the personal background of the adolescents was impossible. The influence of the families which is an important factor, could also not be considered. A deeper understanding of the life of the youth, which would be helpful to holistically and deeply answer the question was impossible.

Although there was the help of a translator, the communication, especially within the group interviews, was difficult. The flow of the conversation was interrupted by the translation, which led to limited and superficial results in the group interviews. The interviews with the youth were held in the offices of the Roma Foundation. The research access was also enabled by the Roma Foundation, who helped to initiate finding groups and established the first contact. The interview with the football trainer took part in his office in the church in Stolipinovo. This interview was held in English without a translator. Framework conditions are represented in the following table:

Table 1 Framework conditions

Respondents	Number of participants	Age	Length
Youth group 1	6 boys at the introduction, 3 at the interview	15-21 (3*15, 1*16, 1*17, 1*19, 1*21)	28 min.
Youth group 2	5 boys at the introduction and the interview	12-14 (2*2, 1*13, 2*14)	25 min.
Expert	Trainer of a football club	/	34 min.

6 Results

The recordings of the interviews were transcribed and analyzed by the qualitative content analyses, according to Gläser and Laudel (2009). At first, a categorical system was developed, based on the guidelines of the interviews. With this, a structural and focused analysis was possible. There were six categories of the interview with the expert that were investigated. On the basis of these, information from the obtained transcript was fundament for the analyses. In the following, the categories will be summarized into three. For the analyses of the interviews with the youth, three categories were developed as well. Their photographs will be shown to underline their statements. The results will be presented in the following. After that they will be summarized again and represented in the macro-micro-macro-model.

7 Results: Interview with the trainer of a football club

7.1 Structure of the organization and conditions for entry

This category has been chosen to point out the organizational structure of the offer. Because the football club is an offer by the Christian Organization, it authorizes them to do social work and produce new opportunities. It is located in Stoliponovo and only youth from the neighborhood are members. It starts when the children are very young (10 years old) and continues throughout the whole adolescence until they finish school. The training takes place every day. This strengthens a close bonding with the youth. Also, the access is free of cost, which is in contrast to most youth clubs in Bulgaria. Furthermore, the trainer provides the equipment such as shirts, shoes and a ball. He also stays in contact in other instances of socialization, for example, he talks to the parents and the teachers regularly. Moreover, conditions and a strong bonding with the youth lead to more positive effects.

7.2 Restrictions of the everyday life in Stolipinovo

This category has been chosen to point out the restrictions of the neighborhood. The football trainer himself grew up in a ghetto (own term) in Nigeria. He points out that he knows "how the ghetto life looks like" based on his own experiences. He also emphasizes the differences between rich people and their environments, and also between the conditions in the rest of the country. He refers to traditions like early marriage, sometimes at the age of 10-12 years. Regarding the neighborhood effects, he hints at the consumption of alcohol and tobacco. The adolescents start smoking, drinking alcohol and taking drugs at very early age. He mentions that they learn this by watching the adults, but also through the influence of peer contacts. Many youths do not go to school and most of those who visit school leave it early in the first five grades. With less education he also justifies the traditional life. Furthermore, he underlines that they have less access to education. They live segregated and very close within their boundaries, which the consequently means less or no contact with people of the Bulgarian majority. Also there is a lack of leisure opportunities. Under these circumstances the trainer tries to operate and create positive effects by being a member in a sports offering.

7.3 Positive effects of being member in a sports offering

This category includes the effects that influence the youth inside the sports club and also in subsections outside the club. The organization of the football clubs tries to influence neighborhood effects positively. By creating new leisure opportunities, it reacts to the restrictions of the neighborhood. Also the trainer wants to prevent negative neighborhood effects by influencing the youth with a combination of strong relationships and rules. He wants to teach discipline in all parts of the young people's lives, but also understandingly helps them if they are in trouble and talks to the parents or teachers. He points out the importance of education and tries everything to make the members of his sports club stay in school. On this basis, there are rules for all the members, one of which is the aim and condition to go to school regularly and finish the twelfth class. With this, he wants to prevent leaving school early and enables them to have a higher education and more chances on the labor market.

He is also in contact during other important instances of the youth's socialization and has very close access to the young people and their environment. Additionally, he wants to influence them in a good way by other rules. This works due to strong relationships and role modeling. The Christian church wants to change the effects of disadvantaged neighborhoods effects by conveying information and the importance of education. He also points to the educational aspect for overcoming poverty. They are not allowed to smoke, drink, take drugs, and steal. Furthermore, the behavior within the group gets better over time. At the beginning there was tension and fighting in the team very often. This changed, which underlines-the positive effect that emerges from this membership in the sports club and that this membership is useful for communication and socialization in the peer group.

8 Results: View of the youth

8.1 Everyday life in Stolipinovo

One the one hand, the youth described their everyday lives as boring. But on the other hand, they emphasized that they do many different things in their spare time. They also explained they have fun every day when they spend time together. They spent their spare time with their friends mostly hanging out in some places outside and drinking something. Moreover, they played a lot of billiard, nearly every day for many hours. Some of them smoked, some did not, because they were in the football club. Their activities were mostly limited to the neighborhood. Sometimes they went to a pool in another district.

Figure 2 Photograph of a billiard table, Group 2, 11.08.2014

8.2 Places they like

Places they liked were closely associated with movement, other activities, and a clean environment. Also they liked their school, because they learned there.

The youth of group 1 spent a lot of time in the gym. Group 2 nearly never spent time there, they pointed to the costs. In contrast, they spent more time with other activities on public spaces. They took photographs of places where they hung out with friends, benches they sat on and a football field where they played football. Both groups took photographs of a green area. One group emphasized the fresh air at this area. Asked to take pictures of places connected to movement or other activities, they expressed that they liked all the places that were connected to movement or other activities.

Figure 3 Photograph of a playground & sports field at school, Group 2

Besides that, they liked playgrounds, especially those you can climb at, because they trained there and did something good. The adolescents tried to keep themselves healthy. They underlined that they do not smoke at places that they connect to sports and pointed out that smoking is the opposite of keeping fit. This shows that they know about the health risks, even if they smoke. Furthermore, they explained that their lives would be boring without football and billiard and they would not stay fit.

8.3 Places they do not like

Places they do not like were closely associated with incivilities in the neighborhood. They took many photos of rubbish and some of ownerless dogs. Not only the rubbish, but also other factors that mirrored an unclean environment were negatively marked. For example, they took a picture of a chimney that is environmentally harmful. They negatively evaluated a place where drugs were taken. In addition, they estimated a horse-drawn carriage, which only poor people and mostly Roma have, as negative.

9 Conclusion

I begun this paper by noting that the effects of disadvantaged neighborhoods influence youth and strengthen disadvantage. Through fieldwork and interviews in Stolipinovo it became clear which neighborhood effects influence the youth there, how their daily life is organized, and how youth work can engage there.

All in all, three important influence mechanisms of neighborhood effects could be differentiated, collective socialization, role models, and epidemical effects and with this, three important factors: the collective norms in the neighborhood, the adult role models, and the peer group.

The research showed that the youth spend all their spare time with their friends. Also their actions are located in the neighborhood with friends from there and they spend most of their time in public spaces. This underlined the social-spatial orientation that strengthens neighborhood effects. Because the circle of friends is located in the neighborhood, norms get transmitted through epidemical effects (Crane 1991; Oberwittler 2004). They are characterized through early alcohol and cigarette consumption, which also arises from collective socialization through segregation. Their subjective point of view on their spare time activities showed that they liked all places which are connected to sports, movement in general or where they spend time with their friends. This showed the high priority of sports for them. Moreover, it underlined that youth specific places and opportunities for activities are needed.

Furthermore, they said that their spare time is sometimes boring. The fact that they stressed at the same time the variety of their activities and pointed out, that they have fun with their friends, showed an ambivalent relationship to their residential area and spare time in these places. They spend most time at local places, but there were not many youth specific places. So the offer was based on the needs of the youth and attracted them, which helped to get access to them.

In summary, it can be said that they have less opportunities to create their lifestyle and leisure activities in their neighborhood. But leisure activities like sports play a significant role in the identity formations of the youth. Offers like the football club can provide new opportunities for organized spare time, in which social learning takes place. The example of the football club shows, that if they spend their spare time in a sports club, this can prevent negative neighborhood effects and influence actions in the peer group. It also confirms that it is possible to prevent negative neighborhood effects through disadvantage by creating new opportunities. The trainer mentioned segregation as a problem, which leads to negative neighborhood effects and was connected to different priorities in the lifestyle and to a higher risk of leaving school early and alcohol addiction. To prevent these negative impacts, the football club contained conditions, i.e. the adolescents are not allowed to smoke and drink and must go to school until they finish the twelfth class. Because they had the chance to be in the football club, they followed the conditions and were disciplined in other areas. Success in this part helped them to create a positive self-perception and to distance themselves from negative neighborhood effects. All in all, different norms were created through the football club. Moreover, the football trainer impacted the negative neighborhood effects holistically through involving other parts and persons that positively influenced the youth and enabled success in school. He also mentioned that members of the football club were even friends in their private lives. So the spreading of delinquent behavior by peers was prevented through rules.

Being a participant in a youth offer also had a positive influence in different parts of the everyday life. The trainer built up a relationship through spending a lot of time in the sports club and provided support for the youth for a long time. The structure and the frequency of it were also important. They meet every day after school. The interviews with the youth showed that if they did not play football, they hung out mostly with their friends in local places. So football replaced this unstructured time on the street. Furthermore, the trainer worked as a role model because of his close relationship with the youth and his abilities at playing football. He used football as medium to communicate and to gain access to the youth. With rules he impacted the collective socialization of the team and created norms that are different from the collective socialization in the neighborhood. The following figure shows the negative neighborhood effects-that result disadvantage and the positive effect of being a member in a football club.

To summarize, the football club helped to regulate negative neighborhood effects and influenced the youth in a positive way. It laid the foundation to reduce and overcome disadvantage and played an important role for positive development in adolescence. Also, it underlined the positive effect of offers from social work to create new opportunity structures and reduce disadvantage.

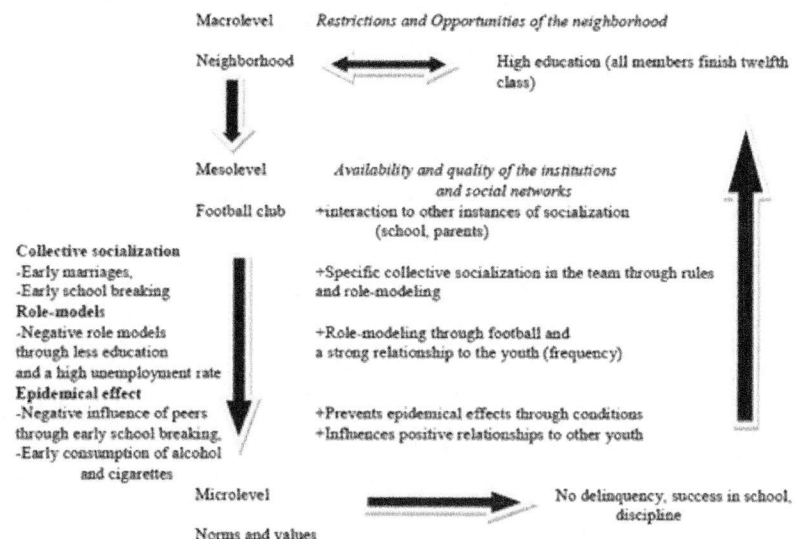

Figure 4 Results

References

Bandura, A. (1971). Social Learning Theory. Stanford: Stanford University.
Benz, W. (2014). „Antiziganismus ist salonfähig." Gespräch mit Romani Rose, Vorsitzender des Zentralrats Deutscher Sinti und Roma. [*Antiziganism is acceptable. Interview with Romani Rose, chairman of the central council of german Sinti and Roma*], in Benz, Wolfgang (ed.) Die unerwünschte Minderheit. Über das Vorurteil Antiziganismus. [*Sinti and Roma. The undesirable minority. About the prejudice antiziganism*], Berlin: Metropol Verlag, pp. 49-63.
Brearley, M. (2001). The Persecution of Gypsies in Europe. American Behavioral Scientist, 45(4), 588–599.
Briggs, X.S. (2007). More Pluribus, Less Unum? The changing geography of race and opportunity, in Beider, Harris (ed.) Neighborhood Renewal & Housing Markets: Community Engagement in the US & UK. Oxford UK: Blackwell Publishing Ltd., pp. 63-86.
Bronfenbrenner, U. (1981). Ökologische Sozialisationsforschung. Konzepte der Humanwissenschaften. [*The Ecology of Human Development. Experiments by Nature and Design*], Harvard: Harvard College.
Castañeda, H. (2014). European Mobilities or Poverty Migration? Discourses on Roma in Germany. International Migration, n/a–n/a.

Crane, Jonathan (1991). The Epidemic Theory of Ghettos and Neighborhood Effects on Dropping Out and Teenage Childbearing. The American Journal of Sociology. 96(5), pp. 1226-1259.
Du Bois-Reymond, M. (2000). Jugendkulturelles Kapital in Wissensgesellschaften. [Youth-cultural capital in knowledge-based society], in Krüger Heinz Hermann, Wenzel Hartmut (ed.) Schule zwischen Effektivität und sozialer Verantwortung. [School between efectiveness and social responsibility], Opladen: Leske und Budric,. Pp. 235-254.
End, M. (2011). Sinti und Roma. Bilder und Sinnstruktur des Antiziganismus. [*Sinti and Roma. Images and meaning structures*], APUZ 22-23.
Friedrichs, J. (2011). Ist die Besonderheit des Städtischen auch die Besonderheit der Stadtsoziologie? [*Is the special of the urban the special of the citysociology, too? The special of the urban*], in Herrmann, Heike u.a. (ed.) Die Besonderheit des Städtischen. [*The special of the urban*], Wiesbaden: VS Verlag für Sozialwissenschaften, pp. 34-47.
Friedrichs, J. & Nonnenmacher, A. (2010). Welche Mechanismen erklären Konttexteffekte? [*Which mechanisms explain neighborhood effects?*], in Becker, Tilo, Birkelbach, Klaus, Hagenah, Jörg, Rosar, Ulrich (eds.) Komperative empirische Sozialforschung.[*comperative empirical social research*], Wiesbaden: VS Verlag für Sozialwissenschaften, pp. 469-497.
Friedrichs, J. & Triemer, S. (2008). Gespaltene Städte? Soziale und ethnische Segregation in deutschen Großstädten. [*Divided cities. Social and ethnical segregation in german large cities*], Wiesbaden: VS Verlag für Sozialwissenschaften.
Friedrichs, J. & Blasius, J. (2000). Leben in benachteiligten Wohngebieten. [*Living in disadvantaged residential districts*], Opladen: Leske + Budrich.
German Association of cities (2013). Positionspapier des Deutschen Städtetages zu den Fragen der Zuwanderung aus Rumänien und Bulgarien. [*Position paper of the German Association of cities to the questions of the immigration from Romania and Bulgaria*], Deutscher Städtetag: Berlin.
Gerull, S. (2011). Armut und Ausgrenzung im Kontext Sozialer Arbeit. [*Poverty and exclusion in the context of social work*], Weinheim und Basel: Beltz Juventa.
Gläser, J. & Laudel, G. (2009). Experteninterviews und qualitative Inhaltsanalyse. [*Expert interviews and qualitatative content analysis*]. Wiesbaden: VS Verlag für Sozialwissenschaften.
Goodwin, M. (2009). Multi-dimensional exclusion: viewing Romani marginalization through the nexus of race and poverty. In: Schiek, Dagmar, Chege, Victoria (eds) European Union Non-Discrimination Law. Comparative Perspectives on Multi-dimensional Equality Law. Oxford: Routlege.
Groh-Samberg, O. (2009). Armut, Ausgrenzung und Klassenstruktur. Zur Integration multidimensionaler und längsschnittlicher Alternativen. [*Poverty, Exclusion and class structure. The integration of multidimensional and longitudinal options*], Wiesbaden: VS Verlag für Sozialwissenschaften.
Harding, D. J. (2009) Violence, older peers, and the socialization of adolescent boys in disadvantaged neighborhoods". American Sociological Review, 74(3), pp. 445-464.
Häußermann, H. & Siebel, W. (2004). Stadtsoziologie. Eine Einführung. [Urban sociology. An Introduction] Frankfurt: Campus Verlag.
Kanev, K. (1996). Dynamics of Inter-Ethnic Tensions in Bulgaria and the Balkans. "Occasional Papers on religion in Eastern Europe", 16(6), 12-45.

Kolb, B. (2008). Involving, Sharing, Analyzing – Potential of the Participatory Photo Interview. In: Forum: Qualitative Social Research. 9(3), Art. 12.
Kronauer, M. (2008). Ausgrenzung und physich-sozialer Raum. [*Exklusion and physical-social space*], in Anhorn, Roland, Bettinger, Frank, Stehr, Johannes (eds.) Sozialer Ausschluss und Soziale Arbeit. Positionsbestimmung einer kritischen Theorie und Praxis der Sozialen Arbeit. 2., überarbeitete und erweiterte Auflage. [*Social exclusion and social work. Position statements from a critical theory and practice of social work.*], Wiesbaden: VS Verlag für Sozialwissenschaften, pp. 181-198.
Kurtenbach, S. Schäfer, I. (2016). Möglichkeiten zur Prävention von Konexteffekten im Jugendalter durch Soziale Arbeit am Beispiel einer Roma Siedlung [*Possibilites for prevention of neighborhood effects of juveniles by social work at the example of a roma neighborhood*.]. Soziale Passagen, pp. 1-16.
Leiserowitz, R. (2010). Die unbekannten Nachbarn. Minderheiten in Osteuropa. [*The unknown neighbors. Minoritys in East-Europe*], Ch. Links Verlag, Berlin.
Lüdemann, C. (2000). Normen, Sanktionen und soziale Kontrolle in der Theorie rationalen Handelns von James S. Coleman. [*Norms, sanctions and social control in the rational-choice-theory of James S. Coleman*], in Peters, Helge (ed.)Soziale Kontrolle. Zum Problem der Normkonformität in der Gesellschaft [*Social control. The problem of non-conformism in the society*], Opladen: Leske und Budrich, pp. 87 – 110.
Marushiakova, E. & Popov, V. (1997). Gypsies (Roma) in Bulgaria. Frankfurt am Main: Peter Lang.
Marushiakova, E., & Popov, V. (2013). The Shades of Incomplete: Roma Educational Policy in Bulgaria. In: Miskovic, Maja, ed. Roma Education in Europe. London: Routledge.
Matter, M. (2015). Nirgendwo erwünscht. Zur Armutsmigration aus Zentral- und Südosteuropa in die Länder der EU-15 unter besonderer Berücksichtigung von Angehörigen der Roma-Minderheiten. [*Nowhere welcome. To the poverty migration from central- and easteurope in the countrys of t he EU-15 under special consideration of persons of the Roma-minority*], Schwalbach: Wochenschau Verlag.
O'Nions, H. (2010). Different and unequal: the educational segregation of Roma pupils in Europe. Intercultural Education, 21(1), 1–13.
Oberwittler, D. (2004). Soziologie der Kriminalität. [*sociology of delinquency*], Wiesbaden: VS Verlag für Sozialwissenschaften.
Pries, L. (2010). Transnationalisierung. Theorie und Empirie grenzüberschreitender Vergesellschaftung. [*Transnationalisation. Theory and empirie of bordercrossing socialisation*], Wiesbaden: VS Verlag für Sozialwissenschaften.
Pries, L. & Kurtenbach, S. (2016). Transnationalisierung als strukturierendes Element des Sozialraums. [*Transnationalisation as structuring element of the social space*], in Kessl, Frank./Reutlinger, Christian (eds.) Handbuch Sozialraum. Grundlagen für den Bildungs- und Sozialbereich. [*handbook social space. Foundations for the education and social fields*] Wiesbaden: VS Verlag für Sozialwissenschaften, *forthcoming*.
Reutlinger, C. (2008). Raum und soziale Entwicklung. Kritische Reflexion und neue Perspektiven für den sozialpädagogischen Diskurs. [*Space and social development Critical reflections and new perspectives for the socio-pedagogical discourse*] Weinheim: Juventa.
Ringold, D., Orenstein, M. A. & Wilkens, E. (2005). Roma in an Expanding Europe. Breaking the poverty cycle. Washington: The World Bank.

Sampson, R. J. & Raudenbush, S. W. & Earls, F. (1997). Neighborhood and Violent Crime: A multilevel Study of Collective Efficacy. Science, 277 (5328); pp. 918-924.
Sampson, R. J., Morenoff, J. & Earls, F. (1999). Beyond social capital. Spatial Dynamics of Collective Efficacy for Children. American Sociological review, 64, pp. 633-660.
Thornberry, T. P. (1987). Toward an interactional theory of delinquency. Criminology, 5(4), pp. 863-891.
Wilson, W.J. (1989). The Truly Disadvantaged – The Inner City, the Underclass and Public Policy. Chicago and London: The University of Chicago Press.

Authors

Svetlana Antova, PhD is a research associate assistant professor at the Institute of Ethnology and Folklore with the Ethnographic Museum, Bulgarian Academy of Sciences. Her research interests are in the field of migration, post-socialist transnational labour mobility, ethno-cultural identity and border-life studies.

Aneliya Avdzhieva, PhD candidate in Social Anthropology in University of Plovdiv Paisii Hilendarski, Bulgaria. Her research focuses on how mobilities and gender influence life strategies and social networks, following geographically, socially and culturally spaced communities, claimed as Roma. Instrument of the study are labour mobilities of women – trade and temporary migration.

Banu Çıtlak, Dr., Associate Professor at the University of Applied Sciences and Arts Dortmund, Germany. Her research interests are migration studies, family studies and social spaces.

Barbara Fulda, Dr., University of Chemnitz, Germany, Postdoctoral Researcher, Research interests: Sociology of the family, Mixed Methods, Urban Sociology,

Maren Hilke, M.A. Social Science, Researcher at the Institute of Social Work in Münster, Germany. Her research focus on early childhood education and family relations.

Sebastian Kurtenbach, Dr, Researcher at the institute of interdisciplinary research on colflict and violence (IKG), Bielefeld University and lecturer at University of Applied Sciences and Arts Dortmund, Germany. His research in urban and migration studies focusses on neighborhood effects, deviant behavior and transnationalism.

Nora Jehles, M.A. Social Science, Researcher at the Research Cooperation of the Technical University Dortmund and the German Youth Institute, Germany. Her research focuses on early childhood education and care as well as social inequality.

Svetoslava Mancheva, PhD candidate in Social Anthropology in the Faculty of Philosophy and History, University of Plovdiv Paisii Hilendarski, Bulgaria. Her research interests are in the field of Anthropology of Childhood, Anthropology of the Body, Anthropology of Learning, Cultural Studies, Social and Cultural Anthropology.

Megan Lueneburg, B.A. Architecture, Fulbright Graduate Researcher, Iowa State University, USA. Her research focuses on the anthropology of domestic architecture.

Rositsa Lyubenova, Phd student at the University of Plovdiv Paisii Hilendarski, chair "Sociology and humanities". Her research interests are socialism studies, family studies and governmentality studies.

Stoyka Penkova, PhD is an Associate Professor at the Department of Sociology and Human Science, Faculty of Philosophy and History, University of Plovdiv Paisii Hilendarski, Bulgaria. She is currently Head of the Department of Sociology and Human Science. Her main areas of research interests include Sociology of Inequalities, Inheriting and Discursive Practices, Performativity and Ideology of the Discursive Practice.

Sascha Riedel, PhD Student at the University of Cologne, Lecturer at the University of Cologne, Germany. His research focuses on the stages and measurement of immigrant integration and quantitative methods.

Ina Schäfer, B.A. Social Work, is graduate student in Empirical Educational Research at the University of Kassel, Germany. She works in a research project, which focus in possibilities to include pupils with disability and their own view on this process. Her research focuses on social work and migration studies.

Meglena Zlatkova, PhD is an Associate Professor at the Department of Ethnology, Faculty of Philosophy and History, University of Plovdiv Paisii Hilendarski, Bulgaria. Her teaching and research interests are in the field of Urban Studies, Visual Anthropology, Borders and Migration, Heritage and Identity.

CPSIA information can be obtained
at www.ICGtesting.com
Printed in the USA
BVOW06s0223180417
481566BV00012B/98/P